UNCERTAIN
★ ALLIES ★

UNCERTAIN
★ ALLIES ★

**GENERAL JOSEPH STILWELL AND
THE CHINA-BURMA-INDIA THEATER**

ERIC SETZEKORN

Naval Institute Press
Annapolis, Maryland

Naval Institute Press
291 Wood Road
Annapolis, MD 21402

© 2024 by the U.S. Naval Institute
All rights reserved. No part of this book may be reproduced or utilized in any form or by any means, electronic or mechanical, including photocopying and recording, or by any information storage and retrieval system, without permission in writing from the publisher.

Library of Congress Cataloging-in-Publication Data

Names: Setzekorn, Eric B., author.
Title: Uncertain allies : General Joseph Stilwell and the China-Burma-India theater / Eric Setzekorn.
Description: Annapolis, Maryland : Naval Institute Press, [2024] | Includes bibliographical references and index.
Identifiers: LCCN 2024017942 (print) | LCCN 2024017943 (ebook) | ISBN 9781682472033 (hardcover) | ISBN 9781682472040 (ebook)
Subjects: LCSH: Stilwell, Joseph Warren, 1883-1946—Military leadership. | World War, 1939-1945—Campaigns—Burma. | World War, 1939-1945—Campaigns—India. | World War, 1939-1945—Campaigns—China. | World War, 1939-1945—Political aspects—United States. | Politics and war—United States—History—20th century. | BISAC: HISTORY / Wars & Conflicts / World War II / Pacific Theater | HISTORY / Military / Strategy
Classification: LCC D767.6 .S456 2024 (print) | LCC D767.6 (ebook) | DDC 940.54/25—dc23/eng/20240730
LC record available at https://lccn.loc.gov/2024017942
LC ebook record available at https://lccn.loc.gov/2024017943

♾ Print editions meet the requirements of ANSI/NISO z39.48-1992 (Permanence of Paper).
Printed in the United States of America.

32 31 30 29 28 27 26 25 24   9 8 7 6 5 4 3 2 1
First printing

All maps created by Chris Robinson.

The views expressed in this publication are those of the author and do not necessarily reflect the official policy or position of the Department of Defense or the U.S. government.

CONTENTS

List of Charts and Maps	*vii*
INTRODUCTION	1
CHAPTER 1. Mission Objectives and Military Authority *January–December 1942*	22
CHAPTER 2. Airpower *December 1942–May 1943*	55
CHAPTER 3. Global Allies *June 1943–November 1943*	74
CHAPTER 4. Leading Allies in Burma *December 1943–May 1944*	96
CHAPTER 5. Directing Allies in Yunnan *March–September 1944*	132
CHAPTER 6. Supporting Local Allies *May–October 1944*	152
CONCLUSION	176
Notes	*187*
Bibliography	*229*
Index	*251*

CHARTS AND MAPS

CHARTS

CHART 1. Stilwell's Command Relationships, 1943–1944   83

MAPS

MAP 1. The Yunnan Campaign   24
MAP 2. The China-Burma-India Theater   37
MAP 3. The 1942 Burma Campaign   107
MAP 4. The North Burma Campaign   142

INTRODUCTION

IN THE LATE SPRING OF 1946, less than a year after the Japanese surrender, the U.S. Army assembled a small team of senior colonels at Fort Leavenworth, Kansas, to assess the China-Burma-India (CBI) theater. These men had all served in the theater for at least a year during the war and had occupied key positions as planners, senior headquarters staffers, and intelligence officers. Although the U.S. Army was still basking in the glow of victory in Europe and the Pacific, the CBI theater had been politically complicated, with seemingly intractable military problems, and these issues had ultimately led to the dismissal of the theater commander, Gen. Joseph W. Stilwell, a four-star general who was widely respected inside the Army. The mission of the assessment team was to use their personal insights into the difficulties and failures in the CBI theater to adapt and revise the curriculum for Army officers attending the command and general staff course. This broad mandate gave the team the freedom to discuss topics not often studied in U.S. Army training manuals, such as managing relationships with allies, the role of politics in Army operations, and the Army's role in shaping American national strategy.

The final report was presented in an "off the record" oral presentation to the instructors and senior leadership at Fort Leavenworth, and only an informal summary has survived in the Army records. The assessment team was sharply critical of the Chinese role in World War II, stating that Chinese leadership was "corrupt, ignorant, untrained, childish, procrastinating, and ineffective." The British role in the CBI theater was also harshly evaluated, with criticism that British imperial interests had been given much greater priority than fighting the Japanese in Allied strategy.[1] The primary conclusion of the team was that U.S. military training and education had not prepared American officers for politics in the CBI theater: "Allied headquarters are ruled much more by political than by military considerations. All U.S. officers should be trained in such considerations." In addition, the team found that the operational strategy of the U.S. Army had been flawed: "The U.S. Army should conduct its wars so as to secure not only military victory but also economic and political advantages for the United States."[2] In contrast to Allied partners, such as the British and Chinese, who "were fighting their war with definite political objectives in view, from which they never wavered. The United States was fighting simply to get the war over with at the earliest possible moment."[3] While this statement has a degree of truth, it might be more accurate to say that U.S. Army officers did not know or understand American political objectives and failed to coordinate tactical and operational plans with long-term national interests. In fact, the American embassy in China had sharply criticized American military officers throughout the war for their unwillingness to consider the political context of their decisions, noting in a cable to Washington that "there is apparently no intelligent recognition of the political aspect of problems which come to them as military matters."[4] This candid assessment highlights enduring issues and difficulties that would frustrate American commanders for the next seventy-five years.

The reasons for the U.S. Army's political failure in the CBI theater are complex and surprising. For much of its history, the U.S. Army had demonstrated an enviable record of success in conducting military actions to secure postwar advantages. In the American Revolution, American forces rarely matched British troops on the battlefield, but through maneuver and avoidance of defeat, they were able to exhaust the British and make a favorable peace. Army campaigns against Mexico, Native Americans, and Spain had added huge areas to the United States, with military commanders often capably serving in the complex role of civilian administrators while local governments were established. In World War I, Gen. John Pershing famously refused to integrate American troops into French and British units, despite their need for replacements during the final German offensive. Pershing's decision, which likely cost thousands of lives and nearly led to a German breakthrough, was based on a political policy that the United States should have an independent military force because it would maximize the bargaining position at a postwar settlement. In these earlier conflicts the U.S. military had been able to shape military operations to achieve the political outcome desired by leaders in Washington, and the U.S. Army had demonstrated a nuanced understanding of long-term American national strategy.

The final report prepared at Fort Leavenworth in the spring of 1946 suggested several radical changes in doctrine and training to address issues identified in the CBI theater. First, the report concluded that the U.S. Army should become more deeply involved in the military affairs of foreign allies, which would become common practice during the Cold War but was an unusual position in the 1940s. U.S. military policy toward allies in the 1940s was dominated by transferring equipment, such as through Lend-Lease. Enmeshing Americans in foreign military organizations was seen as a policy more applicable to European colonial "sepoy" armies rather than those of democracy. Second, the report argued that American military officers needed a more thorough understanding of American political goals and national strategy, that is, political training. The conclusion that the U.S. Army needed more political training also ran counter to established norms. American military officers during the 1940s strove to be apolitical, and many did not even vote in elections to signify their detachment from political affairs. Third, the conclusion that the United States should conduct military operations to gain economic and political advantage was a complete rejection of Wilsonian concepts of promoting freedom and liberty. The report concluded with an assessment that the Army should seek to better understand the American political context because "we can't shrug that off as a job for the State Department."[5] Most important, the underlying concern expressed in all these suggestions was that U.S. military had failed to develop a coherent strategy or provide military personnel with a coherent and achievable mission that was linked to broader American strategy and national security interests.

The Leavenworth study highlights a sharp divergence in American military history and the beginning of new and challenging dynamics in modern warfare that have frustrated generations of American officers.

Since 1945 the U.S. Army has been involved in four major conflicts and dozens of interventions, invasions, and peacekeeping operations. Despite being regarded by many as one of the best military forces in the world, the U.S. Army has often been frustrated by the lack of decisive victories. In addition, military operations in Vietnam, Korea, Iraq, and Afghanistan often seemed poorly connected to the long-term national security goals established by American political leaders. Rather than reflect on their decisions, the response of many Army officers to their inability to achieve complete, lasting victories has been to blame American political leadership, local allies, and interservice rivals for their dissatisfaction with the results of conflict. A wiser and more considered response to the difficulties the U.S. Army has faced since World War II would be to look at the nature of warfare and conflict in the modern era, search for precedents and case studies that can be analyzed for insights and develop more effective strategies. This book examines the role of Gen. Joseph Stilwell in the CBI theater of World War II from 1942 through 1944 because a close examination of the U.S. Army's experience in the CBI theater reveals that many of the dynamics and challenges that vex Army leaders today are not new. The CBI theater brings into focus issues that the U.S. Army, and U.S. military at large, continue to struggle with today.

From the onset of Stilwell's assignment in early 1942, the first challenge he faced was a lack of a clear mission and authority. The United States had been providing military aid and support to China before Pearl Harbor but had vaguely defined these efforts as coordination. Upon being given the assignment to the CBI theater, Stilwell was informed that he should "increase the effectiveness of United States assistance to the Chinese government for the prosecution of the war and to assist in improving the combat efficiency of the Chinese Army."[6] This assistance mission was further emphasized by Stilwell's assignment as Chiang Kai-shek's Allied chief of staff.[7] The negative effect of these ambiguous mission orders was compounded by uncertain political support from Washington, D.C., particularly after the Japanese conquest of Burma (present-day Myanmar) from December 1941 through April 1942, which exposed systemic problems in the joint British-American-Chinese command structure. This lack of clear authority and limited political backing not only impacted Stilwell's relationship with the British and Chinese but also meant that his authority over other U.S. interagency organizations and military services was severely compromised.

Airpower, in the form of close air support and aerial transport and resupply, was vital to CBI in World War II because it compensated for a lack of artillery and logistics support, but despite these advantages airpower was also an existential threat to Stilwell's and the U.S. Army's desired role in CBI. Claire Chennault, famed creator of the Flying Tigers, and other Air Force leaders made a compelling argument in the spring of 1943 that a comprehensive air campaign against Japanese forces could produce results more quickly and efficiently than a land campaign. Airpower, particularly bombing, seemed to offer a way to surmount the challenges of geography, would rely on American faith in technology, and would mean not having to rely on prickly and difficult local allies to strike at the Japanese. This argument found a ready audience with President Franklin D. Roosevelt, who saw airpower as an alternative to ground combat that offered the irresistible combination of faster results with lower casualties. Stilwell, a weak bureaucratic infighter who poorly advocated for his belief in more ground forces, could only point to flaws in the air campaign. In the middle of 1943, Stilwell also faced political difficulties at a series of high-level planning conferences, particularly the Cairo Conference. As the primary military partner linking British efforts in Southeast Asia with the China theater, Stilwell and the U.S. Army role was often caught between the larger U.S. strategic interest to support the British and the CBI theater mission to assist China. With global Allied resources and trained personnel in short supply, the CBI theater could not compete in political importance against the buildup of forces in Britain for a cross-channel invasion or the landings in Italy. In effect, at major planning conferences it was clear that the United States would support the United Kingdom, with which it had an effective partnership across multiple theaters, rather than prioritize the needs of China, which was not only a difficult ally but also a partner who could impact only a single theater.

In December 1943, Stilwell's challenges shifted after he began a campaign in north Burma that was designed to open a land route to China and seize the vital transportation and airfield hub of Myitkyina. Stilwell and the U.S. Army were able to integrate Chinese units that had been trained and equipped by U.S. personnel with local Kachin tribe members led by American officers, with lethal air support. Although the campaign was difficult and fought on a logistical shoestring, Stilwell demonstrated a new model for American military campaigns, with advisory and assistance efforts being more important than having U.S. Army soldiers fighting on the front lines. In later Army campaigns in Iraq and Korea, when U.S. forces relied on local partners, paramilitary forces, and air support to take the place of U.S. brigades and divisions, the results have been mixed. Stilwell's clear success in taking north Burma with few American "boots on the ground" was a clear success that deserves widespread recognition. Stilwell also initiated a campaign from China's Yunnan Province, driving west into Burma, as the second half of a pincer attack, but this effort was less successful. In contrast to the integrated operations in north Burma, American support and liaison personnel in Yunnan could only supply and assist Chinese forces, and the campaign was slow and led to heavy casualties among poorly coordinated Chinese units. Despite the success of the north Burma campaign, Stilwell was soon caught in a severe dispute with Chiang Kai-shek over the conduct of the campaign in China. Tensions between Stilwell and Chiang Kai-shek had been constant for the entirety of Stilwell's tenure. The defeat of Chinese forces in the spring and summer of 1944 during the Japanese Ichi-Go offensive appeared to support Stilwell's advocacy of a deep restructuring of Chinese forces, with Americans assuming a more direct command role. President Roosevelt was initially supportive of Stilwell's taking command of the armed forces of an ally, an unprecedented step for an American military leader. In September and October 1944, though, Chiang Kai-shek, due to political maneuvering and growing opposition within the U.S. military to taking such a direct role in the affairs of an ally, prevailed. Not only was the plan dropped, but Stilwell was relieved of duty.

Throughout this book two key themes are critically important to understanding Stilwell and the American experience in the CBI theater: uncertain allies and ambiguous missions. In the CBI theater, relationships between the Americans and Chinese, as well as between the Americans and the British, were marked by profound uncertainty. Senior leaders did not trust that their counterparts would comply with agreements on a common strategy, leading to hedging behavior and frequent appeals to their respective political leaders to reshape the authorities and responsibilities of the theater. While this dynamic was neither new nor unique to the CBI theater, what was distinctive was Stilwell's reliance on foreign forces. In the CBI theater, most combat personnel under Stilwell's command were Chinese, and uncertainty over his authority and the commitment of allies was not just a headquarters debate but directly impacted tactical and operational planning. Like later American commanders in Korea, South Vietnam, Iraq, and Afghanistan, reliance on non-American forces created a cloud of uncertainty that influenced the entire course of the campaign. The second recurring theme, ambiguous missions, highlights the incredibly subjective and poorly defined goals for the theater. In contrast to traditional military tasks focused on seizing control of a location or eliminating enemy forces, the CBI's mission was relational and diffused. Stilwell and his subordinates had no geographical target, no numerical metric of success, and no other defined objective. Without a clear goal, Stilwell struggled to align his plans with larger strategic operations.

Underlying both themes, uncertain allies and ambiguous missions, is the primary argument of the book: Stilwell failed to fully understand the political context in which he was operating, and his lack of political awareness was the primary reason for his difficulties. Stilwell achieved notable successes in command of the CBI theater and accomplished far more with less reliable forces and problematic authority than most U.S. Army officers could have been expected to achieve, but throughout his tenure in command, he had problems linking his theater efforts to the larger American war effort. When Stilwell understood the political context of his theater's operations he was often able to develop and implement programs that complemented Allied global strategies. In contrast, when he lacked clarity or made no effort to integrate his operational plans with larger strategic goals, he failed to link his efforts to U.S. national interests. If Stilwell had better understood ongoing policy debates in Washington, areas of domestic disagreement, and changing perceptions, he would have been able to more effectively develop operational and tactical programs. Unfortunately, Stilwell's failures were only the start of a frustrating seventy-five years for the U.S. military, as a lack of political awareness, unreliable local allies, and ambiguous missions would lead to personal frustrations and civil-military frictions.

On the surface, political awareness seems like a simple concept: being cognizant of political and social feelings, attitudes, and power relationships. But for an expeditionary military commander, it is an arduous task. At the most basic level, the military as an institution insulates members from society, and senior officers, who likely entered a service academy such as West Point or Annapolis at age eighteen, have spent their life within the military. Senior officers have also spent most of their careers either living on military installations, deployed overseas, or in intraorganizational educational environments, such as the War College, which are all removed from broader currents of American public life. Another key factor is the challenge posed by distance, and even in the twenty-first century, with technology that enables instant global communications, it can be difficult for leaders thousands of miles from the United States to fully understand discussions and debates at senior policy levels in the United States. Third, military commanders are profoundly shaped by their staff, and for most military leaders, their staff is drawn from personnel they have previously worked with or who share similar backgrounds. Although some senior commanders have a small staff section to address "political-military affairs," or at the most senior levels a State Department official assigned to their staff, it is rare for nonmilitary personnel to shape policy in a military headquarters. Last, and perhaps most important, many military officers view any engagement with political life as distasteful and inappropriate. More than fifty years ago, Morris Janowitz cautioned that a professional military's aspirations to be "above politics" should not be taken to the "point of being unpolitical," because this would close off a vital area of understanding that would negatively impact military decisions.[8] Unfortunately, many military officers, such as Stilwell, pride themselves on their distance from the "political swamp."

A key example of Stilwell's lack of understanding of American long-term political attitudes was his continued advocacy for a transactional type of military and political relationship with China despite clear indications that President Roosevelt, other political leaders, and the American public at large desired a long-term cooperative relationship. Particularly during the period from 1941 through 1944, President Roosevelt argued that China would play a vital role, in concert with the United States, in stabilizing East Asia, and he included China as a major world power despite its lack of military power. Members of Congress and American political elites also shared an affinity for China as a prospective long-term partner, and Congress, key media commentators, and nongovernmental organizations, such as Christian missionary groups, all supported sustained engagement. American public opinion at large also demonstrated a deep reservoir of affection and support for a close and enduring bilateral relationship. Public opinion polls clearly showed that prior to Pearl Harbor, the overwhelming majority of Americans, 78 percent, sympathized with China's position.[9] A 1943 poll asking if the United States should make a permanent military alliance with China found 56 percent in favor, and even in 1945, when substantial issues in the relationship had emerged, a *Foreign Affairs* survey found that 86 percent of respondents felt that China could be trusted to cooperate with the United States when the war was over.[10] In this context of deep and widespread public support for forging a close and lasting relationship with China, Stilwell's proposals to make military aid and American support on a quid pro quo basis was an isolated position that was bound to run headlong into opposition. Lacking political awareness of the motivations, interests, and long-term goals of American policymakers, Stilwell was in a poor position to build consensus for his desired theater policies and failed to link the efforts of his theater to American political objectives.

OLD DEBATES AND FRESH PERSPECTIVES

The conduct of U.S. military-political relations in the CBI theater during World War II, the role of personalities such as Joseph Stilwell, Lord Mountbatten, and Chiang Kai-shek, and the war against Japan have been frequently studied in the past seventy-five years. Unfortunately, since 1945 several factors have inhibited accurate and insightful historical studies, and only with the passage of time has politicization decreased. In addition, previous studies of CBI and Stilwell often looked to answer questions relevant for the historical context of their own era, such as Vietnam or the Cold War. This narrow focus obscured the long-term relevance of the CBI theater, downplayed the prominent British role in the CBI theater, and focused on Stilwell's personality rather than his policies. While older assessments are valuable to understanding how the debates and perspectives have evolved, this work will build on older material to develop a better understanding of a broader shift in modern American warfare, take a more holistic view of the CBI theater, and bring our perspective into a post-Afghanistan and post-Iraq era.

This book will contribute to our understanding of World War II, Joseph Stilwell, and the U.S. Army's military experience in three primary ways. First, by integrating previously unused materials it is possible to see a much more balanced and complete picture of not just high-level policy decisions, but the implementation of Army efforts on the ground. Previous studies of CBI have neglected the rich archival materials at Fort Leavenworth, which contain thousands of pages of studies, assessments, and command narratives. These materials were not sent to the National Archives and are not cited in previous works. These materials give us a much better understanding of the tremendous logistical, administrative, and doctrinal challenges in CBI. Unlike American forces operating in Europe, Army leaders in CBI were often forced to "throw out the book" and find new and adaptive solutions, whether it be in medical evacuation from the battlefield, advising Chinese forces, or laying a pipeline through the jungle. A second way this work is distinctive is that it uses a much wider range of non-English materials. As a professional-level reader of Chinese, I can integrate a wide range of Chinese-language documents, memoirs, oral history interviews, and studies into the overall narrative. In the past several decades Taiwan has boldly moved beyond the authoritarian legacies of Chiang Kai-shek and his KMT Party. The impact of these materials is to allow the reader to better understand the complex interplay between Americans and Chinese during a period of close partnerships and high tensions. Japanese records are also accessible and well organized. Unfortunately in the past twenty years there has been no corresponding changes in the People's Republic of China, and archival materials remain tightly controlled. Last, as a former U.S. Army historian, I have experience working with, and understanding of a wide range of, studies, reports, and student papers written on the topics of Stilwell, CBI, and China in World

War II. The Command and General Staff School at Fort Leavenworth and the Army War College in Carlisle, Pennsylvania, require their students to write research papers, and while these papers are not always written to academic standards, they offer insights into how U.S. Army officers, particularly majors and colonels, view the world and the Army's role in conflicts. Many of the dozens of papers cited in this work demonstrate that the worldview and characteristics demonstrated by Joseph Stilwell in the 1940s continue in the Army today. Moreover, by working daily with military personnel and other Army historians I am in a unique position to view the institution of the U.S. Army and understand the distinctive and enduring elements of its culture.

All historians build their work on previous scholarship and the research of others, and this work is no exception. What is rare about historical assessments of General Stilwell and the American role in CBI during World War II has been the extraordinary role of political and personal passions in the historiography. In the immediate postwar period, personal accounts were often highly supportive of Stilwell and damning of Chiang Kai-shek and, to a lesser degree, Mountbatten. Fred Eldridge's *Wrath in Burma* from 1946, which was marketed as "the uncensored story of General Stilwell," concluded that "Joe Stilwell, with all of his vinegar, would have gotten along if the British and Chinese had kept their commitments."[11] First-person accounts by personnel from the CBI theater, such as surgeon Gordon Seagrave, who had walked out of Burma with Stilwell in 1942 and served in the theater throughout the war, lauded Stilwell as a hands-on soldiers' general who pushed forward with a campaign despite receiving little support.[12] The publication of Stilwell's papers, edited and arranged by influential journalist Theodore White, further cultivated the image of a plain-spoken soldier who was defeated in the conference rooms of Washington, New Delhi, and Chungking (Chongqing) but not on the battlefield.[13]

Assessments of the CBI theater and General Stilwell dramatically shifted after the collapse of the KMT government and Chiang Kai-shek's flight to Taiwan in 1949. The outbreak of the Korean War in June 1950 led to renewed American support and renewed cooperation between the Chinese Nationalists and the United States against a shared Communist threat. This rapprochement was accelerated by the actions of the "China

Lobby" in the United States, which supported a policy of close ties with the Republic of China despite Chiang Kai-shek's continued authoritarian politics and instead looked for Americans who had "Lost China." Several of Stilwell's most prominent advisors, such as State Department official John P. Davies, were caught in Senator Joseph McCarthy's anticommunist demagoguery and were fired from the government. A good example of the polemical nature of much of this scholarship is Donald Lohbeck's 1956 biography of Patrick Hurley, the ambassador to China in 1945, which finds that "the record of General Stilwell in China is irrevocably coupled in history with the conspiracy to overthrow the Nationalist Government of China, and to set up in its place a Communist regime—and all of this movement was a part of, and cannot be separated from, the Communist cell or apparatus that existed at the time in the Government in Washington."[14] Many of the assessments of the 1949–1965 period were also written by those who had served in the CBI theater, and they sought to burnish their roles, downplaying Stilwell's importance. Gen. Albert C. Wedemeyer, Stilwell's successor as the senior American in the China theater, repeatedly criticized Stilwell's behavior in his 1958 memoir, *Wedemeyer Reports!* Specifically, he argued that Stilwell had unwisely involved himself deeply with political issues and emphasized the north Burma campaign to open a road to China despite the limited utility of the road.[15] Maj. Gen. Claire Chennault, Stilwell's wartime subordinate and an advocate of airpower, was harshly critical of Stilwell for what he felt was the neglect of the Chinese Nationalists in World War II.[16] Accounts by Nationalist Chinese reinforce the narrative of uncertain American support and Stilwell's incompetence if not overt manipulations as the reason for many of the wartime and postwar reverses. F. F. Liu, a Chinese Nationalist Army officer, concluded that Stilwell had used his control over supplies flown into China to restrict his bureaucratic rivals, such as General Chennault. In addition, Stilwell is criticized for his lack of "diplomacy and tact" in his dealing with Chinese allies.[17] While these first-person accounts are extremely valuable to the historical record, the one-sided nature of the narrative would lead to an equally politicized and distorted response in the late 1960s and 1970s.

Two bright spots during the problematic 1950s were the assessments of political scientists and the official U.S. Army histories. Unlike the personalized and politicized depictions of CBI in the public conversation, political scientists sought to understand how minor powers like Nationalist China, and to a lesser degree Great Britain, had been able to manipulate the United States from 1941 to 1945. Herbert Feis, an academic and State Department employee in the Roosevelt administration, wrote in his 1953 work *The China Tangle* that unrealistic plans, poor communication, and dysfunction in Washington were the source of most of the difficulties. Feis writes that "American diplomacy and military planning got entangled, stumbled; and we failed in our attempt to shape the vast country of China into the image of our desires."[18] In response to the heated political environment of the 1950s, as the official histories of the CBI theater were being produced by the Army, the editors were extremely careful to keep the content focused on factual and operational issues. In 1953 the Army released *Stilwell's Mission to China*, which covered the period from late 1941 through the summer of 1943, followed by *Stilwell's Command Problems* in 1956, which focused on the period from the summer of 1943 through Stilwell's relief in October 1944. A final volume, *Time Runs Out in CBI*, focused on General Wedemeyer's tenure from October 1944 until the end of the war.[19] As official histories, these works were primarily written to provide a historical narrative, with little editorial or analytical commentary. Nevertheless, these three works undercut the notion that Stilwell had sought to establish close ties with the Communist Party, a favorite theme of China Lobby critics of Stilwell. These official histories subtly made a significant critique of U.S. policies in World War II that had favored airpower, pointing out the prohibitive cost and limited direct results of air operations in the CBI theater. While this argument is to be expected from a U.S. Army publication, it did have a positive role in shifting analysis and understanding of the CBI campaign toward more objective and analytical questions, rather than personalized narratives. The official histories also placed a heavy emphasis on the difficulties of coordination and partnership with Allied forces at the tactical and operational level. By broadening the discussion away from high politics and senior military conferences, the official histories revealed tremendous difficulties in training, communications, and logistics throughout the CBI theater. While many of these challenges were to be expected in an area with challenging geography and fragile supply lines, the difficulty of working with Allied military forces at all levels is clearly established by extensive reports and official documentation.

While Feis and the official histories could open the door for a more nuanced and impartial debate, the turbulent 1960s ushered in a new era of scholarship that unfortunately replicated many of the biases and flaws of the 1950s but on the other side of the political and academic spectrum. From the mid-1960s through the 1980s a strongly revisionist school of historiographical writing in the shadow of Vietnam highlighted the corruption, authoritarianism, and incompetence of Chiang Kai-shek and the de facto American support of British imperial ambitions in Southeast Asia. This shift made Stilwell appear to be a noble and honest soldier in his opposition to both Allies, working to fight a war while American Allies focused their attention on acquiring U.S. aid and military support to bolster their own political goals. In 1963, the revisionist shift began with the publication of *America's Failure in China, 1941–1950*, by University of Chicago political scientist Tang Tsou. As a Chinese American academic, Tsou used both English- and Chinese-language sources, and he further developed the ideas presented by Feis that lofty expectations in Washington had been unrealistic and had led to poorly conceived policies. Tsou was blunt in assigning the primary blame for the failures in the CBI theater to senior leaders in Chungking and Washington: "To be sure, Chinese apathy and resistance were the primary cause of Stilwell's frustration. But Stilwell's setback also stemmed from the prevailing [American] attitude that the goal of the war was exclusively military defeat of the enemy, the inability to grasp firmly the political objective of war in terms of a postwar balance of power, and the failure to coordinate military activities with political policy."[20] This controversial and best-selling account opened the doors for a new round of memoirs, personal accounts, and assessments, which now shifted toward blaming Chiang Kai-shek and lauding Stilwell.

Writing in the shadow the Vietnam War, a new generation of academics and policymakers highlighted the contradictions of supporting corrupt and incompetent regimes in the hope that minor reforms or American aid could produce positive outcomes. The dominant narrative surrounding Joseph Stilwell was shaped by Barbara Tuchman's seminal *Stilwell and the American Experience in China, 1911–1945*. First published in 1970, Tuchman's book used Stilwell's lengthy experiences in China to personalize a narrative about larger U.S. involvement. In her account, Stilwell exemplifies American national strengths and weaknesses in dealing with China and Asia at large: being honest and industrious but also prone to favor direct and energetic approaches to large, structural problems. Tuchman concludes that the American mission to assist China "failed in its ultimate purpose because the goal was unachievable. The impulse was not Chinese. Combat efficiency and the offensive spirit, like the Christianity and democracy offered by missionaries and foreign advisors, were not indigenous demands of the society and culture to which they were brought."[21] Her conclusions perfectly matched the sense of frustration and malaise of the late Vietnam War, and the book received the 1972 Pulitzer Prize for general nonfiction.

Stilwell's image was also burnished by the publication of two memoirs by his former subordinates in the CBI theater. John Paton Davies Jr., a State Department official who had served as Stilwell's political attaché from 1942 to 1944, released his account of the era in 1972 with *Dragon by the Tail: American, British, Japanese, and Russian Encounters with China and One Another*. Davies shares Tuchman's assessment that success in the CBI theater, and American policy toward China at large, was doomed to failure. He writes,

> Stilwell's big mistake, in which I sometimes went along with him, was to think that he could strike a bargain with the Generalissimo: Stilwell could arm and train sixty (later ninety) divisions and enlarge the Chinese Air Force if only Chiang would reform his military establishment and take the offensive against the Japanese. Had Chiang been able and willing to do what Stilwell asked, China might well have emerged from the war in fact a great power. And of more primitive concern to the Generalissimo, he might have been able to then fend off the Communists. As Chiang could no more reform his own power base than overcome his idiosyncrasies, the bargain was doomed—as was Chiang.[22]

Stilwell's longtime military aide-de-camp, and later the commander of a force of fifteen Chinese divisions in the CBI theater, joined the discussion in 1971 with his account of the retreat from Burma in 1942, *Walkout:*

With Stilwell in Burma. Frank Dorn is unabashed in declaring that Stilwell "became the scapegoat in an international tug of war in high places," which hinders both our understanding of the man and the issues. In this depiction, Stilwell's personal leadership of a group of 117 men and women fleeing Burma on foot through the jungle was an expression of Stilwell's willingness to share sacrifices and demand integrity and honesty from those he served with. Dorn notes that during the harrowing retreat, Stilwell shared all the hardships of those under his command, and by the time of their arrival in India, the fifty-five-year-old Stilwell had been reduced to 118 pounds, losing almost a quarter of his body weight while on reduced rations.[23] A key aspect of Davies's and Tuchman's revisionist argument was the idea of the "lost chance," that if Stilwell had been better supported in his efforts to engage with the Chinese Communists, led by Mao Zedong, he might have led the United States to be on the "right side" of history. This counterfactual perspective was popular in the 1970s, as President Nixon visited Beijing, and it seemed like twenty-five years of Sino-American history could have been avoided if Stilwell's advice had been heeded, but this conception was based on a limited understanding of the historical context.[24] By the end of the 1970s, Stilwell had been rehabilitated from an overlooked and less-than-successful World War II general into an exemplar of character and a realistic observer of the limits of American power.

The shifting tides of historical reassessment also included academic reevaluation, which also became sharply more critical of Chiang Kai-shek and the Nationalist war effort. Aside from a few remaining defenders in Taiwan and conservative elements of the American academia, English-language scholarship now frequently emphasized KMT weakness and incompetence rather than strength. Lloyd Eastman wrote in *Seeds of Destruction: Nationalist China in War and Revolution, 1937–1945* that by the end of the war the Nationalist government was "utterly debilitated, its weaknesses evidenced by the limited reach of its political sway, the corruption and ineffectiveness of its administration, the self-destructive fighting of its several factions, and the pervasive incompetence and demoralization of its army."[25] An even stronger indictment of the Nationalists and senior American political leaders was in Michael Schaller's *The U.S. Crusade in China, 1938–1945*, which advanced the idea that Stilwell had not only been correct to take a hard line with the Nationalist Chinese regarding military cooperation but also had been prescient in seeking a relationship with the Chinese Communists.[26] In academic articles Schaller was even more blunt, such as in his 1980 article in *Diplomatic History* on Stilwell's relief, "The Command Crisis in China, 1944: A Road Not Taken." Schaller finds President Roosevelt's behavior contradictory and self-defeating, noting that "this continued pattern of approaching the 'brink' and then retreating could only affirm Chiang's conviction that America could not abandon him. While he may have been only partly aware of its implications, Roosevelt's rejection of Gen. George C. Marshall's stiff response demonstrated the American patron's peculiar vassalage to its Asian clients."[27] John K. Fairbank, the dean of American historians of China, was skeptical of conflating history with what-ifs, and he wrote in a sharp review that asking why American military leaders didn't look further ahead and establish postwar policies in China "is a bit like asking why firemen did not deliver the babies in a burning maternity hospital."[28]

In the 1990s, historical studies of World War II and the CBI theater became more balanced and insightful as untapped resources and materials became available that helped to refine and narrow the discussion into more specialized and thoughtful assessments. A major factor in helping to refine the discussion of Stilwell, Chiang Kai-shek, and U.S. policy was the groundbreaking scholarship of Chen Jian in the 1990s. By using Chinese-language sources Chen was able to conclusively demonstrate in a series of articles and books covering the late 1940s that the Chinese Communist Party had no intention of pursuing close relations with the United States and that the "lost chance" of Truman and Mao reaching some sort of stable political arrangement was fantasy. Chen's work decisively ended discussion of what-ifs of the 1940s and refocused research into the complex U.S. relationship with the Nationalist government, which for all its flaws was the only possible ally for the United States.[29] The end of the "lost chance" narrative was a tremendous boost to researchers because it cleared away many of the political implications of their work and allowed for increased specialization. The increased specialization of many recent studies has allowed scholars to slowly close gaps in our understanding of the CBI theater and Stilwell's role. The best example of this trend has been the production of high-quality, professionally researched studies of intelligence. William R. Peers, an American Army officer who later led the My Lai inquiry, published an account of intelligence and guerrilla operations in Burma in *Behind the Burma Road*.[30] Peer's first-person account was buttressed by another memoir, *Behind Japanese Lines: With the OSS in Burma* by Richard Dunlop, but these accounts relied largely on memories rather than archival records.[31] Nevertheless, these two books depicted a highly innovative campaign of sabotage and intelligence gathering carried out against the Japanese in northern Burma by local tribes led by American officers. In the 1990s, specialized studies based on archival research began to appear on this topic, such as David W. Hogan's *U.S. Army Special Operations in World War II* and later academic works, *The OSS in Burma: Jungle War against the Japanese* by Troy Sacquety and *OSS in China: Prelude to Cold War* by Maochun Yu.[32] Since the 1990s, among historians of China, there has been a sharp increase in interest in the 1937–1945 Sino-Japanese War, with many historians focusing more on the lives and experiences of ordinary people as well as presenting a more Sino-centric view of the war.[33]

CHAPTER OUTLINE

This book is structured around six chapters, with each chapter designed to highlight a primary issue and difficulty faced in the CBI theater that has been a recurring concern for the U.S. Army since 1945. To make understanding the lessons of the CBI theater clearer, where possible each chapter has a brief section in the conclusion that will examine comparable experiences in Korea, Vietnam, Iraq, and Afghanistan.

Chapters 1 and 2 focus on Stilwell's tenure from February 1942 through May 1943, when he coordinated with senior American policymakers to define his command roles and authority. Chapter 1 examines the period from January 1942 through December 1942, when General Stilwell was initially assigned to the China-Burma-India theater, and it examines the complex roles he was assigned and ambiguous missions he was formally and informally asked to accomplish. During 1942, the U.S. strategic position in the CBI theater was dramatically weakened by the Japanese conquest of Burma, but by the end of the year Stilwell had developed the foundations for both the reconquest of northern Burma and the development of a model to train the Chinese army. From a strategic perspective, the greatest challenge during this period was the poorly conceived and designed mission for Stilwell and the CBI theater. He was tasked by the War Department to "increase the effectiveness of United States assistance to the Chinese government for the prosecution of the war and assist in improving the combat efficiency of the Chinese Army."[34] Chapter 1 develops an understanding of Stilwell's authorities and responsibilities and the poor coordination by Stilwell and senior American policymakers to establish the CBI theater. Chapter 2 focuses on the period from December through May 1943, when American policy in Asia was the subject of a heated debate between Stilwell and his subordinate, Claire Chennault. As Stilwell sought to gain support for a program of military aid and advice to strengthen the Chinese army, Chennault appealed for support to establish American airpower as the primary military force in East Asia, which he argued could inflict heavy losses on the Japanese from bases in China. This debate in the spring of 1943 was a difficult period for Stilwell, who failed to "sell" his desired programs to national leaders, particularly President Roosevelt, who looked to Chennault's program as an opportunity to accomplish larger national objectives at a lower cost. Stilwell's difficulty in understanding the motivations of political figures was a major problem for his effort to gain support for his initiatives. Chapter 2 highlights Stilwell's failure to defend his programs from competitors, who provided American policymakers with alternative plans that were possibly easier, faster, and more desirable from the perspective of Allied relations.

Chapters 3 and 4 explore the period from June 1943 through May 1944, when Stilwell's relations with the British in India and Burma were critically important. Chapter 3 examines June through December 1943 and focuses on Stilwell's effort to more tightly integrate the CBI theater into Allied global strategy, with significant success. After being defeated in the counsels of war in the spring, Stilwell worked to gain a consensus for his strategy to launch a campaign in northern Burma to open the Burma Road, thereby easing the logistics difficulties in the CBI theater. By working with the British and elements within the U.S. Army, he was able to present his policies as the product of consensus, and he linked his desire to attack northern Burma with larger American and Allied strategic goals.

Chapter 3 demonstrates that with improved staff support, particularly from political advisors, Stilwell was able to reshape and improve his standing among senior leaders, and by the end of 1943 he had successfully linked his desired plans to take the offensive in Burma to Allied global efforts. Chapter 4 focuses on the campaign in northern Burma from December 1943 through May 1944. In this campaign, Stilwell commanded large numbers of Chinese troops, who had been retained and reequipped by the U.S. Army, and these forces were central to his plans to reopen the Burma Road and provide a land route for supplies to reach China by attacking from northeast India. Stilwell's force also included small numbers of Americans, as well as British contingents, and in addition to his command of battlefield operations, he was continually forced to manage the needs and be aware of the divergent interests of his fragile coalition. While Stilwell achieved notable victories and proved that his conception of building Chinese army forces into units capable of fighting and defeating the Japanese was sound, he continued to face severe political difficulties with his British military commander, Lord Mountbatten, and with Chiang Kai-shek. Chapter 4's examination of the north Burma campaign demonstrates that although Stilwell achieved great successes at the tactical and operational level, he was unable to build on these achievements and antagonized both his British and Chinese partners.

Chapters 5 and 6 examine the spring and summer of 1944, as Stilwell was drawn deeper into Chinese politics. Chapter 5 also focuses on operational and tactical issues in the CBI theater and examines the campaign against Japanese forces in northern Burma attacking from China. In contrast to the direct American control of operations in the drive from India into Burma, the offensive launched from China was explicitly designed to have a "light footprint" of American control. While this model for providing military advice and assistance was partly a result of logistics, it was also a way to remove Americans from difficult military and political decision making and thereby minimize friction and de-escalate disputes. Despite these intentions, the campaign of the Chinese Expeditionary Force (CEF) similarly led to intense political maneuvering and negotiation between the Chinese and Americans regarding logistics, air support, time lines, and objectives. Chapter 5's examination of the offensive from Yunnan into

Burma demonstrates a contrasting approach to Allied leadership from the campaign in north Burma, with minimizing friction and de-escalating disputes taking priority, at the expense of battlefield effectiveness. Last, chapter 6 focuses on the China theater, which was only a part of the CBI theater but became increasingly important in the summer and fall of 1944, as Chinese forces suffered a series of defeats. The collapse of Chinese forces in key sectors was a major setback for efforts against Japan, but they also presented Stilwell with an opportunity to gain greater influence and achieve his goal of improving the effectiveness of the Chinese army. Rather than be drawn into complex military and political debates in China, Stilwell steadfastly refused to support regional leaders with American weapons or training despite corruption, incompetence, and authoritarian tendencies in Chaing Kai-shek's "national" government. This decision again highlights Stilwell's limited political awareness, which led to neglected strategic opportunities while continuing the theme that despite difficulties with the British and Chinese, it was Stilwell's interactions with American policymakers in Washington that was decisive for his command.

★ **CHAPTER 1** ★

MISSION OBJECTIVES AND MILITARY AUTHORITY

January–December 1942

My only objective is the effective prosecution of the war, our common cause.
—Gen. Joseph W. Stilwell[1]

AMERICAN INVOLVEMENT IN the CBI theater was profoundly shaped, and in many ways hindered, by a complex and cumbersome alignment of authority and responsibility. Military leaders, most notably Joseph Stilwell, as well as civilian officials such as the ambassador to China, Clarence E. Gauss, were tasked with a wide range of actions that included coordinating overlapping roles with allies, integrating multiple U.S. federal government agencies, and leading the fractious military services. From January through the fall of Burma in April 1941, Stilwell's mission was poorly defined and centered on working with Chiang Kai-shek. Between May and August, Stilwell took a more active role and slowly developed a plan to achieve more limited objectives against the Japanese in Burma. Finally, between September and December, senior policymakers in Washington, D.C., grudgingly gave their support to a limited plan to retake northern Burma and train a select group of Chinese army forces.

The lack of a clear, concise, and actionable mission in the CBI theater has become an increasingly common aspect of American military operations. Rather than territorial objectives or a goal to force unconditional surrender, most post-1945 military operations have been designed around more subjective goals and fluid metrics of success. Most notably in Iraq and Afghanistan, military forces have been called upon to support a wide range of local military and civil authorities and to engage in "nation-building" programs. Another characteristic of the CBI theater that has been replicated in recent conflicts is that while the initial definition of the role of a senior American officer in CBI was defined by Chiang Kai-shek and President Roosevelt, the evolution of the CBI structure after May was often shaped by Stilwell himself. The ambiguities of the CBI theater, its distance from Washington, and its complex command arrangements gave military officers an opportunity to take a more active role in defining their mission. Stilwell did not have a sophisticated theory of organizing the CBI theater, but he was able to slowly build a credible framework of action that won the acceptance, if not the enthusiasm, of political leaders. As a result of nearly a year of refinement and increased specification, Joseph Stilwell had achieved the creation of a functioning headquarters with a direct mission, but the impact of delays and miscommunications were felt for years. A military officer more politically attuned or more capable than Stilwell could have worked through these organizational issues more quickly and with less bitterness. The initial mistrust generated by eleven months of political and military disputes would hinder all later actions in the CBI theater, and a significant amount of time had been lost, which would delay major combat operations in Burma until 1944.

INITIAL PLANS FOR THE CBI THEATER

In early 1941, American goals for China and East and Southeast Asia more broadly were shaped more by the personal feelings of political leaders, most notably President Franklin D. Roosevelt, than by clearly stated diplomatic or military strategic guidance. The Japanese invasion of Manchuria in 1931, the Shanghai conflict between China and Japan in 1932, and the Japanese invasion of China in 1937 had increased tension between the United States and Japan, but this had not been translated into strong

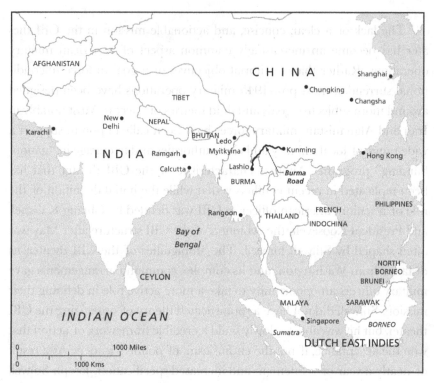

Map 1. The Yunnan Campaign

political support for the Nationalist Chinese government. The American public was sympathetic to Chinese suffering, and American media prominently featured the writings of missionaries, pro-China lobbyists like Henry Luce, and tear-jerker Hollywood films to highlight China's plight, but the general mood of the 1930s was that the United States should remain uninvolved in global affairs.[2] This general sympathy meant that critical stories by reporters in the field, such as of the widespread corruption and smuggling along the vital Burma Road, were often either heavily rewritten or not published by their U.S. newspapers.[3] Problematic statements by Chiang Kai-shek—for example sending a personal congratulations to Hitler after the Austrian Anschluss, endorsing German policies in the 1930s, and repeated attempts to forge a close partnership with Nazi leaders in the late 1930s—were largely unreported.[4]

American military understanding of what would become the CBI theater was limited, with solid intelligence on Chinese issues but more basic knowledge of India and Burma. The U.S. Army Military Intelligence Division had established a Chinese-language training program in 1919 to prepare officers for assignments in the Peking embassy.[5] By the 1930s, a well-informed cadre of Chinese-speaking American military officers were producing extensive intelligence reports, many of them written by Col. Joseph Stilwell, who served as military attaché to the embassy from 1935 to 1939. These reports highlighted a wide range of crippling problems within the Nationalist military and local Chinese forces in unit training and basic tactics.[6] General planning documents produced by the Army staff in June 1940 had placed China in equal priority with support of the British Commonwealth, but without the commitment of definite resources these plans were only a statement of priorities, with no actual policy of providing military aid.[7] The U.S. government's first direct step to assist the United Kingdom and China began with the passage of the Lend-Lease Act in March 1941. By August, the U.S. Army had formed the American Military Mission to China (AMMISCA) to assess and study the possibility of arms transfers and potentially military advisory programs.[8] AMMISCA was commanded by Brig. Gen. John L. Magruder, who had served several tours in the embassy in Beijing. AMMISCA established offices in Chungking, Washington, D.C., and Rangoon (Yangon) to coordinate Chinese requests and the shipment of military supplies in coordination with the British administration in Burma. Initial reports prepared by General Magruder and his staff did not envision a sustained relationship between the U.S. military and Nationalist Chinese forces or an enduring U.S. Army presence in continental Asia. Worn down by years of fighting and politically fractured into regional units, Chinese forces were poorly trained and tactically passive.[9] Magruder, a former attaché in Beijing, was personally skeptical of the announcements of Chinese political and military leaders, who frequently fed stories of great victories over Japanese forces to sympathetic and unquestioning American reporters.[10] Magruder noted, "It is a known fact that the Chinese are great believers in the world of make-believe, and they frequently shut their eyes to hard and unpleasant actualities, preferring rather to indulge their fancy in flattering but fictitious symbols, which they regard as more real than cold facts."[11] Despite General Magruder's skepticism and the lack of indications that military aid would achieve results, American military aid did begin to arrive in the fall of 1941. After shipment across the Pacific, American goods were offloaded in Rangoon, moved by narrow-gauge rail north to Lashio, and then loaded into trucks to be driven seven hundred miles to Kunming, with deliveries reaching a total of nine thousand tons in February 1942.[12]

The Japanese attack on Pearl Harbor on December 7, 1941, radically increased the importance of supporting Britain's position in Asia and China's military capabilities, and subsequent Japanese campaigns in Southeast Asia would make the region a major concern for policymakers in Washington, D.C., during the winter of 1941–1942. But faced with threats to Atlantic shipping from U-boats, German attacks in the Mediterranean, and the need to support the Soviet Union, few American combat units or equipment would be available to directly support Chinese efforts, despite a string of Japanese victories. President Roosevelt, though, desired an American military presence, even if it was primarily symbolic, in China. While Roosevelt's vision was not supported by other Allied leaders, such as Churchill or Stalin, senior American military leaders saw a limited role for China.[13] Secretary of War Henry Stimson envisioned an American role in China that would fulfill the overall American objective of keeping Nationalist Chinese forces at war, which would both tie down the nearly three dozen Japanese army divisions in China and Manchuria and theoretically provide a base of operations for American forces in East Asia.[14] With little war material immediately available for China, Roosevelt was instrumental in having Chiang appointed as the supreme commander, China theater, which provided a grandiose title but no direct control over Allied units operating in China.[15] The title also added to the growing confusion over authority and responsibility of Allied forces in East and Southeast Asia and highlighted Roosevelt's willingness to let political gestures lead to significant military problems. Chiang Kai-shek also sought to increase the American military role in China and appealed to the American ambassador for the dispatch of a new military mission to Chungking.[16]

No senior U.S. Army officer was interested in leading a poorly defined and likely frustrating mission to China, which promised none of the glory or autonomy that came with commanding an American combat unit. Stimson and Marshall attempted to entice Lt. Gen. Hugh A. Drum into the assignment to China despite his lack of experience in the region. He was, however, a savvy bureaucratic operator, and Drum noted the subtle differences in guidance he had received from Stimson and Marshall, as well as the overlapping responsibilities in China that would be performed by units not under his direct control.[17] In a memo on January 5, 1942, Drum accurately described the concept of the mission to China-Burma-India and East Asia as "nebulous, uncertain, and indefinite."[18] Army war planners assigned to assess methods to support China failed to clarify the key issues and could only suggest that an American commander in the region take "such steps as may be practicable and are consistent with other commitments" in other theaters.[19] Even historians sympathetic to Marshall concede that the guidance and command arrangements had "certain inconsistencies" that any career Army officer would find problematic.[20] Drum was also aware that logistical concerns would be a defining constraint for any U.S. policy in the China region. The massive disconnect between American goals for Chinese forces and the limited amount of supplies that could be carried over the fragile Burma Road also caught Drum's attention as an inherent flaw in U.S. war plans. Pentagon planners were already aware that difficulties in China were partly geographic and partly due to the corruption of the Nationalist government.[21] Drum argued that success in the theater would be largely a result of "the development of a Service of Supply, from India, through Burma, sufficient to deliver a greatly increased tonnage into the Chinese theater" that could support more capable ground forces.[22] With no clear mandate of authority and the prospect that the theater would be crippled by poor logistics, Drum declined the command.

On January 14, 1942, Gen. George C. Marshall, chief of staff of the U.S. Army, nominated an old friend, Joseph Stilwell, for the vaguely defined position as commander of American forces in the China-Burma-India theater. Stilwell had been assigned to command an American Corps in North Africa, but Stilwell had a unique background for a senior American Army officer, which made him the only real option for the CBI theater.[23] Stilwell had extensive experience in Asia, and after service in the Philippines during the 1920s, he had served in the 15th Infantry Regiment in Tianjin, where for eight months he had been in the same regiment as then Lt. Col. George Marshall.[24] Chinese-language training was mandatory in the 15th Infantry, and while most officers only learned a few phrases, Stilwell embraced the opportunity to expand his understanding of Chinese culture and customs.[25] Stilwell then served under Marshall at Fort Benning as a key member of the Army's Infantry School. Fluent in Chinese and a skilled tactician, Stilwell was assigned as the military attaché in Beijing in the 1930s and observed closely Japanese military operations and Chinese military dysfunction.[26] While in China, Stilwell also developed a critical attitude toward the British presence in Asia and forged his perception that the British were "smugly complacent about their own superiority."[27] Marshall described Stilwell to British field marshal Sir John Dill as the right man for the job in China: "he possibly understands more of how to do business with the Chinese, particularly in regard to military matters, than any other individual in this country."[28] Throughout the war, Marshall would remain strongly supportive of Stilwell and overlooked any adverse reports of his decisions or behavior.[29]

Unlike Drum, Stilwell unwisely did not play an active role in clarifying his guidance and the mission parameters before leaving Washington, although some progress was made by the newly formed joint U.S./U.K. Combined Chiefs of Staff (CCS). The CCS was formed after the Arcadia Conference in December 1941 and January 1942 in Washington, D.C., and it would emerge as yet another source of directives to senior American military leaders already responsive to U.S. political guidance and War Department orders.[30] Stilwell did recognize the distinctive military/political nature of his assignment and asked for John Paton Davies, a State Department officer he had known in China during the 1930s, to serve as a member of his military staff.[31] In his official orders on February 2, 1942, Stilwell was "designated as Chief of Staff to the Supreme Commander of the Chinese Theater and upon reporting to the Supreme Commander, you are, in addition, appointed Commanding General of the United States Army Forces in the Chinese Theater of Operations, Burma, and India."[32] General Marshall clarified in a message the same day that in this position Stilwell's role was to "increase the effectiveness of United States assistance to the Chinese government for the prosecution of the war and to assist in improving the combat efficiency of the Chinese Army."[33]

Both goals were subjective, with effectiveness and efficiency determined by a wide range of factors such as training, equipment, and leadership, none of which would be under Stilwell's direct authority. The uncertainty of Stilwell's mission guidance was a result of his own reticence to proactively shape the mission, differing assumptions among senior American policymakers, and a lack of firm organizational guidance from the U.S. Army. With American war plans and command structures still being in created in Washington, Army war planners, a nascent United States Joint Chiefs of Staff, and the Anglo-American Combined Chief of Staff were all scrambling for office space and personnel. The U.S. Joint History Office official history of the period notes that due to these administrative issues, "Stilwell embarked on his mission with virtually no strategic or operational guidance. His only instructions were a generalized set of orders issued by the War Department early in February 1942."[34] The broader strategic intent of American, and to some extent British, policy regarding China was even more vague. The CCS used oblique language to identify "several things which are necessary," regarding China, including "closer and more effective liaison with the Generalissimo," and an "increase in Chinese combat strength."[35] None of these vague bureaucratic phrases had any precise goals or any associated plans for logistics, specific instructions or criteria upon which commanders in the China area could base their decisions.

Increasing the Chinese combat strength and improving the efficiency of Chinese forces was a goal that American military planners regarded as difficult, if not impossible. General Magruder reported that military aid would not turn the tide against the Japanese and appealed for more limited objectives. On February 10, 1942, Magruder sent a scathing assessment to the War Department, stating that "assistance, no matter how great, is not to be regarded as having added substantially to China's striking power. The brunt of any offensive warfare in China must be borne by foreign troops sent there by Allied powers, and the only thing which we can expect from the large resources of Chinese manpower is that they will occupy areas evacuated by the enemy and consolidate advances won by others."[36] Pessimism among Americans on the ground in China, Burma, and India was not limited to military personnel. Ambassador to China

Clarence E. Gauss, a career foreign service officer who had extensive experience in China, also saw any American effort in the region to be problematic. Gauss was a well-regarded foreign service official who had worked his way up from being a clerk in the consular service. He had first been stationed in China in 1907 and had returned for multiple postings, giving him an expansive knowledge of local and national Chinese politics.[37] Gauss' reports to Washington and his dealings with Chinese were cautious, and the embassy in Chungking regularly filed reports about the increasingly powerful reactionary elements of Chiang Kai-shek's Nationalist Party and the role of political violence by Chiang's associates such as Dai Li.[38] In the spring of 1942, Gauss reported to Secretary of State Cordell Hull that "China is to us a minor asset at this time. Our task is to prevent her becoming a liability and to raise the value of the asset so far as possible, to encourage resistance and to increase its effectiveness." Gauss stated that American policy and military plans should be formed only after "bearing in mind the limitations on what we may reasonably expect from this country."[39]

Despite the concerns of senior American military leaders and State Department officials, American public support for China was high, and Stilwell overlooked a clear indicator of the political support for China while in Washington. At the same time Stilwell's mission was being developed and structured, China requested a $500 million loan from the United States, and despite strong misgivings by Treasury Department officials and others in the U.S. government, it was approved by the House via voice vote and unanimously approved by the Senate with no debate.[40] The loan had no conditions or specific terms for repayment, and it was a clear indicator of the strong support for China and the limited desire of the public or American politicians to scrutinize the relationship. Stilwell was more attentive, although cynical, about the idiosyncratic role President Roosevelt played in setting military policy, noting that he was a "rank amateur in all military matters," as well as a man who made decisions impulsively.[41] After meeting Roosevelt personally, Stilwell described him in his diary as "unimpressive" and noted Harry Hopkins' unclear role in shaping Roosevelt's thoughts, as well as Hopkins' appearance as a "strange, gnome-like creature."[42] In his brief six weeks in Washington, Stilwell missed an opportunity to better understand the mood, concerns, and flow of policy-making, and he formed sharply critical opinions of many of the key individuals that would profoundly shape his mission.

On February 11, 1942, Stilwell and a small staff departed Washington for China, with uncertain authority, uncertain roles, and ambiguous goals. Stilwell had failed to get his superiors to coherently structure his tasks and align them with broader U.S. interests, and he had little instruction on how to serve as chief of staff to Chiang Kai-shek. This clear failure of guidance would set the table for four months of poorly coordinated and often futile efforts in CBI.

FLAWED COMMAND STRUCTURES AND THE FAILURE IN BURMA

The first four months of Stilwell's tenure in CBI, from late February through mid-May, would see his command role and the larger U.S. effort in the region faced with insurmountable challenges. Poor coordination, vague instructions, a lack of trust between Allied forces, and limited experience all contributed to the ill-fated Burma campaign of early 1942. The resounding defeat of the Allies in Burma helped clarify what was possible and provide the motivation to streamline the mission of the theater. The lessons of the retreat through Burma would profoundly shape Stilwell's conception of his role, and in the summer and fall of 1942 he would work to ensure that what he saw as the lessons of the spring catastrophe were learned and that his authority would be clarified and strengthened.

While Stilwell was en route to the CBI theater, he was given additional personnel for his mission. Col. Clayton L. Bissell was assigned as the senior aviation officer on Stilwell's staff, and he would prove invaluable in improving the organization and structure of air forces in the area. Bissell had a distinguished record in the air service and had served as the aide to controversial aviation pioneer Brig. Gen. William "Billy" Mitchell. Logistics was understood to be especially important in CBI operations, and Brig. Gen. Raymond A. Wheeler was assigned to lead the services of supply in CBI. Wheeler had been assigned to Iran, where he worked to increase Lend-Lease shipments to the Soviet Union, so he was experienced in operating with limited resources and working in an austere environment.[43] These two officers would be integrated into a group of roughly two dozen people that Stilwell had selected to form his initial staff.[44] With few exceptions, the small group of officers assigned to Stilwell in February 1942 would remain the senior leaders of the CBI theater throughout his tenure, and they remained an extremely cohesive and loyal group. Last, Joseph Stilwell received a third star, becoming a lieutenant general on February 25, 1942, giving him a bit more stature and influence to deal with British and Chinese partners. This additional support did not make up for the fact that Stilwell would lack any American ground forces to command and would have to use his limited air assets and supplies and leverage his position between the British and Chinese to make any progress in achieving his goals.

Japanese probing attacks into Burma, coming through Thailand, began in late January 1942, and with the fall of Singapore on February 15, it was clear that Japanese forces would soon be attacking the main port of Burma, Rangoon, in force.[45] The collapse of American, British, Dutch, and Australian (ABDA) command in the Dutch East Indies (Indonesia) had led to a new directive of the CCS making the British general Archibald Wavell the "Supreme Commander, India," which had authority over Burma. American forces in India and Burma consequently reported through Stilwell to Wavell.[46] This decision was made without any input from Stilwell. When Stilwell officially arrived in the CBI theater on February 24, 1942, landing in Karachi, the situation in Burma had degraded rapidly and Japanese forces were rapidly advancing on the main port of Rangoon. Stilwell continued his flight eastward, reaching Lashio in northern Burma, where Chiang Kai-shek and General Chennault were waiting to coordinate Chinese participation in the defense of Burma. Stilwell had briefly met Chiang in 1938, and from their initial meetings in early 1942 it was clear that a difference of personality types would be a constant challenge.[47] Stilwell's aide remarked, "Gen. Stilwell and Generalissimo Chiang Kai-shek were at odds, not only temperamentally, but politically, philosophically in various areas. Gen. Stilwell had very, very high standards of character, integrity, high integrity, high intelligence, and was forthright, impatient, frank, and on the other hand the Generalissimo was a politician. He liked to maneuver people."[48] Stilwell was also at odds with the

British, if not on specific tactics, in temperament. In a report to the War Department, Stilwell lambasted British officers as more focused on the "maintenance of so-called standards of the personal life of an officer," with polo and a retinue of native servants, and that combat operations were seen as a nuisance that "upset the leisurely routine of Empire as prescribed by Kipling."[49] Stilwell also believed the British dismissal of Chinese offers of military forces to supplement the Burma defenses in December 1941 was a decisive mistake, because it robbed planners of time to integrate Chinese forces and caused a lingering diplomatic resentment by the Chinese, which continued to resonate throughout the spring campaign.[50] Less than two weeks after Stilwell arrived in theater, Rangoon fell to the Japanese on March 8, 1942, which meant that the primary supply route for the Burma Road had been severed, and any supplies for China would now need to be flown into Lashio and transferred to trucks.[51]

The fall of south Burma did provide Stilwell the opportunity to have AMMISCA, which had now lost its major base, moved under his authority, and Chennault agreed to move his American Volunteer Group under Stilwell's command as an Army organization.[52] Stilwell's role was also strengthened because he saw an opportunity to use his position as a buffer and intermediary between the British and the Chinese in Burma. Chinese troops entered Burma in late January to assist with the British defenses, but British suspicions that Chinese troops would be poorly disciplined and commanded were matched by Chinese suspicions that the British would use Chinese forces to absorb the brunt of Japanese attacks.

A private message from President Roosevelt to Chiang on March 11, 1942, asking the Generalissimo to "explore the possibility" of placing Chinese troops under Stilwell was sufficient to cut through further political maneuvering.[53] Chiang Kai-Shek authorized six Chinese divisions to serve under Stilwell's command in Burma, with Stilwell reporting to the British general Harold Alexander, and further additions ultimately raised the Chinese contribution to three armies: the Fifth, Sixth, and Sixty-Sixth.[54] With Chinese divisions and British reinforcements, Allied planners hoped that defenses in mid-Burma could hold off the Japanese until the monsoon made further movement difficult, but the plan to have Stilwell command Chinese troops quickly ran into practical difficulties. Chinese divisions were smaller than British and American divisions, which have more than ten thousand soldiers at full strength. Chinese units more often had roughly six thousand soldiers, and they lacked their own supply units, vehicles, or other equipment that could enable rapid movement.[55] Firepower was also extremely limited, with the Chinese Fifth Army of three divisions having only twelve 75-mm howitzers at the start of the campaign, with limited ammunition.[56]

A more enduring problem was that although Chiang Kai-shek had publicly given Stilwell authority in Burma, telephone communications directly from Chiang to the Chinese commanders superseded Stilwell's orders.[57] Chiang's directives called for a defensive approach to military operations, based in large part on Chiang's flawed understanding of the tactics developed by German advisors in China during the 1930s. This often meant attacks ordered by Stilwell never occurred, and unexpected withdrawals made organizing a coherent defensive line impossible.[58] Chiang even specified fixed defensive positions for Chinese divisions, even though these locations were often widely dispersed, with no reserve forces to counterattack Japanese flanking maneuvers.[59] This micromanagement reached such an extent that during the Burma campaign, Chiang sent specific instructions on deployments for the handful of Chinese tanks deployed.[60] Stilwell's aide, Richard M. Young, who was ethnically Chinese, remarked that Chiang's commanders were under orders to report Stilwell's instructions and "to communicate to Chungking by radio and by telephone to tell the Generalissimo what the orders were. If the Generalissimo said, 'Okay, carry them out,' then the commanders will carry them out, but if the Generalissimo withheld or said no or delayed his approval then the commanders would also delay in the field. And you know for a tactical situation that's disastrous."[61]

British accounts shared this conclusion, noting that even if Chiang concurred with Stilwell's orders, the slow process of sending radio messages to Chungking often resulted in a "fatal delay in the execution of urgent movements."[62] General Wavell, in a personal message to Churchill, noted tersely, "Chinese co-operation not easy."[63] Stilwell wrote scathing messages to Washington highlighting the continual interference by Chiang, noting that Chinese commanders could "bypass me for anything they want to do and then blame me for the result."[64] Chiang's habit of subdividing military organizations, meant to limit threats to his sole authority, also meant that messages sent by him to one unit might not be sent to other units, adding a further level of confusion and uncertainty.[65] Chiang was unrepentant about his continual meddling in military operations, asserting that his officers had a limited military education and that "knowing their limited capacity, I plan ahead for them."[66] Historical studies of Nationalist Chinese forces during World War II and the later Civil War have highlighted Chiang's frequent micromanagement of operations, from hundreds if not thousands of miles from the front, as a major reason for losses to the Japanese and later the Communists.[67]

The contribution of Chinese troops to the defense of Burma did not slow the relentless Japanese advance, but isolated examples of cooperation and defensive tenacity did provide Stilwell with a template for future operations.[68] On the outskirts of the city of Toungoo, the Chinese 200th Division, commanded by Dai Anlan, whom Stilwell held in high regard, held for ten days against repeated Japanese attacks before withdrawing in good order on March 30.[69] The Chinese forces had been able to move into a defensive position a week ahead of the Japanese advance, giving them time to prepare solidly constructed fortifications and establish effective command and control.[70] Japanese forces were eventually able to wear down the defenders through artillery and air support, but the tenacity of Chinese soldiers impressed Stilwell and the British. Another bright spot was the skill shown by the 38th Division, particularly its commander, Sun Li-jen. On April 19, Sun's forces attacked the Japanese near the oil fields at Yenangyaung, where seven thousand British soldiers and thousands of civilian refugees had been cut off after the Japanese took control of the road network.[71] Disobeying the orders of his Chinese army commander, Sun personally led a regiment in support of a British armored brigade, which reached the encircled British forces, allowing for an evacuation north.[72] For his actions, Sun was awarded an honorary CBE.[73] British general William Slim wrote of Sun, "I found him a good tactician, cool in action, very aggressively minded, and, in my dealings with him, completely straightforward. In addition, he had a great advantage that he spoke good English with a slight American accent, having, as he was rightly proud to tell, been educated at the Virginia Military Institute."[74] Other British observers shared this assessment, finding Sun to be "straightforward and cooperative," and amid the numerous Chinese generals appointed solely due to their loyalty to Chiang Kai-shek, Sun was "certainly the most competent."[75] American assessments concurred and found that throughout the campaign, General Sun demonstrated that he was the most able Chinese commander, but he was limited by Chiang Kai-shek's micromanagement.[76] That Sun had used his initiative to assist the British position was especially noteworthy to American officers, who were incredibly frustrated that Chinese units would not voluntarily assist other units, even in desperate circumstances.[77]

Amid the retreat from central Burma, a Japanese column flanked Allied positions after moving through the Shan states, an area theoretically defended by Chinese troops, and Allied forces began a full-scale retreat in mid-April. A further strain on the command structure occurred due to looting by Chinese troops for supplies and to the continued interference of Chiang Kai-shek.[78] At a conference on April 25, British generals Alexander and Slim, together with Stilwell, agreed that a complete evacuation of Burma was necessary, with troops withdrawing to India and China.[79] Many senior Chinese military leaders took matters into their own hands and attempted to flee, often ahead of their troops. General Lo Chin-ying infamously had his staff commandeer a train at gunpoint, but most Chinese soldiers had to walk out of Burma. Other commanders, such as Dai Anlan, commander of the 200th Division, chose to disregard all instructions from Chiang or Stilwell and move their troops north at their own discretion.[80] On May 5, Stilwell decided to join the exodus of soldiers and exhausted civilians and began walking out of Burma north and west toward the border of India. Stilwell's decision to personally lead a small party on foot, rather than take an airplane to India, has been criticized as a failure to retain command and control, but at this stage of the campaign communications and effective control had largely evaporated and radio contact between units was nonexistent.[81] Capt. Richard Young, a senior aide to Stilwell, believed that the decision to walk out of Burma alongside Allied units was intended to improve the public impressions of senior leaders, who had often been far in the rear during the campaign, and to cultivate an image of Stilwell as more connected to an ordinary

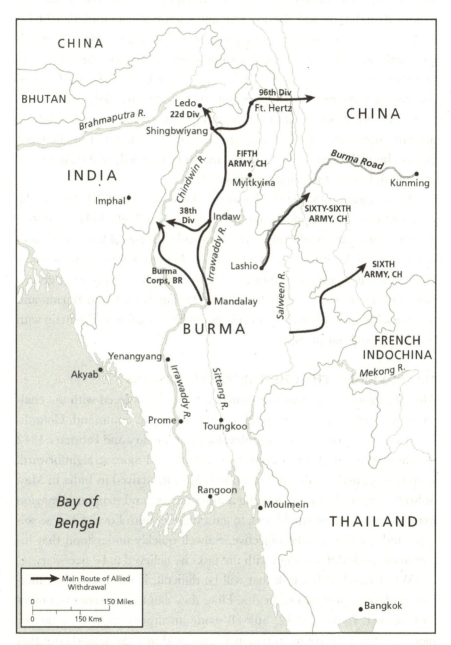

MAP 2. The China-Burma-India Theater

soldier.[82] Stilwell's choice was also motivated by a desire to evacuate the wounded on the last available aircraft, and a sense of camaraderie with his staff.[83] Stilwell's decision to lead a party of 117 men and women through the jungle on a three-week hike was a propaganda coup for his command and sharply contrasted his leadership style with his British and Chinese counterparts. Airdrops of supplies helped keep the party fed, and the support of the local population kept the group safe so that every member of his party survived. After reaching India, Stilwell's frank and public comments about the severe issues in Burma were extolled by the American press as an honest and frank assessment.[84]

More importantly for the future of the war in the CBI theater, the walkout from Burma appears to have crystallized Stilwell's belief that with proper training and leadership, American and Chinese soldiers could function in the jungle. Stilwell believed that with better equipment, more coordinated aerial supply operations, and a network of friendly local groups providing assistance, it would be possible to march back into Burma and take back lost ground, and this deeply embedded belief would remain with Stilwell throughout the war.

MANEUVERING THE CHINESE INTO DECISIONS

After the disastrous retreat from Burma, Stilwell was faced with the challenge of redefining the possibilities and goals of his command. Complicated and overly optimistic plans developed in January and February 1942 in Washington had been overtaken by events, and more straightforward, simpler objectives needed to be defined. After he arrived in India in May, Stilwell's emphasis was on creating a more narrow and structured mission mandate in which he would seek to gain tighter control over Chinese soldiers and a more specific objective. Stilwell quickly understood that his command tools did not align with the tasks he believed to be necessary.

When faced with a task that will be difficult, if not impossible, military leaders employ two strategies. First, they can ask for more resources and support. In May 1942, Stilwell made an urgent request for one or more American divisions to regain Burma and provide a solid core that could "aid me in organizing Chinese forces for decisive offensive operations."[85] This appeal, although logical from Stilwell's perspective, was impractical in the context of overall U.S. resources in 1942. General Marshall responded that this request must be denied on logistics grounds, noting that "the shipping required to transport one or more American divisions to your command and to support them once in your area would involve an undertaking which we are simply not repeat not in a position to make."[86] Second, when faced with overwhelming challenges, military commanders can redefine their mission and objectives. Stilwell's redefinition of his mission to encompass more focused and clearly defined tasks was most clearly seen in his enthusiastic development of plans to equip and train Chinese soldiers with American personnel and then lead these soldiers in a campaign to take back northern Burma.

In contemporary American military operations, military assistance and advisory efforts are common, but in 1942 this was a bold and risky plan. The U.S. Army had some experience training local troops in the Philippines, and the Philippine Scouts, a unit composed of Filipino troops led by American officers, were a reliable and effective unit that fought well against the Japanese in 1941 and 1942. Despite this experience, the Philippine example was not directly applicable because it was a traditional colonial approach to building local military forces. Taking direct control of Chinese military forces, installing American officers, and commanding these forces in battle was not an option that would be approved either by Chiang Kai-shek or by President Roosevelt, who was extremely careful to differentiate American policies from European colonialism. Stilwell also lacked sufficient American personnel for effective command and control. Stilwell needed a way to increase his command authority over Chinese units and increase their military effectiveness, but without requiring a large American Army presence. On April 28, Stilwell requested that a training program for Chinese forces be initiated in India, and the War Department approved provided the "project was feasible and was concurred in by General Wavell."[87]

On June 3, Stilwell flew to Chungking and presented his plan to dramatically reshape the Nationalist forces, purging numerous high commanders, condensing dozens of divisions into more effective and fully manned units, and promoting younger officers.[88] While Stilwell's proposals made military sense, he must have known there was little chance of any

Chinese leader acquiescing to reforms that would impact the byzantine political structure Chiang had created. But it did provide him with political cover. It demonstrated to American policymakers that he had attempted to function in the role of Allied chief of staff to Chiang and increase the effectiveness of the Chinese army as a whole, but his plans and advice were rejected. Just weeks after his proposal had been rejected by Chiang, Stilwell's effort to refine his role in the CBI theater was also given a boost when Chiang Kai-shek made a political mistake and overplayed his hand with President Roosevelt. In mid-June, Chiang's effort to have China added to the Combined Chiefs of Staff was rebuffed for diplomatic reasons (the USSR declined to join the group) and because Chiang seemed less interested in developing strategy and more interested in increasing allocations of Lend-Lease supplies. In late June, the U.S. War Department ordered aviation assets that had been assigned to Stilwell to redeploy to the Middle East, where German units were driving on the Suez Canal. Faced with what he believed to be a personal affront rather than an action driven by military circumstances, Chiang delivered an ultimatum to Stilwell for transmission to Washington. The "Three Demands" stated that at a minimum, three American divisions must be assigned to India, five hundred planes be available in China for military operations, and that five thousand tons be flown into China monthly.[89] Not only were these demands outlandish, but Chiang wanted it done quickly, with the U.S. planes in China within sixty days, tonnage increases starting in August, and U.S. troops in India no later than September 1942.[90]

Stilwell wisely demurred from endorsing the message, recognizing that Chiang's request would be perceived as excessive by Washington.[91] At the same time, opinions of China's worth were shifting. Secretary of War Henry Stimson, who had received Magruder's extremely critical reports as well as frank assessments by Stilwell, increasingly viewed Chiang and his government as "riddled with graft and personal power politics" that shared little with American war aims.[92] Stimson sought to encourage Stilwell to maintain his composure and keep pushing for changes, writing in a personal message in mid-June, "you need have no anxiety as to the support of your own government. You accepted an offer of duty which lesser men would have tried to avoid and have shown the utmost courage and skill against impossible odds."[93] Chiang's assertive message, combined with sober assessments of China's military capabilities, created a feeling that Chiang had overplayed his hand with Washington. Chiang had also isolated himself from the British. In April 1942, Chiang had met Indian Nationalist leaders, including Mahatma Gandhi, in a move that was widely seen as a rebuff of the British.[94] Ambassador Gauss reported that senior Chinese officials routinely made "embarrassingly frank derogatory statements concerning the British."[95] Chiang's behavior left him without friends during the summer of 1942, leaving an opening for Stilwell.

Capitalizing on Chiang's error, Stilwell seized the chance to offer a compromise solution that would benefit him and his plans. On July 18, Stilwell laid out a plan to attack Burma with a force driving southwest from Kunming along the Burma Road and another pincer moving south from India.[96] Stilwell carefully established that the requirements for the attack were achievable in the context of logistics constraints, with two Chinese divisions in India and twelve in Yunnan, which would all receive U.S. support.[97] This plan could provide Chiang a face-saving escape from his "Three Demands," because if he agreed, it would be a sign that he would accept more limited and focused American activity, rather than simply have the United States provide massive amounts of aircraft and supplies. Stilwell timed his proposal to be released in late July, when presidential envoy Lauchlin B. Currie had arrived in Chungking for a three-week assessment of the theater and its command relationships. Currie's role was ambiguous and was part of Roosevelt's habit of using personal representatives, who in the words of Secretary of War Stimson "were usually easy dupes of the wonderfully charming circle around the throne at Chungking."[98] Stilwell described him as naïve and like a "5th grade boy ... [who] jumps from one subject to another" and doesn't really understand the key issues.[99] Currie had also developed the view in 1941 that because of China's dependence on the United States, "it is not anticipated that any difficulty of non-co-operation will be experienced," and to fit this mental schema he ascribed most issues to the U.S. military personnel rather than political or strategic differences.[100] With Currie available as a messenger, Chiang grabbed the political life raft that Stilwell had offered him and accepted the proposal on July 29 in an attempt to demonstrate that he was committed to the war and accepted his role in American offensive plans. Stilwell had now achieved one of his primary objectives and had been able to cajole and coerce Chiang Kai-shek into making a firm commitment on the record, in front of a presidential envoy, that the goal was to retake northern Burma through a two-pronged attack under his leadership.

With renewed political capital, Stilwell now began to place more effort on strengthening the organizational and administrative foundations of his position. An assessment of the Burma campaign prepared by Stilwell's staff concluded that while many Chinese soldiers had performed bravely and several commanders had demonstrated effective leadership, the lack of equipment and especially the limited firepower of Chinese divisions meant that "compared to the Japanese division it is at a hopeless disadvantage."[101] With airlift deliveries via the Himalayan airlift, "the Hump," continuing to fall short of expectations, it was becoming clear that efforts to train and utilize Chinese units would need to be based in India. Two Chinese divisions, the 38th and 22nd, had retreated to India during the withdrawal from Burma, and they were available for training as the nucleus of a larger reform program for the Chinese army. Despite the obvious logistics advantages, basing Chinese troops in India was politically sensitive for the British, who were struggling with Indian Nationalism and limited military resources for their own troops.[102] Stilwell convinced the British to hand over to the U.S. Army a POW camp for Italian prisoners located at Ramgarh in northeast India, where training of Chinese soldiers could be conducted.[103] In his radio messages to the War Department, Stilwell bluntly described his plan for training the Chinese in India as being forced by logistics necessities and that he must "take the Chinese to the weapons since we cannot take the weapons to the Chinese."[104] In private, Stilwell noted that Ramgarh would also be a way to "strengthen our grip on the [Chinese] Army" so that the mistakes of the Burma campaign could be avoided.[105]

The training camp opened on August 26, 1942, and it quickly became the showpiece of Stilwell's command and his training ideas.[106] The heavy investment Stilwell was making in Ramgarh is clearly demonstrated by the fact that he assigned six full colonels and three lieutenant colonels to the training program, a massive percentage of his few senior American officers in the theater in August 1942.[107] Stilwell's concept for this force, codenamed the X Force, was that it would be supplied and equipped by the United States, trained in U.S. Army tactics, and given specialized instruction in combat engineering, field artillery, and medical services.[108] The wide range of schools and specific training programs required to bring Chinese divisions into alignment with American concepts of warfare was staggering. The 38th Division offered courses in jeep driving, radio maintenance, and anti-aircraft firing, alongside training in animal care, engineering, and other programs tailored for operations in north Burma.[109] Jungle training was also a particular focus of General Stilwell, and he gave explicit instructions that Chinese soldiers needed not just familiarization with the jungle environment but training in basic skills like swimming, hunting, and collecting local fruits and vegetables so they could operate independently.[110] In theory, when training was completed, this force would be able to attack northern Burma and defeat the one or two Japanese divisions in the area.

Stilwell's efforts to push forward with the training and support of this small force of Chinese in India was driven by a desire to create a more focused and limited mission. While debates about supplying thirty Chinese divisions continued in Chungking and Washington, Stilwell's Ramgarh camp gave him a prototype he could use to highlight the benefits to be gained by further deliveries of weapons and equipment.

LEVERAGING WASHINGTON FOR SUPPLIES AND ORGANIZATION

Following his successful efforts to increase his political capital in the summer of 1942, Stilwell was in a strengthened position to achieve his goals of increased authority and mission control in the CBI theater. From September through December 1942, he continued to push forward with his program of training Chinese personnel in India, who would be under his direct command. Stilwell also began to tighten the distribution procedures and control over Lend-Lease supplies to ensure he could allocate the type and quantity of equipment throughout the CBI theater. By the fall of 1942, Stilwell began to advocate for a strict quid pro quo basis for negotiation with the Chinese, and access to Lend-Lease supplies would provide him with critical leverage. Last, Stilwell worked to secure American support for his offensive plan in Burma. Chiang's endorsement of the plan in July was useful, but American and British senior leaders at the CCS would need to support the plan with adequate resources for it to be viable.

While Stilwell's concept for training a Chinese force in India was simple, management of the program was challenging. While stationed in India, Chinese officers remained in command of their troops, but these commanders were dependent on the United States and Great Britain for their supplies, equipment, even their military pay, and if they were killed in the line of duty, the U.S. Army would pay a gratuity to their relatives.[111] Chinese units in Ramgarh were designated the "Chinese Army in India" (CAI), and General Stilwell was the senior commander, but day-to-day command of the CAI in Ramgarh fell to Brig. Gen. Hayden L. Boatner, who had a reputation as an intellectual, spoke Chinese, and earned an MA degree in Chinese history from Harvard before the war.[112] One of his first acts as commander was to encourage American personnel to learn the Chinese language and culture to become more effective military partners.[113] At the same time, Boatner shared Stilwell's desire to more closely manage Chinese units, and by retaining control over pay, equipment, and rations, he encouraged his Chinese subordinates to "play ball" with the American program.[114] Like Stilwell, Boatner had no lofty expectations of success and was under no illusions about the difficulties of a Sino-American military partnership.[115] After his initial inspection of the Chinese soldiers in India, Boatner reported that "the condition of the Army troops is pitiful" and that in addition to being disorganized, the men seemed "completely demoralized."[116] Boatner had under him two Chinese division commanders, Sun Li-jen and Liao Yaoxiang, both of whom had been in the Burma campaign and taken their units to India rather than attempt to retreat to China. General Sun had distinguished himself in the Burma campaign, but Liao, who had been educated at a French military academy and spoke to Stilwell in French, had not had a prominent role in the campaign, although he was commended by Americans as one of the few Chinese commanders to be interested in the welfare of his soldiers.[117]

Stilwell's limited pool of American personnel meant that even by the end of 1942 he had fewer than 750 military personnel available to support Chinese ground forces at Ramgarh. Fortunately, the personnel assigned to Ramgarh were often older and intentionally "top-heavy," with 250 American officers and 500 senior enlisted personnel and almost no junior enlisted soldiers. This staff was given the mission of establishing an American training program copied directly from models at Fort Benning. This program included instruction in bayonet attack and hand grenade throwing but also vehicle maintenance and drivers training class.[118] British general William Slim was quick to praise the Ramgarh center and the intensive training methods. He remarked, "Good food, medical care, and regular pay achieved wonders. I have never seen men recover condition as quickly as those Chinese soldiers. Intensive training, under picked American instructors, began on mass-production methods, which were most effective."[119] Training all soldiers together also helped build a sense of camaraderie and ensured an equal level of skills, which eliminated the problem faced by Chinese units that conducted ad hoc forced conscription (*zhua zhuangding*) whereby a unit added untrained and poorly motivated soldiers during operations.[120] Word of the high pay and good conditions in Ramgarh had also reached China, and soldiers were reportedly bribing their commanders to be sent to India for training.[121] With morale and skills improving, Stilwell and Boatner began to develop a small cadre of American officers to be assigned to Chinese units as liaison teams. These liaison teams were given strict instructions that they were not to view themselves as commanding Chinese troops. Boatner's instructions to American liaison personnel were explicit and direct: "You are taking up a very, very difficult assignment.... It will tax your initiative, ingenuity, tact, and spirit of cooperation to the utmost" and that the goal of their efforts was to provide advice and support to their Chinese officer counterparts.[122]

To increase his command autonomy, as well as boost the efficiency of American efforts in the CBI theater, Stilwell kept the American footprint in China deliberately small while expanding the American presence in India. A major reason for this decision was that every American stationed in China required supplies that would have to be flown in via the Hump, so establishing large headquarters elements in Kunming or Chungking would only add to logistical burdens. For the position of Allied chief of staff to Chiang Kai-shek, Stilwell kept his staff to fewer than ten people, not just for logistics reasons but because the Burma campaign had convinced Stilwell of the limited value Chiang Kai-shek placed on his opinions, and the position was essentially a formality by mid-1942. In contrast, the New Delhi headquarters of the CBI theater began to massively expand, as staff support sections were added throughout the fall of 1942. Offices for a theater judge advocate general, surgeon general, quartermaster, finance offices, and other key staff elements were all operational by November 1942.[123] Despite increasing expertise, the challenges of geography and the existing British infrastructure remained an issue. American supplies were often delivered to Karachi, and then had to be transported across India by rail. As Stilwell's administrative structure matured, on September 1, 1942, the CBI theater SOS (Service of Supply), which reported to him, was given authority over Lend-Lease transport and equipment in India. By using shipping priorities and control over inventory, Stilwell attained effective control over all supply shipments into China, which not only streamlined the complicated Lend-Lease organization but provided him with a major point of leverage over the Chinese.

As Stilwell was working to reshape his command by developing his organization and its war plans, senior leaders in Washington had still not responded to either Chiang Kai-shek's truculent Three Demands or the war plan crafted by Stilwell in late July 1942. Army Chief of Staff George Marshall was in favor of rebuffing Chiang's demands and for going ahead on a plan to attack into Burma, with a goal of reopening the Burma Road.[124] Marshall wrote to President Roosevelt personally to argue that in the CBI theater, "our great objective is to re-occupy Burma sufficiently to open up a supply route into China. The British cannot do this alone; the Chinese certainly can't manage it; neither side would admit of leadership by the other. So our only hope as I see it is to secure guidance by an American. He must be a troop leader rather than a negotiator or a supply man who would only serve to promote harmony in Chungking."[125] Marshall also ordered Army planners in the Operations Division to begin work to integrate a Burma operation with other planned offensives for 1943. While Stilwell had the firm backing of General Marshall and Secretary of War Stimson, officials in the State Department and the White House were more skeptical of Stilwell's plans and favored a more conciliatory approach to dealing with Chiang Kai-shek. Complicating the situation was the role of presidential envoy Lauchlin Currie in Chungking. In early August 1942, Stilwell misjudged Currie and, not knowing that Currie had become close to Chiang, had given Currie a memorandum that was sharply critical of the situation in China. In particular, Stilwell stated that "the probabilities are that the CKS regime is playing the USA for suckers; that it will stall and promise, but not do anything; that it is looking for an allied victory without making any further effort on its part to secure it."[126] This broadside attack was not viewed favorably by Currie, who floated the idea of Stilwell's relief, which Marshall dismissed with the support of Secretary of War Stimson. But Currie was successful in blocking Stilwell's plan to put U.S. aid on a quid pro quo basis with Chinese actions.[127]

More significant opposition to Stilwell emerged in the State Department. Stanley Hornbeck, a special advisor to Secretary of State Hull, and Maxwell M. Hamilton, chief of the Division of Far East Affairs, strongly advocated for giving Chiang Kai-shek more support with less American scrutiny over Lend-Lease supplies. In addition to his official position, Hornbeck also had personal connections in Washington and was close friends with prominent columnist Walter Lippman, which would provide him with informal means to shape government policy and public opinion.[128] In the 1930s, Hornbeck had repeatedly clashed with the Army staff, which had wanted to relocate U.S. personnel out of China, and had instead argued that military forces, even if they had no combat potential, were still valuable symbolically and to signal long-term American intentions.[129] Hamilton was a prolific writer of memorandums and assessments, all of which argued for the importance of Chiang Kai-shek and China to the American war effort.[130] Hamilton wrote in July 1942 that after numerous American defeats in Asia following Pearl Harbor, "China has withstood this blow to its morale largely through the great influence and leadership which Generalissimo Chiang Kai-shek—a man who has demonstrated amazing tenacity of purpose—exercises in China." Hamilton dismissed criticisms of the Nationalist government on the grounds that the "Chinese governmental structure is of relatively recent origin" and that this fact led to "more than usual inefficiency in the administration of the central government."[131] Hornbeck and Hamilton also took the position that the threat of Chiang pursuing a separate peace needed to be addressed because it could greatly hinder the Allied war effort, despite Ambassador Gauss reporting that this was an empty threat.[132] During the course of the war, Hornbeck strenuously disagreed with Stilwell's pessimistic reporting and accused him of being a "poor salesman" of policies to support Chiang.[133] While these opponents of Stilwell's plans could not stop the planning momentum in 1942, they continued to write and critique War Department plans and in time would align with airpower supporters to create a significant challenge to Stilwell's authority.

As opinion in Washington coalesced around a Burma campaign, President Roosevelt was now in a position to respond to Chiang's Three Demands. In a message on October 12, 1942, Roosevelt affirmed the importance of Chinese support to the Allied war effort and promised increased air support and expanded airlift operations into China but was vague on specific dates and times of delivery. The demand for American ground forces was rejected, but American personnel would be available to assist, advise, and support Chinese units, such as those at Ramgarh.[134] With both American and Chinese support for a Burma attack, Stilwell could now focus on enlisting vital British support. American military leaders in Washington helped Stilwell build the case for offensive action in Burma by highlighting the dangers of allowing continental East Asia from becoming a quiet, loosely garrisoned sector for the Japanese, allowing them to move troops elsewhere, such as to attack India.[135] Initial feelers put out by Stilwell to the British in August about conducting an attack into Burma were not successful, and Stilwell's political advisor John Paton Davies reported that "the British have no intention of attempting to retake Burma in the foreseeable future" and preferred to wait until 1944 at the earliest.[136] Stilwell's "sharp-elbowed" personal style also contrasted sharply with British norms. The British official history of the Burma campaign describes Stilwell as "outspoken to the point of rudeness" and that "his criticisms were often unjustified and he could be utterly uncompromising."[137]

Before attempting to push his plan for a Burma offensive with the British again in October, Stilwell was careful to line up increased support from Washington. In an October 6 message to Marshall, Stilwell highlighted the difficulties he faced in New Delhi and warned that "if the British obstruct this plan the consequences here will be serious" and highlighted that with the U.S. and Chinese in agreement, the British were now holding up the staff process.[138] Marshall sent part of the message to Field Marshal Sir John Dill and expressed his personal view that the British were now stalling the Burma planning process. On October 18, 1942, Stilwell began a series of conferences with General Wavell in New Delhi, where he presented further details of the planned offensive into Burma.[139] Wavell was skeptical that training and planning could be done quickly and prevaricated, but messages from senior British leaders in Washington convinced Wavell to be more supportive of Stilwell's plan.[140] Stilwell also allayed British fears that the operation to retake Burma would terminate after the reopening of the Burma Road but instead would drive on to reach Rangoon, which was the key British objective.[141] By the time of a second series of meeting, beginning on October 27, Wavell was sufficiently committed to the campaign to begin working out tactical and logistics details.[142]

Refining the specifics of the planned offensive would continue well into December, and Stilwell was forced to repeatedly address adjustments or revisions to the plan raised by Chiang, the British, or American war planners, as supply requirements were refined and developed. A particular area of concern was the decision to build a connector road behind the planned advance in north Burma, with the goal of ultimately linking Ledo with the Burma Road at a point north of Lashio, creating a land line of communication even if the rest of Burma was not taken. Stilwell's plan was also the subject of intense criticism by advocates of airpower, most notably Claire Chennault, who viewed a land offensive as misguided. Instead, Chennault favored enhancements to his air force squadrons in China, which he believed could inflict decisive losses on the Japanese.[143] While Chennault's views slowed progress, they could not stop the forward momentum of the planning process. After receiving Chinese commitments to support the plan in principle at a high-level meeting held in Chungking on December 6, on December 7, 1942, General Marshall formally submitted Stilwell's plans for endorsement by the U.S. Joint Chiefs of Staff and highlighted that a limited campaign in north Burma could provide significant strategic gains with minimal logistical support.[144] These plans were endorsed by the U.S. Joint Chiefs of Staff in late December 1942, highlighting a remarkable turnaround in Stilwell's fortunes over the summer and fall of 1942.[145]

By December 1942, Joseph Stilwell had built a complex organizational structure on the ashes of the catastrophic defense of Burma. He had displayed deft political handling of the demands of Chiang Kai-shek during the summer of 1942 and gained support among American policymakers for taking a harder line with the Chinese. By demonstrating his ability to get training underway at Ramgarh, he had shown the Chinese a model for Army reform they could tentatively endorse. In the fall, Stilwell had been able to generate support among British and American leaders for a limited offensive in north Burma to open a land supply line. By selectively engaging the Americans, British, and Chinese on specific issues rather than broad policy objectives, Stilwell had been able to isolate opposition and prevent a unified opposition to his plans. British general William Slim remarked, "Stilwell was magnificent. He forced Chiang Kai-shek to provide the men; he persuaded India to accept a large Chinese force, and the British to pay for it, accommodate, feed, and clothe it."[146] On the anniversary of the Pearl Harbor attack, Stilwell received a message from General Marshall that expressed the pride in the accomplishments made in the CBI theater. Marshall wrote, "I am keenly aware of the seemingly insurmountable difficulties that you have faced daily in the creation of an efficient striking force to reopen ground communications with China. You have far exceeded our expectations in securing authority for the reorganization which you are now rapidly putting into effect."[147] By November 1942, Stilwell had 15,000 Chinese soldiers undergoing training in India, and this force would be the nucleus of a more effective and more closely managed campaign into Burma.[148]

LINGERING ISSUES

Despite clear successes that reshaped his chaotic assignment and gave it a clear purpose and structure, Stilwell still had three unresolved issues he had not been able to address. While none of these were debilitating, they gradually became sources of criticism and conflict in the CBI theater. In 1943 and 1944, the lack of unity in the CBI theater presented Stilwell with difficulties, as information, assessments, and suggestions were often sent to Washington through channels of communication that left him isolated. Stilwell overlooked the role of Ambassador Gauss in Chungking.

As a career foreign service officer rather than a political appointee, Gauss did not have much political influence in Washington, but he was a talented observer of Chinese politics and shared many of the same views as Stilwell. Despite a mutual dislike of Chiang Kai-shek and pessimism about the Nationalist Chinese government, Stilwell did not take Gauss into his confidence; for example he only told Gauss the contents of Chiang's Three Demands after Gauss had heard of it through the embassy rumor mill. When Gauss asked Stilwell point blank for the dates of these communications, Stilwell avoided the questions by saying he couldn't say without his notes.[149] Stilwell's political liaison, John Paton Davies, felt that Gauss was sensitive to attempts by Stilwell and Chennault to bypass his formal authority as ambassador, but out of pride and professional training he did not take the initiative to develop a good working relationship with the military.[150] Stilwell's failure to cultivate Gauss as an ally was a missed opportunity that would have profound consequences in 1944, when Stilwell would badly need State Department support. Stilwell's relative neglect of the American embassy in Chungking also meant that American Army and Navy attachés assigned to the embassy, who had access to Ambassador Gauss and other senior members of the CBI theater, were not always working with Stilwell. In October 1942, the Naval attaché in Chungking, Colonel McHugh, submitted a report that criticized the Army's theater plans and noted that Stilwell's removal might eliminate several coordination issues in the theater. This report drew a sharp reply from General Marshall in Washington, who felt that the Naval attaché had worked to "undermine both Chinese and British confidence in General Stilwell," and if there was a perceived split within American military ranks, it would "most seriously jeopardize the success of any campaign."[151]

A final area where Stilwell's reshaping of his roles and missions had been less successful was the potential to use Chinese regional forces, that is, local troops nominally under the authority of Chiang Kai-shek but functionally independent. In a region as vast and politically decentralized as East Asia in the 1940s, many local military commanders directly controlled areas up to a province in size and often provided effective leadership. While forces nominally loyal to Chiang probably numbered 900,000 soldiers, forces loyal exclusively to regional and local leaders were much larger, although they were likely to be less well-armed and trained.[152] Lung Yun, a military officer who became the governor of Yunnan on the border with Burma, was a classic example of a local military leader that nominally recognized the Nationalist government in Chungking while retaining de facto independence and rule over his province.[153] Relations between many local leaders and the Chungking government were so poor that if Lung Yun needed to leave his area of control to confer with senior leaders in Chungking, he required a hostage of equal importance, such as Chiang Kai-shek's wife, Mei-ling Soong, to be in Yunnan under guard by his troops to ensure his safe return.[154]

Encouraging and supporting local forces by providing American training or equipment offered a chance to more quickly strike the Japanese in China. The best opportunity for a more decentralized method of improving Chinese military efficiency would have been to support the troops of General Xue Yue, commander of the 9th Military Region, which comprised the important provinces of Hunan and Guangdong. Xue was originally from Guangdong and spent his military career in the area. He had joined the KMT in the 1920s and commanded troops in anticommunist campaigns of the 1930s, while retaining close ties to his home region. In 1937, Xue was appointed to command the 9th Military Region, and through control of local military forces he operated with little oversight by Chiang Kai-shek and the Nationalist government. Two other capable military leaders were Li Tsung-jen and Bao Chongxi, who had a powerful regional force in Guangxi. Foreign military observers characterized Li as "aggressive, ambitious, intelligent, nationalistic, puritanical, efficient, honest, daring and innovative." Bai was described by British intelligence as "a thinker and planner in the realms of both politics and strategy."[155] Both Bai and Li were theoretically part of the Nationalist government, but they ran their provinces independently and had no close connection with Chiang Kai-shek.

Stilwell made no attempt to cultivate relationships with local Chinese military leaders, even those in strategic locations or whose troops defended vital airfields. Part of this is due to Stilwell's strict insistence on providing support only to the "national government," which in effect meant the forces personally loyal to Chiang Kai-shek.[156] While one can denigrate these local commanders as "warlords" who would have requested American arms with scant plans to use these weapons, making connections with subnational leaders might have also provided political leverage against the demands of Chiang Kai-shek.

CONCLUSION

While the campaign in Burma had been a disaster and Stilwell's first eight months in the China-Burma-India theater had been extremely difficult, it firmly shaped his goals and his methods to build political support for his plans. In his assessment of the failures of the 1942 Burma campaign, Stilwell highlighted a lack of offensive spirit by Chinese and British troops, as well as ineptitude among senior commanders.[157] His efforts to develop the Ramgarh training center, with troops under his control, was an attempt to bypass these issues and create an aggressive, reliable source of combat troops. More politically, Stilwell had identified that in the CBI theater, he could act as an intermediary between the British and the Chinese, building his own role as the vital center of Allied strategy. In a message to General Marshall on September 1, 1942, Stilwell noted that "the British will not accept Chinese direction. The Chinese will not accept British direction. . . . The Chinese would accept American direction if the British would and might if they wouldn't. The British would probably resist American direction unless pressure were brought to bear."[158]

A more difficult and lingering problem for Stilwell was the lack of direction from Washington, particularly the vague pronouncements from President Roosevelt.[159] In contrast to Roosevelt's vague desire to assist China and make it a postwar power, driven in large part by his feeling of sympathy, Chiang Kai-shek had drawn up a specific list of territories, political positions, and relationships that he sought to achieve by the end of the war.[160] The failure to establish clear political objectives for American military actions in the China-Burma-India theater not only violated basic strategic principles expressed in Clausewitz and Sun Tzu, but it also meant that American military officers would be operating devoid of a framework to make decisions and establish priorities. While Stilwell had redefined and reshaped his mission by the fall of 1942, he was still operating without constructive engagement from Washington.

Viewed from a larger context, Stilwell's poorly conceived and amorphous orders were the beginning of increasingly subjective and complex military assignments. In late 1943, when being assigned as the supreme Allied commander in the European theater of operations, General Eisenhower was given clear instructions that "you will enter the continent of Europe and in conjunction with other Allied nations, undertake operations aimed at the heart of Germany and the destruction of her armed forces."[161] These clear orders gave a defined scope and clear purpose that could be achieved with defined results. In contrast, since 1945, objectives given to military commanders have often been subjective and undefined, more like Stilwell's than like Eisenhower's. For example, in 2003, shortly before the U.S.-led invasion of Iraq, the end-state established by policymakers in Washington included terms such as, "Iraq retains sufficient forces to defend itself but no longer has the power to threaten neighbors" and that Iraq have "acceptable provisional government in place," both of which are highly subjective and vague goals.[162] As a result of ambiguous guidance, military leaders are forced to make their own assessments and plans, risking a misalignment of national strategy with military operations and plans.

★ **CHAPTER 2** ★

AIRPOWER

December 1942–May 1943

**His [Stilwell's] enemies were of four kinds—
Japanese, Chinese, British, and American.**
—Secretary of War Henry L. Stimson[1]

SINCE WORLD WAR II, airpower has been a tremendous asset for U.S. military operations, and the development of close air support, aerial transport, and resupply efforts in the CBI theater compensated for a lack of artillery and roads. In contrast to Stilwell's reputation as a conventional old-fashioned infantry officer, he quickly grasped the opportunities presented him by airpower. While unique aviation capabilities made Stilwell's tasks and operations more effective at the tactical level, at the strategic level, airpower was an existential threat to Stilwell's conception of operations in the CBI theater and the paramount role he gave to ground forces. In December 1942, despite the apparent success of Stilwell's effort to bring hesitant Chinese and British leaders into his plan to retake Burma, voices within the American military sought to redirect plans and resources to emphasize airpower. In the spring and summer of 1943, Stilwell would be forced to fight a political campaign in Washington, New Delhi, and London, arguing for support for ground operations in the CBI theater rather than a strategy that emphasized aerial bombing of Japanese forces. The most powerful advocate of an airpower strategy was Claire Chennault, the world-famous leader of the Flying Tigers, who made a compelling argument that a comprehensive air campaign could attrit Japanese air forces, bomb vital transportation networks in East Asia, and close shipping routes along the Chinese coast. Chennault argued that airpower could also act more quickly and efficiently using the limited supply resources available, compared to a prolonged land campaign through the dense Burmese jungles. Advocates of an airpower-centric campaign in the CBI theater were responding to severe logistical and organizational constraints. Tonnage flown over the difficult Himalayas continually fell short of expectations in late 1942, and several hundred aircraft would be easier to sustain than a massive effort to improve the training and abilities of millions of Chinese soldiers. Political leaders, always concerned about civilian morale and eager to find strategies that would minimize casualties, were also enthusiastic about the possibilities of airpower. As an additional bonus, an air campaign based in China meant that the United States could limit its role in Southeast Asia, avoiding difficult political issues with the British.

Stilwell and Chennault pursued radically different strategies of engagement with their higher headquarters and political leadership. Supporters of airpower provided a compelling vision that aerial warfare was an idea that could rapidly be turned into reality in the CBI theater, and they articulated in meetings and conferences a plan that offered a high chance of success with minimal risk. President Franklin D. Roosevelt had supported the growth of air forces and naval aviation for many years, and he believed that aerial attacks offered the irresistible combination of faster results with lower casualties. In Chungking, Chiang Kai-shek similarly viewed airpower as a way to achieve results without the difficult creation of ground forces, which might upset the fragile coalition structure of his political regime. In contrast, Stilwell was a weak bureaucratic infighter and was hindered by his natural inclinations to oppose other U.S. military officers in front of American political leaders. Stilwell was also a poor public speaker in high-level diplomatic and military environments, and while he was highly effective in one-on-one meetings or in small groups, he lacked the charisma and showmanship of Chennault to make his points to an indifferent or hostile audience. Stilwell pointed to flaws in an air campaign, but his approach could only slow, rather than stop, the steadily increasing importance of air forces in American national strategy for the CBI theater.

From mid-December 1942 through May 1943, Chennault and his supporters would seek to make supporting airpower in China the primary mechanism of U.S. military support to the CBI theater, and this strategic debate would profoundly shape operations in Asia. Stilwell's inability to defeat Chennault's arguments or silence him through administrative channels not only hindered Stilwell's plans for the theater but highlighted an issue for the U.S. Army that has endured: how to overcome the appeal of airpower. Since 1945, airpower advocates have continued to press for an increasing role for aerial bombing. More recently, the use of unmanned drones in Iraq and Afghanistan has given policymakers an alternative to deploying American "boots on the ground" in dangerous areas. While the effectiveness of air campaigns has not often matched the soaring rhetoric of airpower advocates, they continue to be a logistical and politically expedient answer to military challenges. Stilwell's struggle to integrate an air campaign into his overall plan for the CBI theater highlights the beginning of aerial operations as a potential rival to traditional Army ground operations, which has led to a situation where maintaining a focus on ground operations requires political skills and engagement with senior leaders.

SHIFTING ROLES AND ECCENTRIC PERSONALITIES

Stilwell's difficulty with airpower, and airpower advocates, began in large part because of the ambiguity of roles and functions that had plagued the first nine months of operations in CBI. Chinese officials had been seeking an expanded role for American airpower since 1940, and Stilwell confronted the legacies of previous organizational and bureaucratic compromises when he arrived in the CBI theater in 1942. Compounding these difficulties was a fundamental clash of personalities and strategic outlook. Stilwell and Chennault had not only fundamentally different leadership styles but a different outlook on military operations and goals. Personalities, as much as policy differences, would create underlying tension within the CBI theater, and a lack of a unified plan would provide senior officials in Washington with an opportunity to become involved in military decision making.

After the outbreak of the Sino-Japanese War in 1937, the Chinese Nationalist government had sought foreign military arms, particularly aircraft, from a variety of nations. The Soviet Union and Italy both provided a limited number of aircraft and quickly identified problems in Chinese pilot training that severely limited their air operations. Political difficulties between the Chinese and these nations led to a search for an apolitical and Western source of expertise. Claire Chennault, a retired U.S. Army Air Force officer with widely recognized skills in training pilots and developing tactics for single-engine aircraft, was hired in 1937 to be an advisor to the Chinese air force.[2] After surveying the situation in China, where Japanese planes roamed essentially unchecked and bombed Chinese cities on a daily basis, Chennault led a delegation to the United States in 1939 seeking to buy aircraft and equipment, with limited success. Again, in November 1940, Chennault was part of a Chinese delegation led by Major General Mao Pang-tzo of the Chinese air force that sought to purchase five hundred American combat aircraft.[3] With the massive expansion of the American military after the fall of France in June 1940, Chinese requests were unrealistic, but one hundred fighter aircraft were eventually allocated to China. To alleviate issues with pilot training, in the spring of 1941 the U.S. government allowed for American military pilots to join an "American Volunteer Group" (AVG) on a one-year contract, paid for by the Chinese government, to fly aircraft in China against the Japanese.[4] Throughout this process, Chennault had developed a close working relationship with senior leaders of the Chinese Nationalist government, including Chiang Kai-shek and his wife, and political sponsors gave Chennault a wide range of latitude in conducting operations.

After Pearl Harbor and the assignment of Stilwell to the CBI theater, the status of the AVG became an early source of contention between Chennault and Stilwell. Since the AVG was technically part of the Chinese air force, Stilwell had no formal authority over Chennault or the American pilots. The AVG, known popularly as the "Flying Tigers," had provided close air support to Chinese ground forces in Burma during the spring of 1942 and had reduced the impact of Japanese air raids on major Chinese cities. They had also developed a reputation as a loosely disciplined organization that might be difficult to integrate into a larger Allied war effort. The initial elements of the U.S. Army Air Forces in the CBI theater were the remnants of the U.S. Far East Air Force under the command of Maj.

Gen. Lewis H. Brereton, who had evacuated a small force from the Philippines to Java, one step ahead of the rapidly advancing Japanese, and then relocated again to India. In India, this force was redesignated as the Tenth Air Force, but Brereton was not an effective or diligent organizer, and Col. Clayton L. Bissell assumed the primary tasks of restructuring Tenth Air Force operations in India, establishing a trans-Himalaya air supply route and developing the framework for air operations in China.[5] Chennault had clashed with Bissell earlier in his career and described him as "a cold, meticulous man with a filing-cabinet mind, who sought to cover his inability to cope with people by refuge in strict adherence to Army regulations."[6] Chennault's personal background, as the poor son of a rural farmer and later a factory worker who had entered the Army through an aviation program in World War I, marked him apart from the officers shaped by the puritan and spartan attitudes of West Point.[7]

Stilwell and Bissell's by-the-book approach to handling administrative and organizational issues quickly created tensions with Chennault, who was used to running operations more informally.[8] Stilwell noted in a message to George Marshall that while Chennault might be a fine tactician, "his administration is terrible, and his judgement of men is weak."[9] For example, an ongoing area of disagreement was the Army's approach to fraternization in China. Due to high rates of venereal disease, Chennault, with the support of medical officers on his staff, had established quasi-official brothels, where American servicemen and Chinese women could be regularly screened for infection. Venereal diseases rates fell dramatically. Stilwell opposed the policy on moral and administrative grounds, and for much of the war Chennault's men would be engaged in a cat-and-mouse battle to hide these establishments from Stilwell's inspector general staff.[10]

More substantive than Chennault's personal dislike of Stilwell's attempt to follow a more "by the book" approach to command was a widespread concern among aviators that Stilwell did not fully understand aircraft and air operations. Chennault noted that Stilwell had "a strong prejudice against airpower coupled with a faint suspicion of any weapons more complicated than a rifle and bayonet."[11] Col. Robert Scott, who served under Chennault as a senior member of his staff, felt that Stilwell had limited experience with the capabilities of modern aircraft, remarking that Stilwell was a "dyed-in-the-wool infantryman who, regardless of his three stars, did not have the barest conception of airpower or its potential."[12] Moreover, Scott believed that Stilwell's focus on tactical operations hindered larger efforts, noting, "There was considerable truth in the oft-repeated description of Vinegar Joe as the best damned four-star battalion commander in the Army."[13] Moreover, Chennault, who had clashed with numerous American military officers while in uniform, was exceptionally diligent in maintaining political support with political leaders, in stark contrast to Stilwell. General Arnold, who was not a supporter of Chennault personally, grudgingly acknowledged that Chennault "had the originality, initiative, and drive the Chinese liked; also, a knack of doing things in China that was possessed by very few other American officers.[14] Even Stilwell's supporters, such as Adm. William Leahy, conceded that he lacked solid political judgment and that he was "down in the jungles far away from Chungking. Although tactless and with a tongue too sharp for his own good, he was an excellent fighter and knew what to do on the ground."[15]

On June 23, 1942, Brereton and a large percentage of the bombers in the CBI theater were rushed to Egypt to aid in the defense of the Suez Canal, leaving Bissell in command.[16] This action infuriated Chiang Kai-shek, who saw the reassignment of critical assets as a personal insult, which played a part in shaping his demand for five hundred aircraft as part of his "Three Demands" on June 28, 1942.[17] In July the AVG was formally placed under Stilwell's command, and Chennault was reinstated on active duty in the U.S. Army Air Forces with the rank of one-star general, to command this force. With his new rank and with support from his close personal relationship with Chiang Kai-shek and Mei-ling Soong, Chennault immediately began to lobby for an expanded air campaign in China. In a July 16 proposal to Stilwell, Chennault argued that China-based airpower could effectively target Japanese military installations, interdict railway transport and shipping, and wear down Japanese aviation through aggressive, offensive action. Stilwell rejected Chennault's proposals and instead made defense of the air route from India to China the primary focus of Chennault's forces. In Stilwell's conception, offensive action would be secondary to escorting transport planes and eliminating Japanese threats to the vital airlift effort.[18]

Stilwell's rejection of Chennault's approach in the summer of 1942 reflected the severe resource limitations of the time and the need to stabilize operations in India after the fall of Burma, but in the fall of 1942, added resources became available and reignited the airpower debate. By September 30, 1942, War Department programs to provide the Tenth Air Force with the reinforcements, including heavy and medium bombers, as well as a large number of transport aircraft, had made significant progress.[19] The majority of these reinforcements would be assigned to India, partly because of the logistics barriers to supporting them in China, but also because Stilwell wanted the aircraft to assist his planned offensive into Burma. Chennault clearly saw the plans as an attack on his role and as evidence that Stilwell "thought of himself primarily as a simple field soldier and had little understanding of or patience with his primary duty as a military diplomat."[20] With little support from either his air commander Bissell or his theater commander Stilwell, Chennault began utilizing his connections with Chinese policymakers to promote his plans, and he claimed that if provided with sufficient ammunition, spare parts, and fuel, he could defeat Japan with 105 fighters, 30 medium bombers, and 12 heavy bombers.[21] This outlandish claim was eye-catching and bold and it matched with Chiang Kai-shek's desire for a more visible attack against Japanese forces in China, rather than in the jungles of Burma. Chennault believed that this force, although small, could use air bases in the Chinese interior to conduct raids and attacks on Japanese positions, then relocate to another base, keeping the Japanese guessing and protecting the aircraft from counterattacks.[22]

Chennault also began using personal communications with American policymakers to circumvent Stilwell. In October 1942, Wendell Willkie, the 1940 Republican presidential candidate, visited Chungking as a personal representative of Roosevelt, and Chennault gave him a detailed briefing on the possibilities of airpower in China and handed him a letter for the president that outlined his plan to develop airpower in China to defeat the Japanese, "probably within six months, within one year at the outside."[23] In his memoirs, Chennault defended his use of Willkie to bypass his chain of command by attacking Stilwell's tight control of communications, which he referred to as a "carefully constructed dam of censorship," and he also claimed that Willkie asked him to write the letter outlining an airpower plan for China.[24] While in Chungking, Willkie was also in contact with the naval attaché, Lt. Col. James M. McHugh, USMC, who supported Chennault and criticized Stilwell's understanding of airpower in a report that Willkie included along with Chennault's letter to Roosevelt.[25] In his diary, Stilwell referred to both Chennault and McHugh as "rattlesnakes" and thought Chennault's plan was a "jackass proposition."[26] Willkie's reports were given further reinforcement by Madame Chiang, who visited the United States in November 1942 and similarly attempted to promote Chennault's plan with civilian policymakers within the Roosevelt administration, such as Harry Hopkins.

Among American senior military officers, Chennault's position was viewed skeptically, with respect for his accomplishments tempered by distrust of his organizational abilities and negative assessments of his personality. Chennault was not a respected member of the close-knit group of senior American aviators, nevertheless, Gen. Henry H. (Hap) Arnold, commanding general of the Army Air Forces, noted that China lacked sufficient airfields, stockpiles of aviation gasoline, or the required ground support personnel to make a rapid increase in aircraft logistically possible.[27] In January 1943, General Marshall acknowledged that Chennault had "demonstrated great genius in his operations against the Japanese," but he was concerned that he "appears to disregard the actualities of the logistical problem which our responsible commander, Lt. General Stilwell, is struggling to master by the spring operation in North Burma."[28] In a message to Stilwell, Marshall noted that one way to defuse some of the political pressure would be to approve promotions for Chennault and Bissell, which would give airpower supporters a symbolic victory.[29] Marshall stressed to Stilwell that he needed to consider political factors in Washington because "they are pertinent to the conduct of operations and particularly so in your theater."[30] While pressure was being exerted in Washington, Chiang Kai-shek also worked to focus strategy on airpower and walk back his commitments to support an offensive in north Burma. Citing a lack of British naval support in the Bay of Bengal, Chiang formally withdrew Chinese forces from the planned late-spring offensive in a message to Roosevelt on January 8, 1943. Chiang's message elaborated that rather than a ground offensive, "the remarkable potentialities of an air offensive in China have already been demonstrated by a small and ill-supported force." Increasing support to China-based airpower, Chiang argued, would generate a return "out of all proportion to the investment."[31] By January 1943, it appeared that Stilwell's plan to strike into northern Burma, only recently approved, was already being reevaluated in light of the increasing appeal of an air-centric strategy in the CBI theater.

STRATEGY CONFERENCES AND POLITICAL CONSIDERATIONS

The poor relationship that had quickly developed between Stilwell and Chennault over the role of airpower would play a critical role in two important strategic planning conferences, held in Casablanca and Washington in early 1943, which gave airpower a prominent role in the CBI theater. Stilwell's failure to engage substantively with political leaders and more importantly his failure to understand the political needs and motivations of policymakers left him isolated from important discussions. At the Casablanca Conference held by senior American and British leaders in Morocco between January 14 and 23, 1943, Stilwell's planned spring offensive into Burma was pushed back until later in the year, after the monsoon season, primarily due to British hesitancy in attacking before they had greater resources available in South Asia.[32] Throughout the conference, President Roosevelt made favorable remarks about the role of airpower in China, believing that because air operations caught public attention, even a "small effort to send aid would have a tremendously favorable effect on Chinese morale."[33] More specifically, Roosevelt directly referenced Chennault's argument about China-based aircraft attacking Japanese shipping and believed that if two hundred aircraft were based in China they could "spend most of their time in attacks on shipping, but occasionally they could make a special raid on Japan." In response, General Arnold and General Marshall both highlighted the severe logistics difficulties in the CBI theater and the shortage of transport aircraft.[34] Despite the resistance of General Marshall to reinforcing airpower in China, he understood the president's political logic and intentions. Providing additional air support to China for psychological reasons would be carried out despite the tremendous cost in highly trained personnel and valuable equipment required to support air operations in China.[35]

At the conclusion of the Casablanca Conference, in a joint letter to Chiang from Roosevelt and Churchill, they stated, "We have decided that Chennault should be reinforced at once in order that you may strike not only at vital shipping routes but at Japan herself."[36] Chiang further encouraged Roosevelt's inclination to increase support to Chennault and expand his authority with a letter on February 7, which suggested that Chennault be given one hundred additional aircraft to directly target Japanese shipping and that air operations in China be removed from Stilwell's authority.[37] Despite Chennault's increasing salience in strategy discussions, Stilwell retained the clear support of General Marshall, who sought to temper President Roosevelt's requests and expectations while also moderating Stilwell's anger at Roosevelt, whom Stilwell referred to contemptuously as "Big Boy" in his diary.[38] Marshall had strongly supported Stilwell's efforts to promote a ground offensive and had lobbied his fellow members of the U.S. Joint Chiefs of Staff to focus support on ground operations because "the Chinese soldier will fight, has no nerves, and requires a minimum of food, clothing, and similar supplies. He can endure long marches over difficult country."[39] Marshall was also skeptical that the Chinese army could successfully defend U.S. airfields from Japanese advances, because operations in Burma and Southeast Asia had demonstrated that the Japanese tended to focus ground attacks on airfields.[40]

A significant problem for Stilwell's effort to gain political support in Washington was that he had no larger narrative of China's importance to the United States other than to defeat Japan. Chennault, Roosevelt, and others in Washington, particularly in the White House and State Department, envisioned a close postwar relationship between the United States and the Nationalist government.[41] In March 1943, the chief of the State Department's Division of Far Eastern Affairs, Maxwell M. Hamilton, urged increased support for airpower because it would better support American objectives, including "China's present and post-war attitude" and help with "giving China a greater feeling of joint participation in the war against Axis countries."[42] Hamilton's focus on "attitude" and "feeling" was a direct contrast to Stilwell's advocacy of specific military objectives and a quid pro quo diplomatic arrangement. John Carter Vincent, a State Department official in China, echoed Hamilton's points and specifically linked airpower with an overall goodwill between the United States and China:

> I believe that material aid given should be conditioned upon the theory that it is as much a good will as a military investment, perhaps more so. It should therefore be given in a form most evident to the public. Widespread activity on the part of a strong Fourteenth Air Force under Chennault would fulfill this condition ideally and would be a good military investment as well.[43]

In effect, airpower had symbolic importance to the prestige of Chinese leaders and was useful to many in Washington not because of its military value, but because it helped resolve current and potentially future political issues. Stilwell's inability to present a larger, long-term strategic vision of an enduring and useful Sino-American relationship meant that his policy suggestions lacked an overarching narrative to give them meaning and context. Stilwell's dislike of politics and unfamiliarity with political norms and behaviors was a significant barrier to building opposition to airpower. Stilwell's political advisor, John Paton Davies, wrote in March 1943 that Stilwell, "while he endeavors to avoid playing domestic politics, he cannot prevent politics from being played on him." Davies reported that when he had raised this issue with Stilwell, the general had remarked, "My safest course is straight down the road."[44] Stilwell did allow Davies to organize several informal gatherings with journalists and senators, but these efforts were too limited and only grudgingly accepted by Stilwell to make a significant impact on Washington policy debates.[45] Stilwell's decision to avoid political engagement closed off an avenue for him to improve his understanding of strategic debates and discussions. In contrast, Chennault's aide-de-camp Joseph Alsop was both a former political columnist and cousin of President Roosevelt, and he used his political connections to forcefully promote Chennault's case in Washington.[46]

At the conclusion of the Casablanca Conference, a delegation of senior U.S. and British officers traveled to New Delhi and Chungking to assess the challenges of the region and meet with Chiang Kai-shek.[47]

General Arnold briefed Chiang Kai-shek on the decisions made in Casablanca to increase support to Chennault's air forces, and Chiang seized the opportunity to press for Chennault to be given an independent command.[48] On February 6, 1943, Chiang gave Arnold a list of military consultation points and noted that it was "very important that a separate Air Task Force under Gen. Chennault be formed in China. That Task Force to be under Generalissimo's direct control. No other organization would work. Chennault only air man who understood Chinese."[49] General Arnold confirmed that Chiang was sincere in his beliefs and noted in his memoirs that Chiang's "unlimited confidence in General Chennault complicated the problem terrifically. He believed Chennault to be the greatest air commander the world had ever produced and he wanted Chennault to head up everything."[50] While the notion that U.S. forces would be directly assigned to Chiang's control was unrealistic, when Arnold left Chungking, he carried a letter from Chiang to Roosevelt urging that Chennault be given an independent command. Chiang's appeal, and his savvy approach to base his proposal on the positive impact it would have on Chinese feeling toward the United States, an issue with immense importance for Roosevelt, had a profound impact in Washington.

On March 11, 1943, the China Air Task Force commanded by Chennault was redesignated the Fourteenth Air Force, and on March 14 Chennault was promoted to major general to command this new formation.[51] Stilwell also received guidance from Marshall that he was to support Chennault's operations, which included allocating a minimum of 1,500 tons of supplies a month via the Hump air route.[52] Despite these plans and Chennault's increasing political clout, insurmountable logistics constraints still slowed the buildup of airpower, and although Chennault was a noted tactician, he was not a skilled and experienced administrator and took little interest in logistics.[53] He was now a major general responsible for a large military unit with day-to-day bureaucratic functions, such as personnel assignments and reports and mundane paperwork that was required to support the organization, tasks Chennault largely ignored. Chennault and his supporters used Stilwell as a convenient scapegoat whenever administrative failings and practical issues impacted air operations. For example, due to transportation difficulties, in March and early April 1943, Chennault was so short of aviation fuel that he suspended combat operations of his forces, a move his supporters took as evidence of a lack of support from Stilwell.[54]

In late April 1943, President Roosevelt had another opportunity to assess and redirect CBI strategy when both Stilwell and Chennault were ordered to Washington to participate in the Trident Conference with senior American and British leaders. Chennault was quick to seize the opportunity to present his case directly to senior policymakers, which he knew was a rare opportunity. In Washington he captured the imagination of Roosevelt by outlining a plan, which he had not shared with Stilwell before the conference, to gain air superiority in China by September 1943, which would allow for sustained bombing operations.[55] Chennault's requests for support had now increased from the 105 fighters, 30 medium bombers, and 12 heavy bombers to 150 fighters, 48 medium bombers, and 35 heavy bombers. He also increased his supply requirements from 1,500 tons to 4,900 tons per month.[56]

With this enlarged force, Chennault made the claim that his forces could damage or sink one million tons of Japanese shipping in the area from the Yangtze River to Hainan Island. Chennault was again aided by Chiang Kai-shek, who sent a message to the White House that he would like the entire air transport tonnage for May, June, and July to only carry aviation supplies because of the profound importance of airpower to China. Chiang's message undercut Marshall and Stilwell's argument that increased air attacks would lead to a Japanese response, because Chiang gave his personal assurance that he would stop a Japanese ground advance on the air bases.[57] Chiang's message did not give any indication on how the tonnage flown into China via the Hump airlift would be transferred to Chennault's bases, which were hundreds of miles farther east and which could not be directly supplied via the poor Chinese road network.[58]

In contrast to Chennault's efforts to directly influence political leaders, Stilwell worked through his chain of command, passing on his assessments to General Marshall. Stilwell argued that increasing support for air operations would require curtailing plans to support Chinese ground forces, and expanded air operations would lead to Japanese ground attacks directed against airfields. Stilwell noted that "if we start an air campaign, they may decide they are being hurt to the extent it would be advantageous for them to take Chungking and Kunming. If that is done, we will have to fold up out there."[59] To Marshall privately, Stilwell also argued that allowing Chennault to circumvent the chain of command would negatively impact command and control in the CBI theater and effectively give Chiang Kai-shek a more prominent role in shaping U.S. policy: "Without a general plan, U.S. units in China will be at the mercy of the often whimsical and unsound decisions of a commander whose actions are often dictated by local politics."[60]

Stilwell repeated a request for U.S. combat troops in the CBI theater, two divisions, but since these troops would have come at the expense of other operational areas, he found few supporters for his proposals.[61] Stilwell was also a poor salesman in describing the positive aspects of what he could do with additional assets, instead focusing on highlighting the weakness of airpower and Chinese forces.[62] In contrast, Chennault's positive demeanor and optimism was infectious, and even Army officers critical of the grandiose air plans noted that Chennault "spoke with conviction and expressed confidence in the success of his projected operations," which had a profound impact on political leaders weighing their options.[63] Stilwell's efforts to present his case were ineffective and he lacked the personal charisma and political showmanship to stand out among senior policymakers.[64]

In addition to his flawed personal approach, Stilwell blandly advocated for continuing the established plan to begin a ground campaign into Burma and proposed that pressure be increased on Chiang Kai-shek to fulfill his promises to support an attack into Burma from Yunnan. Neither of these proposals were new or included any innovations that might ease logistics burdens, speed the advance, or reduce casualties. Stilwell settled into a defensive position of pointing out flaws in Chennault's plan to defend support to Chinese ground forces. Despite his plain style, Stilwell retained the support of Marshall, Admiral King, and General Arnold, who were all skeptical of Chennault's questionable and optimistic assertions. Marshall's staff was highly critical of Chennault's plan and produced detailed assessments that concluded that a small air force was "insufficient" to accomplish American strategic goals in China.[65] Admiral Leahy, closely aligned with Roosevelt, supported Chennault's plan because of its political ramifications.[66] Roosevelt stressed to Churchill and senior British military leaders that a Chinese collapse was a very real possibility and that increased military aid and aircraft were needed for political reasons.[67] British strategic planners did not oppose the American emphasis on airpower, and Prime Minister Churchill was in agreement with Roosevelt that airpower was preferable because he could not understand how ground "operations in the swamps of Burma would help the Chinese."[68] British assessments of Chinese ground forces also stressed that the scope of problems in Chinese ground forces showed that any expectations they could be reformed into an aggressive force were unrealistic, leaving airpower as the only realistic option.[69]

Chennault wrote in his memoirs that throughout the Trident Conference in Washington, Stilwell seemed "curt, surly, and short tempered, and even his friends Marshall and Stimson were disappointed by his exhibition."[70] Stimson noted in his memoirs that "if he had been a careful and persuasive advocate, rather than a brilliant soldier with a passionate but inarticulate loyalty to his job, he would perhaps not have failed at Washington in May, 1943, in his greatest single chance to win the President's personal backing."[71] Others at the conference, including President Roosevelt, wondered if Stilwell was ill based on his withdrawn demeanor and passive role in the conference.[72] Stilwell saw it differently, noting in his diary in a sarcastic and bitter tone that "Roosevelt wouldn't let me speak my piece.... What's the use when the World's Greatest Strategist [Roosevelt] is against you."[73] Stilwell's inability, or more accurately a disinclination, to engage in politics to build a consensus for his approach clearly remained an issue, but Stilwell's lack of interest in viewing problems from a political perspective was a more systemic issue. Stilwell failed to fully understand President Roosevelt's sympathies and inclinations, and his behavior had also left Roosevelt with the impression that Stilwell was a domineering and surly martinet. In the spring of 1943, Roosevelt had sent a message to Marshall that noted Stilwell's flawed approach, noting "when he [Stilwell] speaks of talking to him [Chiang] in sterner tones, he goes about it just the wrong way," noting that Chiang was "the Chief Executive as well as the Commander-in-Chief, and one cannot speak sternly to a man like that or exact commitments from him the way we might do."[74]

On May 3, 1943, General Marshall informed Stilwell that Roosevelt had decided to back Chennault based on a political assessment that the low state of Chinese morale after years of war meant that "the air program was therefore of great importance" to boost their flagging spirits. Marshall noted that Stilwell's presentation had failed to capture Roosevelt's imaginations and that the president had "drawn the conclusion from his interview with you that the air activities were in effect largely to be suspended while the more tedious ground build-up was being carried out."[75] Stilwell did not fully accept this explanation and noted in his diary that he felt the conference had been a sham: "F.D.R. had decided on an air effort in China before we reached Washington."[76] Stilwell would be allowed to continue training Chinese forces in India, and a campaign into Burma was still approved, but it would be limited to reopening a land route to China via northern Burma, rather than push the Japanese out of the entire country.[77] The president also gave specific instructions that the Hump airlift would increase deliveries to 7,000 tons in July and 10,000 tons by September 1943. Of this total amount, Chennault would be given priority on the first 4,700 tons per month, with the remainder going to Stilwell's programs.[78] In his diary Stilwell maintained that this supply effort was misguided and that although the Fourteenth Air Force "will do the Japs some damage but at the same time will so weaken the ground effort that it may fail."[79]

The goals outlined by Roosevelt were clarified and expanded by the military staff in Washington, and an internal memorandum by the U.S. Chiefs of Staff now identified air operations in and from China as the number one objective in the Pacific and Far East in 1943–1944.[80] By the end of the first week of the Trident Conference, Chennault's plan was adopted as the basis for more detailed strategy planning, while Stilwell's program was correspondingly reduced in scope. The final wording of the Trident Conference plan was for "land and air operations from Assam into Burma via Ledo and Imphal, in step with an advance by Chinese forces from Yunnan, with the object of containing as many Japanese forces as possible, covering the air route to China, and as an essential step towards the opening of the Burma Road."[81] This plan meant that operations in the summer of 1943 would be limited to the fringes of Burma, and the start date was pushed back to November 1, 1943. Stilwell's plans to rejuvenate Chinese ground forces and his authority, which he had rebuilt in the second half of 1942, were now decisively restricted and relegated to being a secondary effort in the CBI theater.

CONCLUSION

During the period from mid-December 1942 through May 1943, because of Stilwell's failure to engage or convince policymakers of the value of his plans, his authority and influence was gradually reduced, while the prestige and influence of Chennault expanded. Defending the slow, gradual reform of Chinese military forces would have been an arduous task for even the most skilled political leaders, but Stilwell failed to make a compelling case that could persuade policymakers, and he also failed to leverage his support from senior military officers. In contrast, Chennault regularly bypassed senior military leaders, including his direct superiors, to present a case that was based on flawed assessments and overly optimistic projections.

While Chennault had won the political battle in Washington, the decision to support unproven theories of airpower had mixed results in the CBI theater. The fighters and light bombers of the Fourteenth Air Force did have success when they had the element of surprise. Strafing attacks by fighters and bombing from low altitude by medium bombers was also effective in closing the upper stretches of the Yangtze River to Japanese shipping in daylight.[82] Heavy bombers, which Chennault had less experience in handling, were less effective. In an August 21, 1943, raid on Hankow, a force of fourteen B-24 heavy bombers was badly mauled, with two planes lost and ten others severely damaged. A follow-up attack on August 24 by seven B-24 bombers resulted in four more shot down, with one additional aircraft crashing upon landing.[83] In less than a week, the core of the force of heavy bombers requested by Chennault and supplied at great expense with supplies airlifted from India, was destroyed by Japanese air defenses. Moreover, attacks on Japanese oceangoing shipping along the China coast never developed or reached the lofty goals that had attracted President Roosevelt's attention.

A postwar U.S. Air Force study of the Fourteenth Air Force antishipping campaign concluded that "missions against shipping off the China coast, even though claims exaggerated the results, were recognized as not worth the effort expended."[84] Chennault's forces were able to achieve notable tactical successes, but they never evolved into a force that could inflict decisive casualties on the Japanese or make a larger strategic impact on the war. Postwar assessments of the impact of the Fourteenth Air Force show that Chennault's forces regularly overestimated the amount of shipping destroyed by a factor of ten and that Japanese shipping losses in the China theater were negligible until late 1943.[85] Policymakers at the Trident Conference had been convinced by Chennault's charisma and optimism, but he could not deliver on his promises. The political decision to favor airpower also did not result in a significant improvement in relations between the United States and China, and at the Cairo Conference in November 1943, Chiang Kai-shek's continued demands and intransigence would lead to a loss of support for China among senior Allied leaders.

Stilwell's key flaw throughout the spring and early summer of 1943 was his lack of political perspective. As a career soldier, Stilwell lacked the experience and inclination to become involved in what he perceived as political issues, which is understandable, but he also failed to consider political requirements when making his plans. By favoring Chennault's plan for aerial operations, President Roosevelt demonstrated that he favored the plan that appealed to his own political and personal preconceptions. Stilwell's approach offered only more political conflict with Chiang Kai-shek, slow progress, and eventually a costly and difficult ground campaign. The inability of Stilwell to reframe military policies around more attractive and useful political objectives would lead to a diversion of resources in CBI and an air campaign that absorbed precious supplies and resources.

A major reason for Stilwell's lack of political awareness in the spring of 1943 was his decision to form a personal staff with narrow skills and insights. When forming his initial group of officers in early 1942, Stilwell had drawn a disproportionate number from the military attaché program because they had the language skills required for the theater. In late 1943 and 1944, when large-scale conventional operations began with the drive into northern Burma, many of these officers lacked the tactical experience to lead effectively. Col. Charles Hunter, a senior leader in Merrill's Marauders, noted that "General Stilwell had to rely heavily, or let us say, he relied very heavily, on Chinese speaking American officers. Thus, he narrowed his choice to a particular breed of cats who were not always best qualified to carry out his policies and his directives."[86] The insular nature of Stilwell's staff was compounded by his decision to make his son, Joe Jr., the theater intelligence officer, the G-2, despite his lack of experience, and also bring both of his sons-in-law into the senior staff.[87] Maj. Gen. Hayden Boatner, who was himself a former attaché in China, described Stilwell's staff as a "closed shop" and used the term "Royal Family" to describe the close-knit group of China specialists that were with Stilwell from the spring of 1942 until his relief in October 1944.[88] While every commander wants a staff of which they know the strengths and weaknesses of various members and trust in their subordinates, the members of Stilwell's staff had a narrow area of expertise and had often spent years in Asia, rather than as part of regular U.S. Army units or serving in positions in the United States. British officers in particular commented that members of Stilwell's staff, especially when operating from the front in north Burma alongside their commander, were not always efficient in coordinating with the Allies.[89] American commanders in rear areas of the CBI theater pleaded with Stilwell to have his staff prepare more detailed and methodical studies so that decisions didn't seem to be driven by personal assessments and so that they could present a more polished and professional appearance to their counterparts.[90]

Without the background to understand the broader implications of U.S. Army programs and national policies and removed from major debates, it was inevitable that Stilwell would lack the context of national and Army policies being developed during his tenure, which led to poor coordination and unnecessary confusion. An obvious historical parallel to Stilwell's staff selection would be Gen. Stanley McChrystal's staff, which had a similarly narrow range of skills and whose behavior led to McChrystal's removal from command after negative comments made by his staff about political leaders was reported in a *Rolling Stone* article. McChrystal also shared Stilwell's dislike of engaging with political figures and similarly cultivated an impression of being a humble, frontline soldier.[91] In contrast, Gen. Raymond T. Odierno, who commanded forces in Iraq during the troop "surge," included several prominent civilian members on his staff, including non-U.S. personnel, most notably British academic Emma Sky, to provide perspective and insights. Stilwell should have developed a more diverse staff and accepted the importance of nonmilitary considerations and perspectives to better integrate his plans in the CBI theater with global Allied strategy and American political concerns.

★ **CHAPTER 3** ★

GLOBAL ALLIES
June 1943–November 1943

We must all eat some crow if we are to fight the same war together.
—Gen. George C. Marshall, private message to Stilwell[1]

By the summer of 1943, after Stilwell's influence had eroded at the Trident Conference, it looked like his plans for the CBI theater, which centered on opening a land route to China by pushing the Japanese out of northern Burma, would remain permanently stillborn. Chennault's success in crafting a compelling narrative for airpower, continued opposition by Chiang Kai-shek to systematic Army reforms in China, and British reluctance to mount a campaign in Burma, had all combined to thwart Stilwell's plans for the north Burma campaign that he believed was necessary to pave the way for a larger ground offensive in China. Despite these clear setbacks, Stilwell reenergized his authority in the summer and fall of 1943 through arduous work in building forces at Ramgarh and through steady and patient coordination with British military officers to assuage their doubts and fears. While his influence in China was limited and political support in the United States remained uncertain, Stilwell successfully pivoted to build allies within the military establishments of the United States and Great Britain and was able to gain support for a limited offensive in northern Burma to begin in December 1943. The period from June 1943 through December highlights the ability of Stilwell to win the support of British military officers and shape the Chinese army in India into a potent offensive force. While Stilwell's influence declined sharply at the Trident Conference, at the Cairo Conference in late November he had regained influence in Allied Councils of War and began his long-awaited campaign in Burma. The June 1943 through November 1943 period illustrates the political power of building new compartmentalized organizations within a military establishment, not just to add capabilities, but also to shift policy debates.

Stilwell's desire to rebuild his position after Trident would require deft political and managerial efforts. As the primary military partner linking British efforts in southeast Asia with the China theater, Stilwell and the U.S. Army's role was caught between the larger U.S. strategic interest to support the British, and the CBI theater's overarching requirement to manage the tense Sino-American relationship. This difficult balancing act had been a challenge for an apolitical military officer like Stilwell. Stilwell would need to turn his awkward command role to his advantage and find a way to convince the British that their interests in Southeast Asia at large, and more specifically in protecting India from Japanese attack, would best be served by taking the offensive in Burma. Although Stilwell was an unrepentant Anglophobe and took a childish delight in mocking British customs and behavior, he recognized that he needed British support to begin operations in the dry season, which began in December. Stilwell also needed to regain the policy initiative within China and limit the influence of airpower advocates, like Chennault, while working to rebuild his influence and take advantage of missteps made by Chiang Kai-shek. An additional area where Stilwell rebuilt support for his plans in north Burma was through alliances with senior American military leaders, most notably Maj. Gen. Brehon B. Somervell, who saw the CBI theater as an ideal environment to demonstrate American military engineering skills.

Stilwell hoped that with support from key allies within the British, American, and Chinese military commands, a limited offensive would demonstrate that his arduous work and unyielding faith in the Chinese Army in India (CAI) was well-placed. If a road and pipeline were built through northern Burma, Stilwell would be able to transfer the heavy equipment, trucks, artillery, and ammunition needed in China, and he would be able to support a limited modernization of several dozen divisions. Stilwell knew that he could not count on support from senior political leaders in Washington or in London. President Roosevelt had been abundantly clear that he regarded Burma as secondary to efforts in China. Prime Minister Churchill was intently focused on Europe and the Mediterranean and felt that an offensive into Burma would only result in heavy casualties and a slow, brutal campaign through the swamps and jungle. Churchill was also skeptical of Roosevelt's political goal of buttressing China so that it could become a pillar of the postwar international community.[2] Stilwell hoped for more support from military leaders, who might recognize the need to tie down and hopefully destroy the Japanese forces in Burma, which comprised at least four, and Allied intelligence suggested might include as many as eight, of Japan's elite Class-A divisions. These divisions would be a potent invasion force if directed against India, and if redeployed to the Pacific they would undoubtedly make the American island-hopping campaign even more bloody and difficult. Stilwell also hoped that military officers might not share Roosevelt's faith in the Hump airlift to sustain operations in China and would support a limited campaign that would open a land route. By mid-July 1943, as Stilwell's policies and programs took shape, the military training programs for Chinese soldiers continued to progress, and individual and small-unit training of the CAI had been completed, leading to battalion and regimental training exercises to prepare units for tactical maneuvers.[3] Stilwell's efforts to resolve practical difficulties in Burma would demonstrate again that in purely military affairs he was a talented, disciplined, and effective leader, and he skillfully leveraged this success to regain a more prominent strategic role.

Stilwell's actions in the summer and fall of 1943 highlight the multiple factors that are applicable to military operational decision making. First, Stilwell understood that all strategic and policy decisions are temporary and began working to rebuild his position rather than fall in line with the decisions made at the Trident Conference. Second, he was able to develop the Ramgarh training center and engineering projects in the CBI theater as evidence of success and convince senior leaders to build on these tangible successes. Third, he subtly shifted his role in a Burma campaign to emphasize the support it would give to British objectives in

Southeast Asia and logistics objectives to supply China overland. This deftly removed him as the focus of operations and helped include powerful bureaucratic allies who now saw their interests as being supported by a north Burma campaign.

BUILDING HIS OWN ARMY

After the Trident Conference, Stilwell's effort to push forward with a north Burma campaign was built on his argument that it could be conducted without significant American or British combat units. Stilwell's faith in the Chinese soldier led him to believe that he could undertake offensive operations against a division-sized Japanese force using only the two Chinese divisions trained at Ramgarh. In effect, Stilwell was making a virtue out of necessity, because after being denied American forces, he had to seek alternative solutions using resources already in theater. Stilwell's remarkable success in training and developing the CAI led Chiang Kai-shek, British military leaders, and the American Joint Chiefs of Staff to give grudging approval for Stilwell's plans. Stilwell's success in this effort was a result of hard work and his talent for leading combat soldiers. Reflecting on the development of Chinese forces for the Burma campaign, British general William Slim highlighted the energy and enthusiasm of the sixty-year-old Stilwell: "Everywhere was Stilwell, urging, leading, driving."[4] Stilwell's training program for Chinese forces was tailored to support his plan to use Chinese troops in both India and the Chinese province of Yunnan in a pincer attack that would converge on the Myitkyina area of northern Burma. The CAI force of two divisions, along with a range of supporting units, would attack southward from the Ledo area, driving down the Hukawng Valley, while a much larger force would attack southwest from Yunnan, along the route of the old Burma Road. The training experiences of these two forces was radically different, and while the CAI experience in training and later combat was almost universally held to be a success, the difficulties Stilwell and his American staff had in developing and advising Chinese forces in Yunnan shattered American expectations about Chinese troops ever playing a decisive role in the war against Japan.

The Chinese force in Yunnan that was planned to form one of Stilwell's pincer attacks was designated the Chinese Expeditionary Force

(CEF), which was one component of a larger training program in Yunnan, dubbed the "Y Force," that would seek to reshape thirty Chinese divisions. While the Chinese Army in India was built through a military school system, the American role in the Y Force would be built around a short-term training program and small groups of American liaison teams operating with Chinese units. In contrast to Ramgarh, where Americans created a closed system with U.S. control over personnel schedules, pay, and all supplies and equipment, the training program in Yunnan would be much less intensive. Chinese personnel would cycle through American training centers to learn critical skills and would then return to their units. These courses in artillery, communications, and so forth, would consist of only six weeks of instruction by American advisors, after which the personnel would hopefully disseminate their new skills to others when they rejoined their units. The American commander of the Y Force training and supply program was Col. Frank Dorn, a "China Hand" who had served at the Peking embassy with Stilwell before the war and had been alongside Stilwell as his military aide during the Burma campaign and the humiliating walkout to India. In Yunnan, Chinese troops always remained under direct Chinese command, and Dorn had no authority over troops outside of the training centers area. The contrasting approaches of the two forces is clearly seen in the way American guidance was disseminated. At Ramgarh, General Boatner developed a habit of putting all important orders into writing (both Chinese and English) and using his own signature and official seal, which he could then give to his Chinese subordinates.[5] In contrast, Dorn could only submit requests and memorandum to Chinese commanders and hope they acted on his guidance.

In theory, fourteen divisions under General Chen Cheng were assigned to the CEF that would drive into Burma and would receive U.S. Army support and training. A major problem emerged when Chinese units arrived far below their assigned strength for training yet demanded the full allocation of supplies and weapons to be provided by the U.S. Army. General Chen's CEF had less than 50 percent of its assigned 196,000 soldiers in April 1943, and it was suspected that this was intentional, with any extra weapons supplied being quietly diverted to Chinese units elsewhere, primarily to Chiang Kai-shek's most trusted units surrounding Communist areas.[6] In addition, many of the troops were hastily collected from a variety of different factions within the Chinese army. Col. Walter Wood, a senior U.S. liaison officer, assessed that the potential of the training centers was wasted: "the sad thing was that it did not teach. No one fired on the ranges. No one maneuvered on the training areas. Haphazard lectures, or to be more accurate, speeches were the order of the day."[7] These problems were well-known to American military leaders, but after the Trident Conference, Stilwell believed he had no support or authority, writing, "It seems absolutely impossible to do anything. The President has undercut me and the Chinese resist manfully every attempt to help them fight."[8] Without the clear support of a powerful political patron in China, the Y Force and the critical China Expeditionary Force, which was meant to attack into Burma, continued to go through the motions of training and preparation, with little actual progress. Stilwell would need to perform better at the Cairo Conference and win support for operations in northern Burma and gain political pressure to improve conditions in Yunnan.

In contrast, the early investment in training Chinese soldiers that had retreated to India in mid-1942 had now paid large dividends, and these troops increasingly were rated as capable of aggressive, offensive action. The 38th Division, under Sun Li-jen, had been brought up to full strength with more than 12,000 personnel, and the 22nd Division under Liao Yao-xiang had slightly less. These two units would outnumber their opponents in the 18th Japanese Division, which was stationed in northern Burma. Transfers of heavy weapons, particularly machine guns and mortars, would also enable the units of the CAI to gain a firepower advantage over Japanese forces. As CAI units moved out of training areas and into camps nearer the front, American advisors were assigned to positions down to the battalion level to provide assistance and coordinate air supply and artillery support. General Boatner, as commander of the Chinese Army in India, made it clear to American advisors that they needed to adjust their military behavior to succeed in their new role. In his instructions to liaison officers, he stated, "You are taking up a very, very difficult assignment. . . . It will tax your initiative, ingenuity, tact, and spirit of cooperation to the utmost," and he cautioned advisors to always think through a situation from the point of view of their Chinese officer partners.[9] The role and authority of American liaison officers operating in Chinese units required delicate calibration to ensure both Chinese and Americans worked toward a productive relationship. General Boatner's instructions to liaison officers highlighted that American officers need to accomplish two goals: improving their assigned units' effectiveness and providing accurate information to higher U.S. headquarters. Boatner noted, "Your duty is to make the organization to which you are assigned the most effective battle unit possible" but also to serve as "the connecting link between this headquarters and the Chinese unit concerned." Boatner stressed that liaison officers would maintain an independent system of communications to send tactical information to headquarters independent of their Chinese host unit. This would ensure that American headquarters had accurate and verifiable reports to shape plans. This placed liaison officers in a difficult position of having a dual loyalty: they were being asked to integrate their efforts with a Chinese unit but were also responsible to a second chain of command. Boatner also cautioned liaison officers to guard their conduct with the Chinese, noting, "Do not take part in 'politics.' Be sparing in both criticism and praise of subordinate officers for your motives can easily be misunderstood."[10]

The development of an American-led Chinese force in India provided Stilwell's most important ally, General Marshall, with a valuable card to play in negotiations with the British. When faced with British hesitancy to begin an attack into Burma, Marshall cited the success of efforts at Ramgarh.[11] Through slow and steady efforts to train and develop the Chinese Army in India, Stilwell had created a critical point of leverage in favor of an attack that could be used in strategic discussions. The force in Yunnan, although much less capable, also provided Stilwell with an existing organization that he could argue needed just supplies and personnel to become more effective. This leverage would be especially important at the upcoming Cairo Conference, where Stilwell's role was subject to further revision, and his plans for Burma were the subject of intense debate.

WINNING OVER THE BRITISH

While Stilwell was refocusing his attention on a limited offensive into northern Burma, the CBI theater was also changing due to Prime Minister Winston Churchill's restructuring of the British command relationships in India and Burma, and this would be a tremendous opportunity for Stilwell and his proposed north Burma campaign. At the Trident Conference in Washington, the discussion of airpower in China had been the primary focus of Stilwell's attention, but discussion of operations in Burma, which was vitally important to British imperial interests, had continued to develop. The British continued to be opposed to a major campaign in Burma, and Churchill had stated in May that he opposed devoting resources to "swampy jungles in which operations could be conducted for only five months of the year."[12] Any Sino-American operation in Burma would also require close coordination of British forces, ideally by conducting simultaneous amphibious landings along the Arakan coast. Unfortunately, a full-scale invasion of Burma would require a sizable portion of Allied transport aircraft and landing craft, which were the two pieces of equipment that were vital in the planned invasion of France. In particular, the poor transportation network in central and northern Burma would require many Allied troops to be supplied via airdrop of supplies, a costly and time-consuming method of logistics support. Diverting landing craft from the buildup for a cross-channel attack in Britain or reallocating transport aircraft from the Hump airlift to support a drive into Burma contradicted two long-established American goals. British military leaders, particularly General Sir Alan Brooke, appeared to take a great deal of delight in pointing out these plainly obvious contradictions and the stark inconsistency in American plans for an invasion of Burma.[13] The consensus reached at Trident was that a campaign in north Burma was an option to reopen land communication and supply routes with China, but it was deliberately vague on the timing of any offensive in light of the equipment and logistical requirements. In this context, Stilwell had an opportunity to build support for his plan for a limited offensive because it would allow both British and American senior leaders to take action in Burma while not jeopardizing their more important strategic plans.

To streamline operations in Burma, on June 19, 1943, Churchill proposed the creation of a new Southeast Asia Command, which would integrate Anglo-American efforts in continental Asia. After American requests, primarily voiced by President Roosevelt, that China be excluded from this command area and that Americans be given at least several of the key command positions, the proposal was put on the agenda for the upcoming strategy conference in Quebec. The Quadrant Conference, which began in Quebec on August 19, 1943, was primarily focused on Europe, where the recent surrender of Italy required revisions to the plan to attack Germany. The discussions at Quadrant did continue to develop the basic strategic concepts that had been formulated at the Trident Conference in May, which called for an invasion of Japan following an "overwhelming air offensive from bases in China." While U.S. planners continued to argue for an offensive along the Arakan coast to support Stilwell's planned attack in north Burma, British planners noted in classic bureaucratic delaying tactics that "the form of this decision must await on the outcome of discussion," considering other strategic considerations.[14] More importantly for Stilwell and the CBI theater, senior leaders at Quadrant approved Churchill's proposal and appointed Vice Admiral Lord Louis Mountbatten as supreme commander of a newly established Southeast Asia Command.

Mountbatten was a rising star in the British military, with both an aristocratic background and expertise in amphibious operations, and unlike many British officers, he made an effort to charm Americans.[15] His command would have responsibility for the areas of Burma, Sumatra, Malaya, and Ceylon (Sri Lanka) and was created to conduct "vigorous and effective prosecution of large-scale operations against Japan in Southeast Asia," as well as allow the British authorities in India to focus on civilian administration.[16] Churchill was pleased with the acceptance of his proposal, believing a new command led by Mountbatten would provide the stimulus of "a young and vigorous mind in this lethargic and stagnant Indian scene."[17] General Marshall concurred, and he radioed Stilwell that while the new command arrangement was "illogical," he would find Mountbatten to be "a breath of fresh air."[18] General Marshall recommended Mountbatten highly in his communications with Stilwell: "Mountbatten is full of energy, drive and imagination to a point that irritates staid British high officials. He is very likeable and has enthusiastically entered cooperation with American proposals time after time."[19] Mountbatten's appointment would provide Stilwell with an opportunity to impress Mountbatten with his plan and energy, arguing that his north Burma offensive could achieve solid gains with a minimum investment of resources.

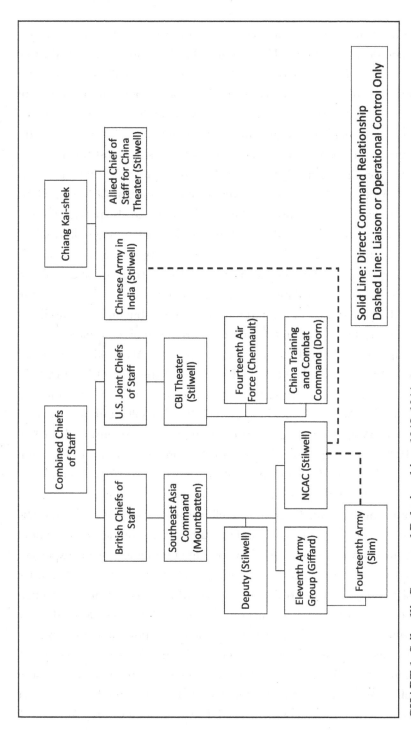

CHART 1. Stilwell's Command Relationships, 1943–1944

Stilwell also gained unexpected support for his plans from a new bureaucratic ally within the U.S. military. The drive into northern Burma, which appeared to senior policymakers to be a potentially useful but not urgent effort, received unexpected and significant support at the Quadrant Conference and in the Pentagon from U.S. Army logistics officers. Ironically, the extremely challenging and difficult climate and terrain in northern Burma was seen by American logistics leadership, most notably Maj. Gen. Brehon B. Somervell, as an opportunity to prove the skill and enterprise of American engineers. Not only would the support of Somervell be vital to accelerating operations in the field, but it would also provide Stilwell with solid support when dealing with the British and among policymakers in Washington, D.C. The price of Somervell's support was that a sizable portion of the praise and media coverage of the Burma campaign focused on the achievements of American military engineers, and while the praise was undoubtedly earned, it did diminish the contributions of Stilwell, his staff, and most important the Chinese troops under his command.

Maj. Gen. Brehon B. Somervell was a career Army officer who had graduated from the United States Military Academy at West Point in 1910 near the top of his class. After choosing to become an engineer, Somervell served in the Punitive Expedition against Pancho Villa and distinguished himself in World War I. After rising through the ranks during the 1920s and 1930s, Somervell played a role in the construction of the Pentagon and was chosen by General Marshall to lead the U.S. Army Services of Supply in 1942, which had far-ranging power over logistics, construction, and transportation functions. Somervell was widely seen as a bureaucratic "empire builder," seeking to expand his authority and influence throughout the Army. He was also not afraid to advocate for building overly expensive projects that had dubious military utility, such as the extremely expensive Canol Road project in northern Canada, which was a triumph of engineering but had negligible impact on the war.[20] Somervell believed that the construction of a road linking Ledo in India to a point along the Burma Road would allow supply convoys to reach China without the necessity of liberating all of Burma. A pipeline adjacent to the road could also supply sufficient aviation and motor fuel for Chennault's aircraft as well as for trucks brought into China via the road. British general Claude Auchinleck opposed a major land campaign in northern Burma and construction of a road on the grounds that the supply line into the Ledo area of Assam, northeast India, was already overburdened.[21] The Assam region of India, a region bounded by the Himalayas in the north and dense vegetation of what is now Bangladesh on the west, bordered Burma but was isolated from India, and it relied on a network of narrow-gauge railways and river barges to ship cargo into the region. British planners highlighted that with construction units focused on expanding airfields for the Hump airlift, developing a transportation network to reach Ledo, let alone push a road and pipeline network into Burma, would entail massive expense and would likely be very slow to have an impact.[22] To support his arguments, Somervell used optimistic, if not outright fabricated, statistics to justify the massive investment, and he openly dismissed British concerns about insurmountable difficulties.[23] At the Quadrant Conference, he argued that a Burma road would be able to supply 65,000 tons a month to China by 1945 or 1946, an estimate that exceeded the eventual capacity of the road tenfold.[24]

At the Quadrant Conference, the final conclusions of the Combined Chiefs of Staff blandly supported opening a land route to China, but the British reluctance was only overcome in large part because the United States agreed to provide the necessary personnel, equipment, and supplies to develop the logistics route in Assam.[25] Moreover, the United States would provide all necessary men and material to meet logistics goals for the Ledo Road and the north Burma campaign effort.[26] Plans also called for a network of pipelines to be built from Calcutta to airfields in India, on through Assam, and, eventually alongside a road, into China at an undetermined date in the future.[27] General Somervell saw the results of the conference as a vindication of his organization, writing that the logistics and line of communications from India to China would be "the greatest engineering undertaking of the War and perhaps the major effort insofar as supply is concerned."[28] For Stilwell, Somervell's "hard sell" of the Burma road plan provided the north Burma campaign with a vital inroad into the overall Allied strategic war plan.

In the CBI theater, moving from plans to reality was always difficult, and in October 1943, Somervell visited India, seeking to negotiate with the British to either massively increase their efforts on the Assam logistics corridor or fully hand over the responsibilities to American Army units.[29] At a conference in New Delhi on October 23, 1943, to discuss logistics, Mountbatten, Stilwell, and Somervell met with Auchinleck, who now commanded the India Command, and Somervell promised to reach the 50 percent increase in shipments if U.S. personnel were given authority over the route and U.S. railway troops brought in to operate the trains.[30] Mountbatten deferred a decision, but Somervell knew that Auchinleck could not match the offer of American troops and equipment. These negotiations highlight the extraordinary lengths taken by Somervell to gain acceptance for a campaign in north Burma because it would provide a way to showcase the engineering and logistical talents of his organization, not because of any affinity for Stilwell or the CBI theater mission. Throughout this process, Stilwell was sufficiently savvy to recognize that Somervell, in the same way a blocker in football will open a path for a runner, could help him achieve his goal of attacking into Burma and deflect British opposition to the offensive. Somervell would put tremendous resources to work to bring about his vision of an engineering triumph of a road linking India to China, and while the road was completed, the cost in terms of money, personnel, and time was exceedingly high. The faith of Somervell and his engineers in their talents and equipment led them to estimate that by the fall of 1945 a two-lane all-weather road could be built that could carry 65,000 tons per month to Kunming.[31] This ambitious goal did not account for Japanese resistance, and it considered issues like dense jungle, monsoon rainfall measured in the hundreds of inches, and widespread malaria-infested valleys, as technical issues to be solved.

DEMONSTRATING CBI CAPABILITIES AND THE CAIRO CONFERENCE

In October and November 1943, Stilwell ordered a series of probing attacks and movements by the Chinese Army in India across the border into Burma. These operations were designed to push forward the area under Allied control, which would enable the construction engineers to make forward progress and to seize key geographic positions for the launching of the overall north Burma ground offensive. More importantly for the CBI theater, these attacks demonstrated to Mountbatten and senior leaders at the Cairo

Conference the capabilities of American-supported Chinese forces in Stilwell's command. On October 5, 1943, General Sun was ordered to begin moving Chinese soldiers forward, down out of the Naga Hills, an area of high ground south of Ledo, and into the Hukawng Valley. Plans called for the 112th Infantry Regiment to seize crossing sites on the Tarung and the Tanai rivers. Allied intelligence was poor, and it was believed that Japanese forces might have small reconnaissance elements at the northern end of the Hukawng Valley but that no units of more than platoon size would be in the vicinity of the Chinese advance. Units only began to reach the rivers on October 30, and they ran into their first Japanese resistance. After pushing through Japanese forward positions, the Chinese advance bogged down when they encountered well-constructed Japanese fortifications, and it became apparent that the Japanese intended to defend river crossing of the Tarung with a battalion-sized force spread across multiple locations.

Stilwell's limited offensive occurred just as Vice Admiral Lord Louis Mountbatten was arriving in the region as supreme commander of a Southeast Asia Command, giving the British naval officer a first impression of energy and offensive spirit. Mountbatten's arrival would prove to be a major boost to Stilwell's fortunes and tremendously increased the chances that a north Burma campaign would take place in 1944. Stilwell was always uncomfortable around political figures, preferring the manners and narrower worldview of military officers, and with Mountbatten's role focused on combat operations, rather than Indian administration, Stilwell developed a better relationship than he had with previous senior British leaders. In addition, Mountbatten's expansive statutory authority enabled him to focus and shape the bland, compromise language produced at the major combined chiefs of staff conferences. The Trident and Quadrant Conferences had identified general programs, but without specific dates, orders, or assigned units, these plans carried little weight. This is shown by Stilwell's lack of support in London or Washington, even though a limited offensive into north Burma was technically approved policy. For the first time since the war began, Mountbatten would provide clear guidance, establish a workable organizational structure, and specify priority tasks to commanders. If Stilwell could convince Mountbatten that the American interest in Burma was related to more than reopening the land route to

China (the stated American objective) and help Mountbatten achieve the British political goals in Southeast Asia, he could form the basis of a mutually beneficial relationship.[32]

While the appointment of Mountbatten was a welcome change for many Americans in the CBI theater, the creation of yet another level of command authority compounded the already complicated command relationships. General Marshall wrote that the creation of a new Southeast Asia Command was "an abnormal arrangement but everything connected with this theatre has of necessity been set up frankly on such a basis because of Indian government considerations and the Generalissimo's position and methods."[33] As the senior American officer in the region, Stilwell was appointed as the deputy supreme Allied commander of the Southeast Asia Command (SEAC). Stilwell's subordinate, General Wheeler, was appointed as the SEAC G-4, to oversee supply issues.[34] The immediate task Stilwell began after Mountbatten formally took command as supreme Allied commander, (SEAC), was to revise the plans for an offensive developed under Auchinleck. The proposed offensive in Burma in early 1944, code-named Operation Champion, was extremely complex, with an advance on the Arakan peninsula and a landing on the Andaman Islands, called Operation Buccaneer, to be coordinated with an offensive in northern Burma under Stilwell, called Operation Tarzan. In addition, a series of deep penetration raids into the interior of Burma would distract the Japanese and disrupt communications and supply lines.

While Stilwell worked to improve his relationships with British leaders, he also took steps to improve his coordination with the State Department and better understand the political context in which he operated. In June 1943, Stilwell passed a request through the War Department for the assignment of four mid-level State Department officials to be attached to his command staff. The request sought to integrate "trained political observers" into the CBI theater staff so that they could "be of service to commanders in the field in matters affecting relations with the various Burmese factions, British colonial administrators, the Free Thais, the French in Indo-China and the Indo-Chinese."[35] The request was approved on August 17, with the quid pro quo caveat that the State Department wanted this new arrangement to initiate "the direct exchange at frequent and regular intervals of views and of information between General Stilwell and the ranking political representatives of the United States in India and in China."[36] The role of Stilwell's new State Department advisors would be especially important at two Allied strategy conferences planned for the late fall of 1943 because Stilwell desperately needed to avoid a repeat of his poor performance at the Washington conference, and solid political advice would be essential.

The Cairo Conference, which began in late November 1943, was attended by Roosevelt, Churchill, and Chiang Kai-shek. Amid the larger discussion of global policy, the conference sought to solidify policy objectives in East Asia, because the defeat of Germany looked increasingly certain by early 1945. Prior to the meeting, American strategic planners assessed the rapid advance by the forces of Adm. Chester Nimitz in the central Pacific, along with the forces of Gen. Douglas MacArthur, as offering a more direct route to attack Japan than a route through China.[37] When the conference began on November 23, Mountbatten's updated plan for an attack into Burma along multiple avenues, Operation Champion, was seen by Stilwell and Chiang Kai-shek as a continuation of the British emphasis on defense of India, and a slow, complicated plan to attack into Burma. Operations were planned to begin on January 15, 1944, with all efforts made to achieve decisive results before the rainy season began in May.[38] Chiang Kai-shek was particularly critical of the diversion of transport aircraft from the Hump airlift to support the offensive, after laborious improvements to the airlift facilities were finally beginning to increase the tonnage delivered to Chennault's airplanes.[39]

Despite the critical importance of the Cairo Conference as an opportunity to advance his agenda, Stilwell's old habits almost led to disaster because he initially neglected to have a well-developed counterargument and alternative plan. Stilwell's political advisor John Paton Davies wrote that on the flight to Cairo, "I was astonished to discover that the General [Stilwell] had no prepared statement or plan ready for the conference."[40] With Davies' frantic assistance, Stilwell crafted a two-page memo while en route that listed eight objectives that could be targeted by military operations in Southeast and East Asia. Despite its brevity, the plan was a major improvement from Stilwell's stance at the Trident Conference, when rather than present a detailed argument, he futilely sought to block Chennault. Davies also noted with pride that the plan was aligned around supporting the already existing positions of many senior leaders, writing, "The beauty of our little plan is that it appeals to so many—Ernie [Admiral King], Hap [General Arnold], the Gimo and FDR."[41] Stilwell continued to press for U.S. ground forces in the CBI theater, requesting one U.S. infantry division by March 1944, with two additional divisions later in the spring.[42] On November 25, Stilwell had another opportunity to meet directly with President Roosevelt, and, accompanied by General Marshall, he made the case that the United States should push for increased American authority over Chinese forces. Continually frustrated by the factionalism and obstructionism, Stilwell argued for "U.S. command, with real executive authority" over a force of at least corps size.[43] Like his earlier meetings with Roosevelt, Stilwell did not establish a good relationship with the president and his proposals were politely noted but did not make an impact on Roosevelt's agenda for the conference. Stilwell continued to travel with the U.S. delegation to the Tehran Conference, which included Soviet leader Joseph Stalin in addition to Churchill and Roosevelt.

The Cairo Conference was also Roosevelt's first opportunity to meet with Chiang Kai-shek in person, and the result of the tense and challenging meetings between the two leaders was a diminished American optimism for relying on China in Asia. Chiang's habit of agreeing to decisions, then reversing himself exasperated Roosevelt's advisors and senior American and British military officials. Chiang's continual demands that the British take action in Burma before he would commit the Chinese Expeditionary Force in Yunnan struck many observers as little more than strategic blackmail.[44] One British observer noted that Chiang's preferred habit was to agree to a policy, then a day later, upon further reflection, demand that "unless several impossible conditions could be fulfilled, he refused to play his part in the operations."[45] Gen. Hap Arnold, the senior American Air Force officer, also found that Chiang was "not realistic. He brushed too many important things aside. He cast aside logistics and factual matters as mere trifles."[46] Stilwell noted tersely in his notes that Chiang gave a "terrible performance" in key meetings and during interactions with senior British and American officials.[47] Mountbatten concurred and noted that senior

British and American leaders, after coming face to face with Chiang, "have been driven absolutely mad" by his behavior and limited understanding of global issues.[48] Even Chiang's fervent supporters, such as State Department advisor Stanley Hornbeck, whom Stilwell's political advisor John P. Davies pithily summarized as "starchy," grudgingly admitted that during the fall of 1943, "the Chinese are apathetic as regards engaging in or preparing for offensive operations on a substantial scale."[49]

In addition to private concerns, by the time of the Cairo Conference, Chiang's status in the eyes of the American public, which had been supplied with a steady diet of pro-Chiang reporting since 1937, was threatened by increasingly critical reporting from the China theater. In August 1943, Hanson Baldwin, a reporter for the *New York Times*, authored a scathing essay about China and Chiang's leadership titled "Too Much Wishful Thinking about China," which depicted Chiang as an opportunistic and repressive warlord, rather than a progressive and staunch ally committed to fighting the Japanese. A congressional delegation of five U.S. senators visited China in August 1943, and Stilwell personally escorted them in Kunming and Chungking, continually highlighting his command difficulties. Henry Cabot Lodge, one of the five senators on the tour, gave a speech later in the year noting that U.S. policy should not be formed on the basis of "sugary propaganda about China," highlighting the marked shift in American perceptions.[50]

Chiang had also hurt his public image with the publication of a book, *China's Destiny*, that outlined his thoughts on the world and China's global role but which was seen as reactionary and authoritarian.[51] The book emphasized the superiority of Chinese traditions and blamed foreigners for China's economic and political issues.[52] A British Foreign Office assessment concluded acerbically that "large parts of [*China's Destiny*] might have been written by Hitler or at least by Franco."[53] Increasingly, Chiang was being perceived as less of an embattled democrat fighting fascism and more of, in the words of Secretary of War Henry Stimson, an "ignorant, suspicious, feudal autocrat" with a focus on political machinations rather than military affairs.[54] By late 1943, Roosevelt had invested a massive amount of political capital in promoting Chiang as the indispensable leader of a global power, but like any political leader, Roosevelt was keenly aware of shifting attitudes and opinions about Chiang, as well as making his own assessments of how useful Chiang would be to his policies.

As Chiang's political influence evaporated, reports about serious issues in the Chinese army were also slowly eroding American faith in the future utility of Chinese operations, and the mediocre performance of senior Chinese military officers at the conference reinforced American concerns. In the briefing material prepared for the Cairo Conference, an assessment of Chinese capabilities and intentions prepared by the U.S. Joint Chiefs of Staff dramatically downgraded their assessment of Chinese forces. The report noted that

> not more than one-fifth of the Chinese Army is currently capable of sustained defensive operations and then only with effective air support; we believe that with the possible exception of the American-trained Chinese divisions, no large number of troops can be expected to undertake more than very limited objective offensive operations, at the present time.[55]

In strategy discussion, Chiang's senior officers made a poor impression on British and American general staff officers. Many of the general officers in the Chinese army had been selected because of their loyalty to Chiang rather than their competence, and by the later years of war, the majority of senior Chinese generals had received only rudimentary military training at the KMT's own Whampoa Academy, rather than at a traditional specialized military school.[56] Even Chiang's close advisors knew they were not selected for their skills and talents, and Wu Tiecheng, a member of Chiang's inner circle, commented without shame that "whether we get any work done or not, as long as we keep our leader pleased, everything is possible; otherwise, it is not beneficial just to get work done."[57] At Cairo, John Paton Davies found that the Chinese military officers were woefully unprepared and that "they do not know how to go about the business of a conference. Too many high-ranking officers, not enough colonels for running around, doing contact and spade work. The generals sit around completely uninformed and out of touch."[58] In planning sessions, British general Sir Alan Brooke noted that the Chinese contributed little and asked very basic questions that were already fully explained in the prebriefing reading material, but when asked about Chinese plans, the result was a "ghostly silence" of officers fearful of making statements that might offend Chiang.[59]

Chiang's officers also lacked the authority to make even minor decisions without his personal approval. A common phrase used by the Chinese to defer making a decision was that they "had not had sufficient time to study these plans," a blatant stalling technique that greatly frustrated American and British officers.[60] After one particularly vapid meeting with the Chinese generals, Brooke was reported to have said to General Marshall, "That was a ghastly waste of time," to which Marshall is said to have replied, "You're telling me!"[61] Chiang's military staff also attempted to surreptitiously modify the language of a meeting document after one of the strategy sessions, drawing a swift rebuke from American senior officers.[62] In another case of poor Chinese military staff work, Chiang argued for a naval component to conduct operations against Burma in order to stop Japanese reinforcements from reaching Burma. Mountbatten referred the Generalissimo to the recent completion of a railway route through Thailand, which would allow the Japanese to reinforce Burma even if they lost control of the Bay of Bengal, showing an embarrassing lack of preparation by Chiang and his staff.[63] In a discussion on Thanksgiving Day 1943, Chiang further embarrassed himself by arguing that the advance into north Burma should seize a line running east to west through Mandalay, an off-the-cuff idea that ignored the mountain ranges, river valleys, and transportation network of Burma, which all run north-south.[64] Chiang's failures at Cairo would lead to a continued erosion in the importance placed on China in the defeat of Japan by the Combined Chiefs of Staff and senior leaders like Roosevelt, Marshall, Churchill, and Brooke.[65]

The steady erosion of trust in Chiang Kai-shek's honesty and the competence of Chinese military leaders was exacerbated by increasing doubts about Chennault's air program. By the Cairo Conference it was clear that his Fourteenth Air Force had been efficient in shooting down Japanese aircraft and striking local shipping, but this had not significantly altered the strategic picture in China. In response to increased aircraft losses, the Japanese simply reinforced the China theater with better aircraft.[66] Within the military it was also widespread knowledge that Chennault's laissez-faire attitude to management and administration had led to substantiated reports of Fourteenth Air Force personnel being involved in smuggling gold, PX supplies, and medicine on U.S. airplanes for sale on the Chinese black market.[67] In addition, Chennault's continued efforts to bypass Stilwell and other senior leaders in order to argue for yet more increases in his air force rankled Army leaders. In September 1943, Chennault sent one of his staff officers to Washington to hand deliver personal letters to President Roosevelt and Harry Hopkins that sought to shift blame for the lack of success in air operations, claiming he not "been given the tools to do the job."[68] That same month, General Marshall received word that Chennault was attempting to pass information to British officers on the Combined Chiefs of Staff without informing any Americans. Marshall bluntly informed Field Marshal Sir John Dill that "General Chennault is an intrepid and inspiring leader who can direct very efficiently the operations of combat aircraft; but his methods of influencing his proposals present a very serious problem for me. His action results in indirectly subverting Stilwell."[69] Chennault's support of Chiang also led him into difficulties with Washington when he advocated that the United States pay for airfields in China rather than have the Chinese provide them as agreed. Chennault's stance was not perceived favorably, and Stilwell commented that "Chennault of course is being used" by the Chinese to advance a position not in U.S. interests.[70]

Stilwell did not emerge from the conference unscathed. In Cairo, General Marshall gave Stilwell blunt advice to be more considerate in his language and behavior toward Chiang and his inner circle. In a postwar interview, Marshall recounted that he had instructed Stilwell to "stop your outrageous talking" and that he was to "stop talking to your staff about these people," because the use of terms such as "Peanut" inevitably leaked to the press.[71] Stilwell was not the only leader to have a difficult experience in Cairo. Mountbatten's plans to attack into Burma were put in jeopardy with the formal cancellation of Operation Champion and the diversion of landing craft from the Indian Ocean to the European theater. Mountbatten continued to advocate for a more general offensive into Burma, rather than just into a portion of north Burma, and he remarked to his staff that "the quickest and most efficient way of taking supplies on a large scale into China is through a port rather than by a long and uncertain land route."[72] Despite these lingering issues, Stilwell had achieved his long-cherished goal of getting approval for an offensive, and with Chiang's permission to use Chinese troops in north Burma he had achieved what General Marshall described as "a milestone in the prosecution of the war in the East."[73]

CONCLUSION

Looking at the period from June through early December 1943, Stilwell's strategic goal did not change, and his continued focus on developing a land offensive into northern Burma remained constant. In contrast, his relative position in Allied plans improved dramatically because he was able to better align his campaign plans with the British and U.S. military leadership. He was also able to exploit the opportunity created by problems within the Allied coalition. The failure of the British to present a coherent plan to attack into Burma, and the missed opportunity of Chiang Kai-shek to win further American support in Cairo, left Stilwell as the only person with a credible plan in the CBI theater. Stilwell's Chinese Army in India, although small in the context of the war, was trained and already engaged in operations. Rather than take a chance on uncertain plans that existed only on paper, Stilwell had created a tangible asset that could attack into Burma immediately, and he offered senior political leaders a tangible success that could be further expanded.

★ CHAPTER 4 ★

LEADING ALLIES IN BURMA

December 1943–May 1944

This is the start of a great experiment.
—Stilwell before the north Burma campaign[1]

BY THE LATE FALL OF 1943, the steady buildup of Allied military forces had finally reached a critical mass, and the slow process of driving the Japanese out of Burma could begin. Stilwell's patient marshaling of Chinese forces had created two completely retrained and fully equipped Chinese divisions, the 38th and the 22nd, which had the skills to attack Japanese units head-on. The addition of an American infantry regiment, the 5307th Composite Unit (Provisional), commonly known as Merrill's Marauders, provided a versatile tool to outflank and infiltrate Japanese lines.[2] The refinement of aerial resupply and close support operations could now provide units moving through the jungle with alternatives to road-bound supply lines and artillery. Behind Japanese lines, forces of local Burmese, armed and led by American OSS officers, provided critical intelligence and attacked Japanese units whenever possible.[3] Working in conjunction, these elements would lead a campaign to capture the vital north Burma town of Myitkyina, site of a critical airfield. Throughout the campaign, which began in December 1943 and lasted until July 1944, Stilwell's polyglot forces struggled to overcome geographic challenges that limited their mobility, and stubborn Japanese defenses slowed the advance. In addition, Stilwell's forces would need to learn to work as a team, with different organizations and different nationalities held together into some semblance of order by Stilwell's mercurial leadership. The modern U.S. Army devotes significant attention to what it defines as "interoperability," which includes not just specific issues like establishing communications with allies and partners but also understanding differences in doctrine.[4] In north Burma, it quickly became apparent that even when British, American, and Chinese units agreed on objectives and timelines, differences in tactics and concepts made interoperability a continuing challenge. The north Burma campaign would succeed in taking Myitkyina in July 1944, and with the vital airfield in Allied control the Hump air route was able to massively increase deliveries. Despite this success, the conduct of the campaign was often difficult, with missed tactical opportunities, personal animosities, and questionable decisions that gave Stilwell political difficulties with British and Chinese leaders.

The campaign in northern Burma highlights three main factors that help us understand Stilwell and the trends in modern generalship that he was struggling to understand and overcome. First, Stilwell would need to rely on foreign troops to take the fight to the Japanese and find ways to convince, cajole, and coerce Allied forces to follow his orders on the battlefield. The overwhelming majority of Stilwell's combat power was in the Chinese units trained at Ramgarh. Chinese units were the largest in terms of personnel strength, had the heaviest firepower, and throughout the campaign they would inflict the heaviest casualties on the Japanese but would also take the most casualties among Allied units. Another source of combat soldiers was the British Long-Range Patrol Groups, informally known as "Chindits" after a mythical Burmese beast (and later renamed the "Special Force"), which came under Stilwell's command but were not trained or equipped in accordance with American doctrine. Second, Stilwell, who all observers noted was a dyed-in-the-wool infantryman with notions of combat that seemed more rooted in the nineteenth century than the mid-twentieth, would need to adapt to the local environment and cultural context. In northern Burma, control of territory and fixed lines of battle were less important than attacking enemy units and seizing the terrain that controlled movement. Third, and most important to the future of Stilwell's command, the north Burma campaign would be a fight for relevance in the headquarters of SEAC and Washington, as well as the minds of the American public. Throughout the six-month campaign, questions would be raised about the expense and effort directed to gain control of an inhospitable area with unpronounceable locations. Chinese units, while under Stilwell's command, also reported and received instructions directly from Chiang Kai-shek, whose enthusiasm for the campaign shifted numerous times. Throughout the campaign, Chiang Kai-shek and Chinese advisors pointed to questionable intelligence estimates that eight Japanese infantry divisions were in Burma as a rationale for postponing the offensive.[5] Even Stilwell's superior, Mountbatten, the commander of SEAC, attempted to restrict the offensive in order to use the resources for his own planned invasion of Sumatra. Stilwell would need to continually look over his shoulder, away from the fighting, to gauge his level of support and make military decisions that could maintain the theater.

INITIAL PLANS AND CAPABILITIES

The forces Stilwell had at his disposal in the fall of 1943 were drawn from a range of sources, including British, Chinese, local Kachin communities, as well as American soldiers and flight crews. While language and cultural barriers were a challenge, they could be overcome; more enduring were differences in doctrine and organization. Units would be asked to fight alongside each other but often had radically different training, command structures, and conceptions of how to defeat the Japanese. For example, while Chinese units had been trained and equipped along American patterns and were expected to engage the Japanese in conventional attacks, British Chindit units were designed to conduct raids. Using either of these types of units in ways they were not designed to operate would waste their specialized skills and potentially lead to heavy casualties, which would have severe political consequences for Stilwell.

When the Chinese 38th Division began moving out of its Ramgarh training area in October 1943, crossing over the border from India into Burma, it was well-supplied, trained, and equipped for combat. The 38th Division, under Lieutenant General Sun Li-jen, had been completely reorganized after its chaotic retreat from Burma in 1942. The core of its strength was three infantry regiments, the 112th, 113rd, and 114th, each of which had three rifle battalions. To provide greater firepower, each infantry regiment now had a mortar company with twelve 81-mm mortars, in addition to an antitank company with eight 37-mm antitank guns, which were small enough to be maneuvered through difficult terrain. The division also had two artillery battalions, including a number of immensely powerful 155-mm howitzers, while engineer, transportation, and signal battalions provided support.[6] American medical liaison officers were also assigned to Chinese units, both to provide direct medical care and to arrange for evacuation of soldiers to hospitals in the rear areas.[7] The 22nd Division, commanded by Lieutenant General Liao Yaoxiang, had a similar organizational structure, with three infantry regiments, the 64th, 65th, and 66th. In total, the 38th Division and 22nd Division each had roughly 12,000 personnel, and when support troops were added, the total strength of the Chinese Army in India was slightly more than 32,000 personnel.[8] During the course of the campaign, additional regiments from the Chinese 30th Division, as well as regiments from the 50th and 14th Divisions, would be flown into the theater from China in early April 1944.[9] Stilwell concluded that they were "well trained and in good shape" and had all the needed skills for the upcoming campaign.[10] Perhaps most critically for the operations of Chinese units attacking south into Burma, on December 18, 1943, Chiang Kai-shek gave Stilwell full authority, both verbally and in writing, over these Chinese units in combat.[11]

Supporting the Chinese divisions were two specialized American-led units to provide armor support and light infantry capabilities. The 1st Provisional Tank Group was a hybrid force composed of both American and Chinese personnel and was led by Col. Rothwell H. Brown, with a Chinese vice commander, Colonel Chao Chen-yu. Colonel Brown had served in China from 1930 to 1934 as an officer in the 15th Infantry Regiment in Tianjin.[12] The unit would serve as the spearhead of the Allied drive into north Burma and was equipped primarily with M3A3 Stuart tanks, a light tank that mounted a 37-mm gun, which was sufficient for the close quarters fighting encountered on the campaign. While the Japanese had few tanks in the northern Burma area, the M3 lacked the armor and firepower to attack Japanese fortifications directly and would need to work in conjunction with supporting infantry.

The second specialized unit added to Stilwell's command was the 5307th Composite Unit (Provisional), code-named Galahad. Stilwell had been requesting American combat units since he arrived in the CBI theater in 1942, but his efforts to get a U.S. Army corps or even a division had been rejected. The creation of a Southeast Asia Command under a British-dominated command structure made it politically valuable to have a token U.S. contribution, and in September 1943 General Marshall directed that three thousand "rugged jungle tested volunteers" drawn from units in the South Pacific and Caribbean be sent to Stilwell.[13] The inspiration for this small unit was British major general Orde Wingate, an unorthodox officer who had created a raiding force that had conducted deep-penetration raids to attack Japanese communications and supply lines in Burma. Churchill and Roosevelt were fascinated by unconventional operations, and at the Quadrant Conference the British had discussed a plan for Wingate's groups to operate ahead of an Allied advance, to flank Japanese strongpoints, and to "reach far into the area of the Japanese lines of communication," theoretically speeding the advance.[14] While Wingate's experiences with these raids had led to some successes, they had also led to extremely heavy casualties for his forces, either from Japanese action or disease.[15] This American unit was envisioned to be used in a deep-penetration attack ahead of Chinese troops operating from Ledo or Yunnan.[16] After arriving in India in late October 1943, the American unit, designated the 5307th Regiment, trained according to Wingate's doctrines that emphasized light infantry tactics, jungle field-craft, and reliance on airdrops rather than conventional supply lines.[17] Personnel for this unit were volunteers, drawn primarily from soldiers assigned to units in the Caribbean or New Guinea, where it was hoped they would have developed jungle experience.[18] It was noted by American medical officers that many of the men who "volunteered" for the 5307th had cognitive difficulties and preexisting health issues, suggesting a time-honored U.S. Army technique of ridding a unit of unwanted personnel by getting them to volunteer for a new unit.[19]

The 5307th was organized, in accordance with British general Orde Wingate's Chindit concepts, into three battalions, each of which was subdivided into two "combat teams."[20] In theory this organization was designed to allow for greater dispersion and flexibility. Each combat team could function independently, with its own fire support, including four 81-mm mortars, two heavy machine guns, and three "Bazooka" rocket launchers, which were not expected to be used on enemy tanks but were useful in destroying bunkers.[21] Each battalion also had an air liaison team to coordinate close air support and airdrops of supplies.[22] Two Japanese American personnel, fluent in Japanese, were assigned to each combat team to provide an intelligence collecting and translation capability.[23] The downside of this light infantry structure developed by the British was that it was not aligned with U.S. Army organizations, leading to unfamiliarity, and the decentralized structure meant it also required a greater degree of coordination by American officers to fully maximize the assets of the six combat teams. The unit was also rushed through training, and most of the personnel had arrived in India on October 31, 1943, after a forty-day cruise from California.[24] Training in India was brief, and the unit entered Burma on February 21, 1944, less than four months after arrival in theater. Command decisions also hindered the development of cohesive units. On January 4, 1944, Stilwell unexpectedly assigned Col. Frank D. Merrill (soon promoted to brigadier general), a trusted member of his staff, to command of the 5307th Composite Unit.[25] Merrill was a skilled Japanese linguist and a former military attaché at the American embassy in Tokyo and had been with Stilwell during the initial walkout of Burma in 1942, but he had limited command experience and had served primarily as a military attaché or staff officer before the war.[26]

Stilwell could also plan on support from several light infantry British brigades. These units, commonly called Chindit forces, had been trained and organized in accordance with Wingate's principles that emphasized mobility as the answer to Burma's challenging terrain and to overcoming Japanese interior lines in Burma. Wingate's skills for self-publicity overshadowed the tenuous military accomplishments of his Chindit forces, and after successfully winning political support from Prime Minister Winston Churchill and President Franklin Roosevelt at the Quebec Conference, he was promoted and given approval to train a larger force. The introduction of American aircraft into SEAC in large numbers meant that instead of marching into Burma, Chindits could be landed by glider and resupplied by aircraft flying into crudely built jungle airfields built in "stronghold" positions. Growing Allied airpower would also provide Chindit units with fire support in the form of strafing attacks and bombing of Japanese positions.[27] Wingate could call upon a dedicated U.S. Army Air Force "Air Commando" unit of twenty-five cargo planes, twelve B-25 Mitchell medium bombers, thirty P-51 Mustang fighter-bombers, and more than a hundred light planes to support his units.[28] In the north Burma campaign, Stilwell could plan on the British Chindit forces helping to isolate the north Burma sector from the rest of Japanese-held Burma by conducting blocking operations that disrupted communications and transportation networks. He would not have direct control of the forces, which remained under Wingate, but in theory the five Chindit brigades assigned to the north Burma fighting could shorten the campaign.

Logistics would play a key role in the campaign, and access to supplies and heavy equipment, such as tanks and artillery, was a major Allied advantage over the Japanese. To speed the advance and compensate for the lack of roads or rail lines in the area, the Allied forces could rely on U.S. and British aircraft to drop supplies, provide close air support, and conduct medical evacuation.[29] Despite Stilwell's personal animosity toward Chennault, he was open to the possibilities of airdrops and close air support for ground forces. In the spring of 1943, Stilwell's staff conducted detailed studies of how airdrops and ground attack aircraft could accelerate the planned offensive into northern Burma. Stilwell requested Army Air Forces officers be assigned directly to his staff to coordinate planning and develop procedures.[30] With artillery support limited, Stilwell's forces could call on P-51 fighters to strafe and bomb Japanese positions. Medical evacuation was another important element of the campaign, and small single-engine aircraft operating out of crude landing strips hacked in the jungle would evacuate more than 18,000 casualties between December 1943 and August 1944 in north Burma, and during the peak of the fighting in May 1944, more than 6,000 soldiers were evacuated by air in one month.[31] Most important, Allied cargo aircraft, flying from all-weather airfields in India, had developed, through a lengthy process of trial and error, efficient methods of airdropping supplies. Procedures to drop cargo had been refined with experienced pilots and well-trained liaison teams operating with combat units on the ground. In November and December 1943, more than a thousand tons of supplies were delivered to forces in north Burma via airdrop, and this tonnage increased rapidly, reaching almost six thousand tons in April 1944.[32] While airdrops could not supply fuel and artillery ammunition in large quantities, they could supply food, animal feed, and small arms ammunition, which could keep Allied forces moving forward. In postwar analysis, Japanese military commanders maintained that the ability of aerial supply to support forces moving around Japanese flanks was the most threatening factor of the campaign because it allowed Allied forces to maintain operations regardless of the terrain constraints.[33]

While aircraft could supply some of the needed material by troops on the front line, the creation of a road network would enable a more sustained advance. On October 16, 1943, Col. Lewis A. Pick had assumed command of the road construction effort, replacing Brig. Gen. John C. Arrowsmith, whom Stilwell felt lacked the drive and enthusiasm needed for the project.[34] Pick convinced Stilwell that rather than a simple "jeep road" through the center of the damp valleys, a more developed military highway on higher ground could better support the offensive, and a more substantial road would remain useful during the monsoon season.[35] By December 1943, U.S. Army engineering troops had gained valuable experience in jungle construction and had pushed the road network from the Ledo base in India into the Hukawng Valley. Like all operations in the north Burma campaign, the construction effort was shared by multiple nationalities and ethnicities. Many of the U.S. Army construction and transportation units were made up of African Americans, collaborating with Chinese army engineers, and laborers hired in India.[36] The construction process was laborious, with tree-cutting, blasting, and grading teams all working around the clock. American engineering reports noted with great detail that clearing one acre of jungle required 200 hours of work by engineers, another 200 hours by Chinese engineers, 250 hours of work by contracted unskilled labor, and 40 hours of work from a tractor to clear one acre. The road distance from Ledo to Myitkyina was 271 miles and would require clearing 4,929 acres just to allow construction crews to begin working on the road.[37] Adjacent to the road would be a four-inch pipeline, providing gasoline to tanks and trucks, and a telephone network. Even a simple task like placing telephone poles and stringing wire was impacted by the Burmese climate. One American communications technician remarked that north Burma was "a part of the world where everything that doesn't rust quickly will corrode or rot away even faster, where batteries have less than half the normal expectancy, and insects do everything but march away with your [telephone] poles bodily."[38] Like frontline soldiers, engineers were exposed to malaria, scrub typhus, and other diseases, making a grueling construction task even more difficult. During the dry season, on average terrain, the road could advance two or three miles a week.[39]

A final element in Stilwell's battle plan was the local Kachin population of north Burma, many of which had been armed and organized by American OSS officers. Many Kachin had turned against the Japanese, and American OSS officers provided weapons, money, and opium to those willing to assist Allied efforts.[40] A small training school had been established in April 1942, and Kachin were given a rudimentary understanding of demolitions, radio communications, and intelligence gathering.[41] Thousands of rifles and submachine guns had also been distributed to the Kachin, and, combined with their native knowledge of the area, the force could be a valuable supporting element to an Allied drive. The Kachin lacked heavy weapons and their motivations were partly mercenary, so they could not be expected to take a direct role in large-scale operations.[42] The Kachin also did not work with the Chinese, partly for cultural reasons but primarily as a consequence of widespread Chinese looting and brutality during the 1942 retreat from Burma.[43]

Opposing these polyglot Allied forces was the Japanese 18th Division, which, like the American and Chinese divisions, was built around a core of three infantry regiments. Each of these regiments theoretically had 2,800 soldiers, but disease and limited replacements would have reduced actual numbers. The 18th Division also contained a separate Mountain Artillery Regiment, with howitzers and cannons specially adapted for difficult terrain.[44] The division was well-regarded and had participated in the successful campaign in Malaya that led to the Japanese capture of Singapore, as well as the invasion of Burma in 1942. Soldiers in the 18th Division were primarily recruited from the island of Kyushu, which gave the unit a shared sense of identity and cohesion. The commander of the 18th Division was Lieutenant General Tanaka Shinichi, and at the beginning of the campaign his headquarters was in Kamaing, in the Mogaung Valley in north Burma.[45] Although the Japanese had five divisions in Burma in December 1943, one division was assigned to stop the Chinese forces on the Salween River, and the other Japanese forces were preparing an invasion of India, scheduled to begin in March 1944, leaving the 18th Division alone to oppose Stilwell's campaign.

The Allied plan for retaking north Burma was profoundly shaped by the difficult terrain of the north Burma area. The goal was to open a land route to China by building a road from India south through the Hukawng Valley and then into the Irrawaddy River Valley, seizing the towns of Mogaung and Myitkyina. The straight-line distance from the India-Burma border to Mogaung was 130 miles, with Myitkyina another 30 miles northeast, but in addition to the Japanese defenders, Stilwell's forces would face a series of geographic obstacles. First, after coming down from the hills along the India-Burma border, the Tarung River flowed across the line of advance. Once over this river, the Hukawng Valley stretched south, with the winding Tanai River running down the center of the valley. The Hukawng Valley was extremely damp; even in the dry season it was covered with dense vegetation.[46] At the southern end of the valley, an area of high ground, the Jambu Bum, marked the end of the Hukawng Valley. Moving over the crest of the Jambu Bum, the terrain opened into another densely vegetated valley, passing through a series of small villages before reaching Mogaung. Mogaung was connected by a road and rail line to Myitkyina, thirty miles away. In effect, Stilwell needed to conduct a three-phased attack. The first hurdle was to get his forces across the Tarung River and through the Hukawng Valley and seize the Jambu Bum high ground. The next hurdle would be to drive down another valley to Mogaung, attacking the heart of Japanese defenses. Last, Stilwell would need to turn his forces ninety degrees and make a final dash east for Myitkyina before the monsoon rains arrived.

While Allied forces had numerical superiority on the ground and far greater resources in the air, the terrain gave the defender a number of advantages. Heavy rainfall during the monsoon season, with more than an inch of rain a day being average in this part of Burma, made campaigning impossible from July through early December, and mudslides and flash floods threatened the still tenuous road network.[47] The moist and humid climate also supported a dense ecosystem of insect life, with malaria-carrying mosquitoes, three kinds of leeches, and biting flies, all of which would slowly degrade the health of any unit operating in the valley.[48] The only road through the Hukawng Valley was essentially a dirt trail, and Allied forces would need to build their logistics route as they advanced. In addition, as the Japanese conducted a fighting withdrawal south, their supply lines would shorten, while in contrast Allied supply lines would be extended ever farther from their base. The rivers and streams also allowed for natural defensive positions, where heavy machine guns and mortars could inflict heavy casualties on attacking units. Overall, an assessment of Stilwell's command in the fall of 1943 reveals that although Stilwell had significant combat forces for the campaign, he would need to carefully and judiciously use them in specific situations where their advantages could be fully exploited. Using British or American light infantry forces in positional warfare, where they lacked firepower, or asking conventional Chinese units to move through the jungle, would negate their individual skills. Stilwell also needed to manage the political implications of tactical decisions. If a unit from one nation took heavy casualties while another unit took noticeably light casualties, questions about burden sharing could quickly lead to political recriminations.

PRELIMINARY ENGAGEMENTS:
BATTLES ALONG THE TARUNG RIVER
Preliminary movements for the campaign began in October 1943, when the 112th Regiment of the Chinese 38th Division began to move into Burma, providing protection for the engineers building the road. The 112th was ordered to advance until it met resistance and proceed south to the Tarung River. Allied intelligence reports prepared in September 1943 found no evidence of Japanese troops in strength in the Hukawng Valley and only one battalion based ten miles north of Mogaung, more than fifty miles from the Allied advance units. In fact, General Tanaka fully expected an Allied attack, and he accurately forecast that Stilwell would attempt to

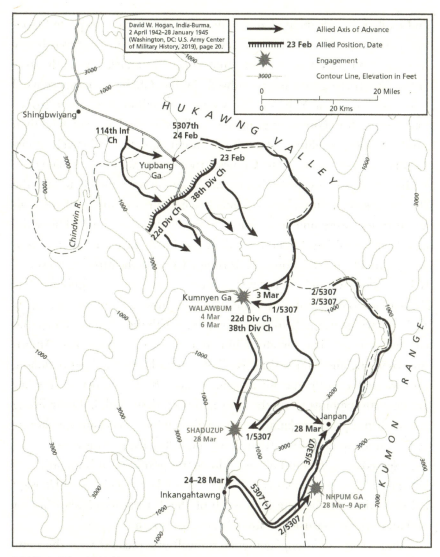

MAP 3. The 1942 Burma Campaign

move through the Hukawng and Mogaung valleys. In the early fall, the Japanese 18th Division began to move forces north into the Hukawng Valley to be in place to block an Allied campaign, which was expected to begin once the monsoon season had ended.[49] On October 24, units of the Japanese 56th Infantry Regiment reached the Tarung River and began building a series of fortified positions at key positions to control river crossings.

On October 30, advancing Chinese units ran into these unexpected Japanese positions, and over the next several days and nights suffered heavy casualties from Japanese machine guns and night attacks. An early crisis for the Allied drive, and a test of Stilwell's faith in Chinese troops, occurred at the small town of Yupgang Ba, where a battalion of Chinese troops from the 112th Regiment were unable to dislodge the Japanese, who then counterattacked, skillfully establishing strongpoints that effectively encircled the Chinese troops.[50] The Chinese troops were not in immediate danger, being supplied by airdrops, and the Japanese were unable to take the Chinese positions with a head-on attack, while other elements of the Chinese regiment were unable to relieve the encircled battalion.[51] This stalemate lasted until late December, when the 114th Regiment of the 38th Division finally arrived along the Tarung River and the growing power of Allied artillery was able to isolate and destroy Japanese strongpoints. The 114th attacked the Japanese positions on December 24 and after a lengthy artillery barrage was able to establish contact with the Chinese troops that had been cut off. The forceful Chinese attack greatly impressed American observers, and Major Peng Ke-li, commander of the lead battalion, was awarded a Silver Star for his leadership.[52] By December 31, the last Japanese strongpoints along the river had been destroyed, but by splitting into small groups, many Japanese forces were able to successfully withdraw south, setting up defenses farther down the valley. Despite these issues, the battle served as the first test of the Chinese troops trained at Ramgarh, and they gave a solid performance.[53] By the end of January, the 38th Division had cleared the immediate area south of the Tarung River, allowing for road and bridge construction units to advance south.[54]

After these initial engagements, Stilwell was pleased with the newfound confidence of the Chinese troops and messaged General Marshall that "they now know they can lick the Japs and have their tails up" and that the men were "keen and fearless" in the jungle fighting.[55] The battles along the Tarung River had demonstrated that Chinese forces were capable, but they still lacked the command and control skills to fully exploit tactical opportunities and flank Japanese positions. Casualties had also been heavy, with the 38th Division suffering 17 officers and 298 enlisted personnel killed, with an additional 400 wounded.[56] This rate of casualties was unsustainable, and new tactics would need to be devised. American liaison officers praised their Chinese units but noted, "We must admit frankly, however, that the enemy has out-maneuvered and out-witted us in the jungle. Many of our men have died bravely, but not intelligently, and hence we have not extracted from the enemy the maximum casualties." Poor usage of firepower and slow coordination of reserve and follow-on forces, both areas where the Allies had major advantages over the lightly equipped and thinly stretched Japanese, needed to be improved.[57] The battles also showed that the Japanese were well prepared to fight a delaying action and were keenly aware that using the terrain and fortified strongpoints could stall the Allied advance until the monsoon rains made further progress impossible. The slow pace of the Chinese advance was also a cause of considerable concern for Stilwell. U.S. commanders relied not just on reports from Chinese officers but could also examine reports from the U.S. liaison teams that were attached to every Chinese regiment.[58] These liaison teams were led by a lieutenant colonel and had a separate radio team to provide direct communication with U.S. headquarters.[59] Maj. Walter S. Jones, who worked with Chinese units extensively during the Burma campaign, noted,

> One of the most serious defects of the Chinese military machine is the general low standard of education, which is reflected in the quality of NCO and junior officer personnel. This not only makes for dubious leadership, but is an impediment in such simple matters as routine correspondence, and in the transmission of messages and orders. As a result, there appears a system which has always existed in illiterate armies. This is a composite of rigid channels of command, refusal to permit initiative in NCOs and junior officers, and centralization of responsibility at field grade or higher levels. A machine built out of this material is bound to be slow, uneven, and awkward in action. Chinese soldiers have been accused of being balky, when the obvious thing to do is readily apparent. The reason for this is simple. Chinese conscripts have been so steeped in the concept of fixed command channels, that they hesitate to take orders from strangers. They may even refuse to obey officers of adjacent Chinese units. They wait until the Old Man talks; and sometimes they are waiting after he is dead.[60]

Major Jones was accurate in noting the losses among command personnel being especially important. The number of Ramgarh-trained personnel was limited, and firepower and innovative tactics needed to be used rather than rely on "straight-ahead" infantry attacks.

NEW METHODS: CLEARING THE HUKAWNG VALLEY

While the Japanese forces encountered around the Tarung had been defeated, the pace of the advance was behind schedule. During late January and early February, Allied forces in north Burma were organized for a drive that could clear the southern end of the Hukawng Valley, and the arrival of the 1st Provisional Tank Group and the Merrill's Marauder light infantry force in late January gave Stilwell two important new tools. Moreover, in late January 1944, engineers had completed the construction of a 470-foot pontoon bridge across the Tarung, allowing vehicles and equipment to move forward.[61] To improve American command and control over these newly arrived elements and improve the supervision of Chinese forces, the Northern Combat Area Command (NCAC) was created on February 1, 1944.[62] General Boatner was appointed the commanding general of NCAC, although he was not a natural field commander, and this combined with Stilwell's habit of micromanaging meant that Stilwell continued to exercise de facto direct command, even on deployments at the company level.[63] OSS forces and Kachin auxiliaries also reported directly to NCAC headquarters, but Stilwell retained direct command authority over their actions.[64] By mid-February 1944, Allied forces had also been bolstered by the addition of the Chinese 22nd Division, which was massing along the Tarung River preparing for the drive on Walawbum, on the southern end of the valley.[65] In contrast to the positional fighting in December, this would be a war of maneuver.

To prevent the Japanese from slowly ceding ground, falling back from one fortified position to the next, Stilwell wanted to envelope at least one Japanese flank. His plans called for a hammer-and-anvil approach to the offensive, using the 1st Provisional Tank Group and fresh regiments of the 22nd Division to push the Japanese defenders south.[66] While this advance was holding Japanese attention, the 5307th would conduct a flanking movement, marching around the Japanese right and occupying a position overlooking the main road near Walawbum. It was hoped that this two-pronged attack would not only speed the Chinese advance but cut off Japanese units attempting to withdrawal. Allied assessment of Japanese tactics found that it was extremely likely that the Japanese would launch an "immediate counter-attack on any penetration of their defenses" and attempt to hold their positions as long as possible.[67] Japanese forces were already preparing a main defense line along the high ground of the Jambu Bum, which marked the southern edge of the valley, and stopping any defenders from reaching these fortifications was critical.

The plan was complicated and relied on each element of the offensive to play its assigned role to engage and block the Japanese forces. Stilwell's plan reflected his years of experience in teaching tactics in the U.S. Army, and the flanking maneuver was the orthodox tactical solution to the problem of an entrenched defender. The key difference between the tactics Stilwell had taught at Fort Benning and the operational level of warfare being practiced in north Burma was the scale and complexity involved. Coordinating military forces in an area of dense vegetation and difficult terrain, compounded by a lack of accurate maps, would lead to frequent communications challenges. Radios carried in the back of jeeps or on the backs of soldiers had a range of only five to ten miles, and transmissions via Morse code by more powerful transmitters could only be conducted when movement stopped for the day. Stilwell's unique style of command, relying on frequent close contact with senior leaders, also meant that guidance shared with one subordinate was often not known to others. While Stilwell's plan made effective use of the different strengths and weaknesses of the diverse elements of his command, command and control was an enduring issue. Dispersing Allied forces also meant that the numerical superiority and massed firepower of the Allies was not focused, limiting the ability to strike a decisive blow.

With the 38th Division recovering from its losses in combat and the hundreds of troops stricken by tropical illness, the 22nd Division under Liao Yaoxiang would take the lead, with the 65th and 66th Infantry regiments deployed on the front lines. These two regiments moved forward on February 23, but movement was slow and cautious. Like the 38th Division along the Tarung River, the Chinese units did not seek to move around the flanks of Japanese positions and often pulled back at night. Communications problems also led to difficulties, with the only landmarks in the valley being abandoned villages or tributaries, both of which were difficult to see at a distance due to the dense vegetation. On March 3, the 1st Provisional Tank Group took the lead and made good progress, advancing several miles before pulling back to establish a nighttime perimeter.[68] At the front, the method and pace of the attack was often decided by the individual commanders of companies and battalions, regardless of how fast Stilwell wanted the advance to move.[69] Engineering personnel were attached to the tank units to help the armor cross obstacles and clear difficult terrain, and over the next few days the tanks continued to make steady progress despite the soggy terrain and the thick vegetation.[70]

While Chinese troops were advancing down the valley, the mission given to the 5307th was to move along a series of trails that followed the high ground on the eastern edge of the valley, then attack Walawbum from the east. It was hoped that these American troops would be able to establish a blocking position behind Japanese lines. Despite the need to get the advance moving quickly, with every day of dry weather being priceless, Merrill, with the concurrence of Stilwell, had the 5307th march from Ledo to their positions in the Hukawng Valley, more than a hundred miles, rather than use trucks, to acclimate the unit to the terrain in the area. Consequently, the grueling march took a week, compared to a one-day truck ride.[71] After finally reaching their staging areas in northern Burma, on February 24 all three Marauder battalions began marching through the dense jungle, which shielded them from Japanese observation but also slowed their movement.[72]

Merrill's forces reached Walawbum on March 2 and established blocking positions overlooking both the river and the main road. The positions were to be held until the advancing 38th Division could make contact. The Japanese became aware of the Marauders flanking force on March 1, although they believed it had been landed by parachute, and had begun organizing a counterattack, pulling forces from the front lines.[73] Beginning on March 3, Japanese forces began a series of attacks on the American positions, but the attacks were successfully driven off with heavy casualties. On March 4, the Japanese attacks continued, increasing in size and with better coordination and artillery support, and American plans to hold the blocking positions until relieved needed to be reassessed. Intelligence reports also warned that a large Japanese force was moving into position to attack the blocking positions from the south. By March 5, machine gun and mortar ammunition was running low, and the two Marauder battalions blocking the road began disengaging that night and withdrew northeast, eventually meeting with Allied forces moving south down the valley.[74] The remaining Marauder battalion, holding a position overlooking the river running through the center of the valley, remained in place and held off continued Japanese attacks. While the Marauder units were moving off the roadblocks, and the Chinese infantry and tanks moved slowly south, General Tanaka ordered his forces to slip around Allied positions and move south. As a result, most Japanese forces were able to move around the scattered Allied forces, and while some were killed in jungle ambushes by OSS-led Kachin forces, the majority made their way to the prepared fortification on the Jambu Bum high ground.[75]

The Allied advance to Walawbum demonstrated that the north Burma campaign could be accelerated by integrating the different skills and capabilities of each Allied unit, and the front line moved forty miles south in only a couple of weeks. Despite this seeming success, most of the Japanese 18th Division had escaped from the attempt to block their retreat and now occupied a stronger position at the end of the valley. Moreover, the costs to the Allies, particularly among the Chinese infantry, was high. By the end of the Walawbum operation on March 18, 1944, the 38th and 22nd Divisions had suffered a combined total of over 800 killed in action, with 1,500 wounded. Most of these casualties were in the 38th Division, which had now been in combat for four months. While Stilwell's use of the Marauders clearly helped loosen the Japanese hold on the Hukawng Valley, the supply difficulties that had forced the blocking forces to redeploy illustrated the limits of light infantry forces to operate behind enemy lines. While Stilwell and his staff would use the basic framework of a hammer and anvil attack in their next operation, the method had clear risks, and it further highlights the shoestring nature of the campaign.

STALLED IN THE MOGAUNG VALLEY

With the Hukawng Valley now in Allied hands, planning began to focus on seizing the Mogaung Valley, which if taken would provide access to the Irrawaddy River and the vital town of Myitkyina, only thirty-five miles away. Stilwell's forces still faced several challenges. The Japanese defenses on the Jambu Bum pass needed to be eliminated to allow road access to the Mogaung Valley. This critical high ground was protected against flanking attacks by the mountainous terrain, and the Japanese had built well-constructed positions, including artillery emplacements for their 155-mm artillery, which had been held in reserve during the Hukawng Valley fighting. In addition, a flanking movement around the Japanese right flank, such as Stilwell had ordered at Walawbum, would be forced to make an exceptionally long march through dense jungle. Moreover, once in a blocking position along the road and river at the center of the Mogaung Valley, Marauder forces would be dozens of miles from the nearest Allied unit, a potentially vulnerable situation.

Stilwell's plan was for continued pressure by the Chinese 22nd Division and the 1st Provisional Tank Group to fix the Japanese in place on the Jambu Bum. The 5307th would then execute not one but two flanking maneuvers to cut the Japanese communications and supply line in the Mogaung Valley. One detachment, composed of the Marauder 1st Battalion and the 113th Regiment of the Chinese 38th Division, would move around the Japanese flank to the village of Shaduzup, five miles behind the Japanese defense line, and block the road.[76] This force would be led by Lt. Col. William Osborne, and his movement around the Japanese flank would require a march of thirty miles through the jungle. A second force, composed of the Marauder 2nd and 3rd Battalions, would also move around the Japanese right flank to seize a blocking position in the village, ten miles south of Shaduzup. This second force would take a much longer route and pass through more than seventy miles of jungle. Merrill would lead this second force despite lingering health problems. For both flanking forces, medical evacuation would only be possible from small landing fields hacked out of the jungle, and airdrops were their only source of supplies. Another major problem that would confront the flanking force was communications, because the farther into the jungle they marched, and more radio signals were absorbed by the jungle vegetation, and units frequently lacked the ability to talk to each other, let alone the distant headquarters.[77]

The plan suffered from several limitations. All Marauder battalions had now been in Burma for more than a month and could no longer be considered fresh, with disease and injuries beginning to cause a large number of noncombat casualties. Intelligence on Japanese deployments and the terrain of the area was also extremely limited. General Stilwell had appointed his son, Joseph W. Stilwell Jr., as his G-2 responsible for intelligence, despite his limited experience, and estimates of Japanese strength were often grossly incorrect.[78] The command staff of the 5307th was also unaware of the full extent of OSS efforts to mobilize the local Kachin inhabitants, and the NCAC staff did not supply any details or suggest that these forces could assist the Marauder plan. The official U.S. Army history, which rarely judges key decisions, concluded that this clear oversight was due to "extremely faulty co-ordination and what might be termed a hoarding of information."[79] The decision to have Chinese troops accompany the shallower flanking movement, aimed at Shaduzup, provided reinforcements for the Marauders, but Chinese forces would need to leave behind many of their machine guns, mortars, and antitank weapons, valuable firepower that was the real comparative advantage of the Chinese infantry battalions in the campaign.

Both flanking forces began their long approach marches on March 12, less than a week after the Walawbum battle.[80] Progress by both columns was slow, with soldiers often forced to hack their way through dense bamboo groves, a time-consuming and exhausting task. It was not until March 28 that Osborne's force, with a shorter route, was in position to attack the village of Shaduzup, and he was successful in establishing a blocking position by the late morning. The 1st Marauder Battalion was able to establish a temporary perimeter and hold off initial Japanese counterattacks during the remainder of the day, before allowing the 113th Infantry Regiment, with its heavier weapons, to reinforce and strengthen the blocking position during the night.[81] This blocking force was not in position for long because pressure from the advancing 22nd Division was already pushing the Japanese off the Jambu Bum.[82] While the Marauders were moving around the Japanese flank, on March 15 the 22nd Division had begun moving forward with two infantry regiments on the front lines, with the third in reserve.[83] The 1st Provisional Tank Group again served as the spearhead, pushing forward to force the Japanese defenses to open fire, allowing for air strikes, artillery, and tank cannon fire to destroy bunkers and fighting positions. Japanese minefields and the simple yet highly effective tactic of felling trees on key approaches slowed the tanks, and point-blank fire from Japanese antitank guns put several out of action on March 23.[84] The Chinese 65th Regiment, which had been held in reserve, was now brought up to maintain pressure on the Japanese and push through the remaining defense lines on the Jambu Bum. Chinese troops were moving slowly but steadily forward when Japanese forces began to withdraw south of the Shaduzup roadblock. By the late afternoon of March 29, Chinese soldiers reached Osborne's forces. While the flanking operation was successful, it also made little contribution to the speed of the Allied advance and failed to trap the retreating Japanese.

The experience of the second flanking force, led by Merrill, was much more challenging. After departing on March 12, the 2nd and 3rd Battalions first marched east before turning south, and Marauder forces reached the objective, Inkangakwawng, on March 23, but noted a strong Japanese presence in the area. An attack on March 24 was driven back by determined Japanese defenders, and a rapid counterattack forced the Marauder unit to withdraw. Alerted to the Marauder presence, a strong Japanese force was sent to isolate the Marauders, and by using the road network in the area the Japanese were able to assemble forces much more quickly than expected. Without heavy weapons and with limited ammunition for a sustained engagement, the Marauder force withdrew back toward the northeast along their approach march. Moving rapidly to stay ahead of the Japanese, Merrill's 2nd Battalion stopped at a small airstrip at Nhpum Ga and developed a hastily fortified perimeter on March 28.

NCAC headquarters was now concerned that Japanese reinforcements trailing the Marauders might use the terrain to their own advantage and push around the flank of the oncoming 22nd Division. To stop the Japanese advance, the Marauders were ordered to hold Nhpum Ga and stop any Japanese advance.[85] Amid this crisis situation, Merrill suffered a heart attack on March 28 and was evacuated, leaving Col. Charles N. Hunter in command.[86] The Marauder position at Nhpum Ga was centered on a thin ridgeline, which provided clear fields of fire but lacked access to water. The perimeter was also exposed to artillery, and the Japanese brought in 75-mm mountain guns and heavy mortars to bombard the two-hundred-by-four-hundred-yard perimeter. Relying on airdrops for food and ammunition but desperately short of water, the 2nd Battalion was surrounded for more than a week. Medical and sanitary problems within the tight confines of the perimeter became a serious issue, with human waste, dead animals, and unburied human corpses leading to widespread dysentery and illness.[87] On April 8, the Japanese forces, who were suffering from their own supply problems and limited reinforcements, withdrew back toward the Mogaung Valley, leaving the Marauders at Nhpum Ga, exhausted and weakened by hundreds of casualties, to rest and regroup. In total, 59 personnel had been killed and another 314 wounded, with most of the force also suffering from at least one tropical disease.[88]

The complicated fighting to gain a foothold in the Mogaung Valley was further evidence of the strengths and weaknesses of Stilwell's approach to the overall Burma campaign. While the Chinese divisions and tank units made slow but not spectacular progress, Stilwell attempted to use his only American unit to achieve a more rapid victory. The decision to use the Marauders as a flanking force, which was successful in the Hukawng Valley, was clearly less successful in the Mogaung Valley. Differences in the terrain, poor communication, and flawed tactical decisions all led to the Marauders being exposed to a coordinated and effective Japanese counterattack that led to heavy casualties. As a light infantry unit designed for raids, the Marauders lacked the firepower to stand and fight Japanese infantry units on even terms. Putting the only three American infantry battalions into a high-risk situation with little possibility of decisively impacting the Mogaung Valley operations was a gamble with little chance of paying off. With the departure of the Marauders for an attack on Myitkyina, the Chinese 22nd and 38th Divisions had continued to press forward, but the Japanese 18th Division held a series of fortified strongpoints blocking their advance south. In mid-April, the Chinese 22nd Division was still forty miles from Mogaung and advancing slowly, with only six more weeks of clear weather before the monsoon season brought an end to large-scale combat operations. Between late April and the end of May, the Chinese units made little progress, with frequent admonishments from Chiang Kai-shek to exercise "caution." Despite Stilwell's continued attempts to push forward, these messages led to both Lt. Gen. Liao and Sun limiting their advance.[89] The drive to seize the southern part of the Mogaung Valley was also supported by British Chindit forces entering the NCAC area, who now came under Stilwell's command and who required their own complex political and military management. The battles of the Mogaung Valley illustrate the extreme difficulties an American commander faces when they must rely on foreign troops, who have their own doctrine, organizational culture, and political goals.

After seizing Shaduzup and the Jambu Bum, Stilwell faced a key tactical decision. The Mogaung Valley widens as it moves south, and the Japanese sought to defend the narrow portion of the valley as long as possible. At the northern end of the valley, which was less than three miles wide, Japanese artillery and an integrated network of bunkers presented a solid front line. The Jambu Bum, although cleared of Japanese forces, still presented a logistics barrier to the engineers of NCAC, and it would take several weeks for crude landing strips to be hacked out of the jungle near the front lines. It quickly became apparent to Stilwell and other American liaison officers that both Liao and Sun had been in contact with Chiang Kai-shek, and between April 23 and May 27, the front line moved forward only five miles.[90]

By early May, Stilwell had moved his headquarters to Shaduzup and would frequently travel forward to the regimental command posts to try to cajole and talk the Chinese commanders into moving forward more quickly. On May 20, General Sun proposed a bold plan to move all three of his regiments around the Japanese flank.[91] Americans suspected he had received approval for the operation from Chiang Kai-shek because while Sun had previously opposed advances of more than two miles a day, he now wanted to send his regiments deep into the Mogaung Valley. The 22nd Division, reinforced by the fresh 149th Regiment, would launch a simultaneous attack on the Japanese front. After several days of marching, Sun's 112th Regiment emerged from the foothills along the Japanese right flank, blocking the road and cutting the Japanese forces in the valley into two elements.[92] Chinese troops were able to fight off a series of Japanese counterattacks, and it became apparent that the Japanese, forced out of their defenses, were suffering heavily from disease and a lack of supplies, blunting the impact of their counterattacks.[93] With the Japanese forces in the north end of the Mogaung Valley increasingly dispersed, short on supplies, and hounded by Chinese forces, Sun sent the 114th Infantry Regiment due south toward the town of Mogaung, where it could establish contact with British forces.

In mid-May, the British 77th Indian Infantry Brigade played an important and controversial role in the seizure of Mogaung, which solidified control over the valley and secured the vital road network. At the beginning of the campaign for north Burma in December 1943, plans called for three British Chindit brigades to move into Burma and establish blocking positions so that the Mogaung and Myitkyina areas could not be supplied or reinforced. Wingate's orders specified that he was to "help the advance of Stilwell's forces to the Myitkyina area by drawing off and disorganizing the enemy forces opposing them, and preventing the reinforcement and supply of these enemy forces."[94] Stilwell was skeptical of Wingate's "blocking position" concept and wrote in his diary that "L.R.P.G.s [Long-Range Patrol Groups] can't hold a place where artillery can be brought in."[95] On the night of March 5, 1944, the 77th Indian Infantry Division Brigade was landed by glider fifty miles south of Mogaung. After several days to reorganize and fly in additional forces, the 77th moved west to block the Japanese road and rail lines that were supplying Mogaung and Myitkyina.

The other two British brigades assigned to the northeast Burma campaign were the 16th and 111th Brigades. The 16th was ordered to march through the jungle overland from its base area around Ledo, India, to the town of Indaw, a straight-line distance of over two hundred miles through dense jungle and difficult terrain, which doubled or tripled the distance traveled. After suffering heavy losses from disease, a greatly reduced force was able to attack Indaw, but the road and rail lines were not blocked. The 111th Brigade was flown into an area farther south of the 77th Brigade but was delayed due to scattered airdrops. Neither the 16th nor the 111th Brigades would play a significant role in accomplishing the objectives of the campaign despite their laudable efforts and the heavy casualties they suffered. In effect, two tremendously valuable brigades did not impact the outcome of the campaign due to poor planning and a lack of Allied coordination.

The death of Chindit commander Orde Wingate in a plane crash on March 24, 1944, led to a change in their role and closer integration into the NCAC chain of command. While Wingate had been directed to support Stilwell, he had maintained close personal control over British forces and planned their operations in accordance with his unconventional concepts. Upon his death, the Chindit brigades became increasingly subject to direct orders from General Stilwell, who looked upon the Chindits as an infantry force that should engage the Japanese rather than disrupt communications and supply lines. On May 17, the 77th, 111th, and 16th Brigades, now designated as the "Special Force," all came under Stilwell's operational control.[96] In late May 1944, the 77th was given instructions to take Mogaung, abandoning any blocking positions and using the entire available force. The commander of the 77th, Colonel Calvert, objected to using his force in a conventional operation for which it was ill-equipped, but he was overruled by Stilwell (although Calvert diplomatically blamed Stilwell's staff for poor communication).[97] Stilwell subsequently complained to Mountbatten that British units disobeyed his orders to advance, and General Slim visited NCAC in an effort to adjudicate the dispute between Stilwell and his British subordinates, but ill feeling remained between senior British commanders and Stilwell.[98]

Despite these command difficulties, by early June 1944 the 77th had moved into positions south of Mogaung and reorganized into a more conventional infantry force of centralized battalions rather than columns so that it could better attack the fortified Japanese positions. By this time, the 77th had been operating behind Japanese lines since early March, and many of the soldiers were suffering from tropical illnesses, had lost weight, and were fatigued after numerous strenuous marches. When the attack on Mogaung began on June 2, 1944, the 77th had only two-thirds of its original three thousand personnel still with the unit, the others having been evacuated, and it would be badly outnumbered by the Japanese defenders, who had been reinforced in late May with elements of the 53rd Division. In addition, the 77th lacked any organic artillery and relied on 3-inch

(81-mm) mortars and close air support.[99] Their attack began on June 2 and quickly turned into a slog, and despite tens of thousands of mortar rounds being fired, they had negligible effect on the Japanese positions, which were often built with substantial overhead cover. It ultimately took more than three weeks of steady pressure and the arrival of Chinese units, who had their own artillery to provide fire support, coming south down the valley to eventually push the Japanese out of Mogaung on June 16.[100] In total, the 77th Brigade suffered a casualty rate of more than 50 percent during the attack, which, along with the effects of widespread disease, meant that at the conclusion of the battle on June 27, it had fewer than three hundred soldiers fit for duty.

THE RACE TO MYITKYINA
In mid-April, one month before the start of the monsoon season and with his forces still more than twenty miles from Mogaung, which was only an intermediate objective, Stilwell was prepared to accept further risk by dispersing his forces to reach Myitkyina. In addition to the monsoon timeline pushing Stilwell, he was also being pressured by General Marshall, who reiterated that the capture of Myitkyina was an essential part of the U.S. strategy to increase Hump tonnage to China. With increasing pressure to show results and a closing window of opportunity, NCAC headquarters created a plan to take Myitkyina that again placed the Marauders in a critical role. Faced with what many Americans perceived as continued stalling, the drive to Mogaung, led by Chinese infantry and tanks, would now become a secondary effort, holding Japanese forces in position. The main effort would be a light infantry force that would march east over the Kumon Mountains, then turn launch an attack on Myitkyina, thus bypassing the major combat units of the Japanese 18th Division. Allied intelligence of Japanese 18th Division deployments remained poor, but it was hoped that with attrition and combat losses, the garrison as Myitkyina would be unable to stop an attack in strength.

The decision to make the Marauders a key part of this plan was extremely risky because by late April the Marauders had been in the field for eighty days, living mostly on a diet of prepared rations and whatever fruits or vegetables they came across in local villages. Tropical illnesses such as malaria and scrub typhus also compounded the nagging health issues caused by dysentery and leech bites. When combined with the combat casualties, these health issues meant that the 5307th was at less than 60 percent strength before the operation began. To compensate, two Chinese infantry regiments would be attached to the drive on Myitkyina. The 150th Regiment of the 50th Division, and the 88th Regiment of the 30th Division, were both newly arrived in the theater after being flown over the Hump airlift to India.[101] Both of these regiments had not gone through extensive retraining or been provided with a full set of American equipment, and their officers had little experience working with Americans. To help this force reach Myitkyina, Stilwell added groups of American-led Kachin, who could serve as valuable auxiliaries but were not trained and equipped to engage large Japanese units.[102] With Merrill still recovering from a heart attack suffered in late March, command of the expedition fell to Colonel Hunter. Hunter divided his forces into three elements, each with American Marauder forces and Chinese or Kachins commingled. The only artillery support for the expedition would be mortars, and a small number of 75-mm howitzers that were carried on mules. Air support was available, but the increasing distance of airfields in India from the front lines meant that the loitering time of close support aircraft was extremely limited.

Hunter's column departed on April 28 and followed a series of trails through the mountains, and it took a week for the first two columns to hike the twenty miles over the Kumon range. As part of efforts to confuse the Japanese but also because of poor coordination of the separated elements, one portion of the expeditionary force attacked multiple small Japanese garrisons in the area, while Hunter led his column south to Myitkyina as fast as his exhausted troops could march.[103] Initial scouting of the Myitkyina area found few Japanese troops, and further reconnaissance on the night of May 16 showed that the vital airfield was only lightly guarded. On May 17, Hunter sent in the Chinese 150th Infantry to seize the airfield, and it swept aside sporadic resistance to gain firm control by late morning. With the airfield in Allied hands, reinforcements could be flown in and supplies airlifted directly to the front lines, and one battalion of Chinese infantry was flown in on the afternoon of the 17th. Although command of the airfield satisfied one of the main strategic aims of the campaign by eliminating the threat of Japanese fighters to the Hump airlift, thereby allowing for increased tonnage to be flown to China, the town of Myitkyina was still occupied by a strong Japanese garrison. Merrill flew into Myitkyina on May 18 to take command of the fighting, but he immediately had another heart attack and was evacuated on May 19. Colonel Hunter had developed a plan to attack the town using Chinese infantry units, and Stilwell flew in to observe the attack, which soon bogged down when faced with Japanese strongpoints, and the units withdrew to establish their nighttime perimeters.[104] Allied coordination failed to exploit the capture of Myitkyina's airfield, and the Japanese responded swiftly, reinforcing Myitkyina and abandoning many of the smaller garrisons throughout the Irrawaddy Valley. These reinforcements were arriving faster than the Allies could fly in fresh troops, giving the Japanese a temporary numerical advantage, which they used to push back Allied attacks and fortify the town. The Allied failure to capitalize on the sudden capture of the airfield and push into the town would lead to a seventy-eight-day siege. The shoestring nature of the Myitkyina expedition, as well as fatigue and heavy casualties due to disease, meant that the victory could not be fully exploited before the monsoon rains arrived.

On May 21, a Marauder Battalion, now reduced to several hundred men, attempted to seize an auxiliary airfield and were not only stopped by Japanese defenses, but they were driven back by a counterattack.[105] Faced with the possibility of a complicated and prolonged fight for the town, Stilwell ordered that American road construction troops be pressed into service as infantry. While construction personnel were often trained in basic combat tactics, their skills were sorely needed for road building and airfield development, and these tasks were delayed while they were sent to Myitkyina to reinforce the attack. Two battalions of engineering personnel, the 209th and 236th, were flown into Myitkyina, as well as 5307th personnel that were returning from the hospital, but all these troops needed to be organized for combat.[106] Further slowing the buildup of Allied strength was the fact that the airfield, while operational, was an unimproved facility, and with increasing rainfall due to the monsoon season, the number of flights it could support was limited. By early June, the

Allied force in Myitkyina was down to one day's supply of rifle ammunition and limited food.[107]

Despite these limitations, Stilwell was desperate to maintain pressure on the Japanese, and on May 25 an attack was launched by two Chinese infantry regiments, the 88th and 89th, which had been flown into Myitkyina. Although these units were fresh, they had not completed the rigorous Ramgarh training sequence and were much less aggressive in pressing their attacks than were veteran units. On June 3, attacks by two additional Chinese regiments, the 42nd and 150th, were also driven off by the Japanese with heavy losses and no gains.[108] By mid-June, the Allied advance had slowed to a crawl, with units moving forward only a few yards a day, as individual Japanese strongpoints were patiently reduced. With poor medical care, limited ammunition, and the effects of the monsoon all hindering operations, morale became a critical factor. U.S. troops, particularly the engineers thrown into the battle, suffered heavy casualties, and Japanese ambush techniques, which more experienced infantry soldiers might have spotted, took a heavy toll.[109] The two American engineering battalions suffered 127 killed and 321 wounded during their time at Myitkyina.[110] Throughout the fighting, Stilwell also kept the Marauder units engaged, although the majority of their personnel had now been evacuated due to illness or wounds.[111] Chinese units, flown into the airfield and assigned a sector of the front, were extremely scared of Japanese night attacks, and American liaison officers greatly feared uncontrolled firing by Chinese troops in all directions.[112] American officers, who led a multinational force, were concerned that "the impression be created that we were withholding U.S. troops from combat in a sector whereas an Allied commander Stilwell was keeping British and Chinese troops in combat."[113]

On June 27, Mogaung fell to British and Chinese forces, removing a threat to the rear of the Myitkyina force, but a major attack on July 12, which was supported by B-25 medium bombers and artillery, failed to move more than a couple of hundred yards into the Japanese perimeter. Close air support was useful in eroding Japanese strength, and during June and July, P-40 fighters flew more than 2,500 sorties against Japanese forces in Myitkyina and were extremely useful in demolishing individual positions through close air support missions.[114] It was not until July that the Allied forces began to notice a weakening of Japanese resistance, as a lack of food, disease, and the slow weight of Allied firepower had slowly ground down the defenses. In late July, Japanese troops began to evacuate Myitkyina, using the Irrawaddy to move downstream on August 1, leaving only a small group of sick and wounded to hold the town, which eventually fell on August 3, 1944.[115]

The cost of the Myitkyina siege was 972 Chinese and 272 Americans killed, with 3,184 Chinese and 955 Americans wounded. The harsh climate also led to 980 Americans being evacuated for medical care. Despite their larger numbers in the area, only 188 Chinese were medically evacuated.[116] Explanations for the slow Allied seizure of Myitkyina have varied, often depending on personal assessments of Stilwell's decisions. Brig. Gen. Boatner highlighted that the Allied troops at Myitkyina were an ad hoc force that came from four Chinese infantry regiments that had been pulled out of three different divisions, together with two battalions of American combat engineers and the exhausted force that had marched over the Kumon range. Lacking cohesion and experience working together, Allied attacks were piecemeal and uncoordinated. The lack of artillery support was also noted as a major problem, as light 75-mm guns, mortars, and strafing attacks by aircraft were unable to dislodge Japanese defenders. Both difficulties can be traced back to the initial organization of the expedition, which had set out on April 28 on what was essentially a raid, with little organic support or ability to hold seized terrain. Stilwell's plan was extremely successful in reaching one objective, capturing the airfield, but he was unable to achieve the larger objective of eliminating Japanese strength in the Myitkyina-Mogaung Valley.

CONCLUSION

Looking at the combat operations of the north Burma campaign, it is evident that political considerations remained a salient factor, even on the battlefield, and profoundly impacted all decisions throughout the campaign. Out of a total force of more than 50,000 ground troops, Stilwell had fewer than 4,000 American combat personnel, concentrated in the 5307th and the 1st Provisional Tank Group. American airpower played a vital role in providing an alternative to artillery and provided critical logistics support, but it could not be the leading edge of the offensive. Similarly, American engineering skills were critical to developing the road and pipeline network that supported the advance. Despite these U.S. accomplishments, the fight against the Japanese 18th Division was won and lost through the actions, and blood spilled, of Chinese and British soldiers. To a great extent, Stilwell was working through Allies to accomplish the goals he had been given by his American chain of command. British leaders, including both Mountbatten and Churchill, remained skeptical throughout the campaign, and Chiang Kai-shek maintained his measured and frustrating indifference to Stilwell's approach. In this context, Stilwell's skills as a battlefield tactician needed to be balanced with an operational perspective that understood the possibilities of his Allied units. British observers, and later postwar assessments, were especially critical of Stilwell's use of Chindit units to perform infantry assaults, most prominently at Mogaung, for which they were not trained and equipped, and they were angered by Stilwell's dismissal of their tactical challenges.[117] On the other hand, American observers were skeptical of both British and Chinese units for their seeming indifference to the issue of time. Stilwell's actions were not perfect, and his decision to send the Marauders on a desperate gamble to take Myitkyina made headlines but did not end the campaign, but in an overall sense he was able to accomplish his core objectives. By June 1944, the Japanese 18th Division had been destroyed as a fighting force, and while it would take another six months to connect the Ledo area to Kunming by road, northeast Burma was under Allied control.

Examining the campaign in north Burma also highlights that Stilwell was given a set of tools, primarily light infantry, to assist the Chinese units he had so carefully trained at Ramgarh, and to a great extent he did not use them effectively. During the course of the campaign, the 5307th suffered 80 percent casualties, with 93 deaths in combat, 293 wounded, and a staggering 2,000 casualties from disease, and the official U.S. Army medical history concludes that "sickness and exhaustion, not enemy weapons, had destroyed Old Galahad."[118] Part of the issue was that the concepts developed by Wingate were based on an unrealistic set of assumptions about the role and use of light infantry in Burma. Deep-penetration raids did not dramatically hinder Japanese operations, and whenever the Chindits or Marauders were assigned to a direct attack or prolonged defense, they suffered heavy losses due to their lack of logistics and firepower support. Reports and assessments by American medical personnel targeted even Wingate's basic ideas, such as the ability of soldiers to march long distances through the jungle carrying packs with fifty pounds or more on limited rations without an inevitable loss in weight, increase in disease, and eventual loss of combat abilities.[119] Light infantry forces in the Burma campaign were too lightly armed, too dispersed, and too oriented to conduct hit-and-run actions to decisively impact the outcome of the fighting.

Compounding these military challenges were cultural challenges that arose from the light infantry style of warfare. Throughout the campaign, light infantry forces failed to work constructively with other units and were not inclined to ask for technical assistance. For example, after repeated communications problems between the 5307th and headquarters, it was suggested that highly trained experts for the Signal Corps assist in handling the radios, but the condescending response was that "Sig corps personnel are undesirable and that better results can be obtained from key-clicking dough-boys who know their basic branch."[120] The light infantry concept in Burma suffered from what a British medical officer described as "ignorance, indifference, and intransigent prehistoric attitudes towards hygiene, sanitation, and medical discipline."[121] This was especially true in the 5307th, which suffered tremendously from diseases and illness. In his memoirs, Colonel Hunter describes American personnel drinking frequently polluted water, resulting in high rates of disease, while by contrast, nearby Chinese units routinely boiled their water.[122] Even British officers, who had developed the Chindit model, became more cautious about the use of light infantry after repeated attempts to use them to attack conventional forces led to heavy casualties.[123]

Being assigned units with highly specialized, and limited, capabilities presented Stilwell with a series of difficult choices that led to higher casualties and slower achievement of the campaign goals. In his retirement, General Boatner, commander of the CAI, was critical of Stilwell's decision to focus on light infantry maneuvers and calling the overland drive on Myitkyina a "desperate gamble" that almost ended in disaster. In contrast,

Boatner argued that "it is entirely possible that both time and excessive casualties would have been saved had JWS [Joseph W. Stilwell] kept his forces, firepower and airpower concentrated to first capture Kamaing, then continue on to take Mogaung, some 20 miles south, and then up the railway, about 20 miles with all his power, to capture Myitkyina."[124] Concentrating his forces would also have allowed them to best utilize the massive construction program that followed the leading troops, with supply dumps, hospitals, and airfields all being built to support the advance.[125] Failure to exploit these advantages led to a more costly and slower campaign. It also appears that Stilwell had second thoughts about reliance on infantry forces, and in July 1944, after continued failures to break the siege of Myitkyina, he ordered the formation of six Chinese tank battalions to provide the CAI with more mobile firepower.[126]

In contrast to the difficulties that British and American light infantry forces faced in prolonged combat, Chinese forces, which had taken most casualties during the campaign, had gained valuable experience and confidence. American medical liaison officers and medical doctors were especially impressed by the hygiene and mental health among Chinese soldiers.[127] An American medical assessment notes that "The very low incidence of functional nervous disorders, and especially the almost complete absence of 'battle exhaustion' among Chinese troops is worthy of mention. Although many thousands of Chinese lived and fought in the jungle for a full year and a half, the morale was unquestionably high throughout the period and was higher at the end of the campaign than at the start."[128] American analysis of airdrops to Chinese units concluded that Chinese rations were lighter and could be more easily free dropped, rather than parachuted, and that "once Chinese units are fully equipped little was ever heard from them except requests for ammunition, rations, medical supplies and certain short-lived items."[129]

In the context of the overall mission of the CBI theater, the seizure of the Myitkyina airfield had immediate ramifications, with transport tonnage increasing dramatically on the Hump airlift. Even as late as April 1944, War Department planners had set a target date for the capture of Myitkyina as January 1, 1945, a target that was achieved nearly five months ahead of schedule.[130] By the end of July 1944, Myitkyina was the busiest airfield in the theater, with a plane landing or departing every two minutes.[131] Average monthly tonnage during the monsoon season of 1943 had reached a peak of 8,632 in October 1943, and it grew steadily throughout the dry season from November through May. Despite the 1944 monsoon season, which began in mid-May, tonnage grew from 12,848 in May to 17,090 in June to 22,148 in July and to a staggering total of 27,125 in August 1944 despite the poor weather.[132] These statistics show that the capture of Myitkyina enabled a massive increase in the total amounts of supplies delivered to China. By the summer of 1944, for the first time since the war began, significant support was arriving in China to reform and improve military forces.

While Stilwell's overall success in the campaign in northern Burma earned him political capital, his handling of the Marauders, in particular their prolonged employment during the siege of Myitkyina, led to significant bad press in the United States. In August 1944, *Time* magazine published an attack on Stilwell's handling of the Marauders titled "The Bitter Tea of General Joe," and the story was also picked up by the *New York Times*.[133] While some negative coverage and criticism is inevitable, Stilwell lacked the acumen and political knowledge to limit the damage, and during questions about his command role, negative press only emboldened his critics. Stilwell's habit of spending extended periods on the front lines, to the point that he was called the "the best three-star company commander in the U.S. Army" by critics also meant that he was often not fully aware of how his operational decisions were presented in the media.[134]

The greatest failure of Stilwell's campaign in north Burma was the level of acrimony that it created among the British, Chinese, and even American units involved. Rather than pull these Allied forces into a more cohesive and united group that had all shared in the destruction of the Japanese 18th Division, the campaign led to ill feelings and recriminations. For example, Chinese officers felt that their units, which had suffered the largest numbers of casualties, were being asked to fight costly battles against Japanese defenders and were called upon to assist British and American light infantry forces when they got into trouble.[135] Stilwell's personality and lack of transparency in his decisions was often a primary cause of friction within the command. Col. Charles N. Hunter, who was so instrumental in the operations of the 5307th, wrote after the war that Stilwell's behavior was idiosyncratic:

> Military education and training is conducted to ensure that officers and men subjected to the stress and strain inherent to combat operations will react, think, and conduct themselves according to proven principles, precepts and doctrine. But I soon learned that there was a 'Stilwell way' and an 'Army way.' [Frank] Merrill understood the 'Stilwell way,' but I was never able to comprehend it.[136]

Stilwell's decision to launch the attack against Myitkyina over the Kumon range was done without coordination with Mountbatten, and although he was successful in taking the airfield, it reaffirmed fears that Stilwell was not always integrating his tactical decisions into a larger strategic framework. Charles Hunter remarked that Stilwell's penchant for personal involvement in operational plans, rather than a more formalized staff-centric system, became a concern, and "as time wore on and it became more obvious that we were working from an artist's sketch of the campaign rather than from architectural drawings by one who knew the details of construction, General Stilwell became known as the 'Musette Bag General.'"[137] General Boatner concurred and remarked,

> Although Stilwell became famous as a trooper commander in the field, and as a tenacious unrelenting general, there was a lack of coordination amongst his various headquarters which caused confusion and conflict. The general had a tendency to render important decisions to subordinate commanders on field trips without letting his staff in on the secret. This caused planners to work in the dark. He detested all paperwork.[138]

Charleton Ogburn, a member of the Marauders and later a senior State Department official, remembered that

> An important factor in the confusion and air of improvisation that prevailed during the critical phase at Myitkyina, one is forced to believe,

was Stilwell's practice of running the theater from his field bag and leaving his headquarters (of which it has to be remembered he had several) to its (or their) own devices while he busied himself at the front.[139]

In effect, each national element in the north Burma campaign believed that they had suffered disproportionate casualties and been forced to carry a heavier burden than their counterparts. Better planning, more transparency, and integration of subordinate unit leaders into decision-making processes could have helped alleviate these concerns and ease fears of mistreatment. As a result, Stilwell's tactical accomplishments were often overshadowed by political friction, leaving a legacy of distrust among key political leaders that was critically important to his continuing campaign plans.

★ CHAPTER 5 ★

DIRECTING ALLIES IN YUNNAN
March–September 1944

Establish the Chinese ground forces on a more dependable basis.
—General Marshall, private message to Stilwell[1]

While the campaign in northern Burma slowly but steadily drove the Japanese forces south, Chinese forces in Yunnan, the second component of Stilwell's plan to retake north Burma, remained ensconced in their positions on the east bank of the Salween River. The development of a Chinese military force in Yunnan, identified as the "Y Force" in American plans, initially included thirty Chinese divisions and quickly ran into problems due to Chinese political constraints and logistical constraints. Between December 1943 and the summer of 1944, Stilwell worked to convince Chinese military and political leaders that they should invest military assets in the Burma campaign, but while Stilwell did receive intermittent support from American political leaders, progress was slow and uncertain. Examination of the Chinese drive into Burma from Yunnan highlights that in contrast to the direct leadership role Stilwell exerted in northern Burma, in Yunnan Stilwell utilized liaison officers, control of supplies, and political pressure to shape the campaign. At the tactical level, Stilwell and American officers in Yunnan needed to adjust the successful policies they had developed at Ramgarh because the Chinese forces in Yunnan were not under their direct control. At the operational level, without direct command of Chinese forces, American military liaison officers could only apply indirect pressure to encourage Chinese military actions. The most common method used to pressure Chinese military commanders was by providing resources, such as artillery, supplies, and air strikes, to encourage action, and correspondingly withdrawing or denying supplies to coerce activity. At the strategic level, Stilwell attempted to work through the constraints of the Chinese political system because his military plans upset the fragile balance of power among Chinese leaders.

The Yunnan campaign also highlights three considerations that have applied to the American way of war since 1945. First, airpower based in China was not under the direct command of the American ground commander, Frank Dorn, which led to a disorganized and less effective force than if it had been integrated into the campaign plan. While Chennault's Fourteenth Air Force provided notable assistance with close air support and resupply, coordination and planning of aerial operations was lacking, and American liaison personnel could only request assistance and hope assets were available, resulting in miscommunication and lost opportunities.[2] Second, the tactical model developed in Yunnan relied on American liaison teams and a network of American supporting technical assets, such as hospitals, engineering support, and logistics specialists, as part of an effort to improve the effectiveness of the Chinese forces. These personnel were effective in improving the medical care and supply operations, but they did not radically change how the Chinese forces operated, and these highly trained personnel were expensive and likely could have been more effective in other roles. Finally, while the American effort to improve the Chinese forces in Yunnan was effective in adding new capabilities to the Chinese army, such as increasing firepower, it was unable to make a significant impact in changing the organizational culture. Short training programs and the introduction of new equipment did not change the way the Chinese army maneuvered and fought the Yunnan campaign. In repeated engagements, Chinese forces undertook frontal assaults, coordinated their efforts poorly, did not flank Japanese positions, and remained wedded to tactical behaviors deeply ingrained by habit and experience. In contrast to the Chinese forces in India, which Stilwell was able to compartmentalize from Chinese political factors, the Yunnan campaign would force Americans to directly engage with Chinese political issues. Stilwell's desire to avoid politics and focus on military issues led to an indirect advisory approach that still led to political frictions without the military effectiveness demonstrated by Chinese forces in northern Burma.

ESTABLISHING THE Y FORCE
Less than two months after Allied forces had been pushed out of Burma in 1942, tentative plans were being made for a Chinese drive from Yunnan back into Burma. Chiang Kai-shek made assurances in August 1942, and again in November, that a force of fifteen Chinese divisions would form a "Chinese Expeditionary Force." But Yunnan was controlled by Long Yun, a military officer who had seized control of the province in 1927. Far removed from the KMT's area of control along the Chinese coasts, Long Yun had controlled his isolated and undeveloped province independently of the central government, and moving large numbers of troops loyal to Chiang Kai-shek into Yunnan would be a direct threat to Yun's continued rule. Moreover, Chiang Kai-shek had a limited ability to order troops to redeploy from the front lines in east China to Yunnan because by late 1942, many Chinese regional commanders had developed strong local powers and loyalties. Generals such as Xue Yue in Hunan, war zone IX, would not respond to orders to send troops to Yunnan. Another key issue that would stall an offensive in Burma was the tense political and military negotiations over the levels of American military support to Chinese operations. American military assessments in the summer of 1942 noted that Chinese forces had sufficient equipment, if properly organized, to fully equip a force in Yunnan with effective weapons, but Chinese leaders saw American supplies and modern weapons as a prerequisite to any action. The compromise position reached was for American supply efforts to focus on specialized equipment, such as light machine guns, submachine guns, mortars, and light artillery, which would increase firepower.[3]

Small numbers of American military advisors began arriving in Yunnan in January 1943, as Stilwell attempted to convince Chiang Kai-shek that with retraining and a limited number of American weapons and equipment, Chinese units could take the offensive into Burma. Despite setbacks to his plans in the spring of 1943, Stilwell pushed forward with plans to develop the Chinese Expeditionary Force into a thirty-division-strong "Y Force," and hundreds of American officers and technical specialists were flown over the Hump and prepared for assignment as liaison personnel.[4] From the outset of this effort it was clear that while the Chinese Army in India (CAI) had the supplies and American personnel to support a comprehensive military school system, the Y Force would have to rely on targeted, focused training and more indirect liaison techniques to improve key areas of Chinese military capabilities.[5]

The American commander of the Y Force training and supply program was Col. Frank Dorn. Dorn was a seasoned "China Hand" who had served at the Peking (Beijing) embassy with Stilwell in the 1930s.[6] As Stilwell's aide during the Burma campaign, Dorn had been part of the humiliating walkout to India. While Dorn had exceptional language skills and was an experienced staff officer, his background was primarily in intelligence work, and he was not prepared to exert any tactical guidance or operational direction. From the outset of his assignment, it was clear that Dorn would have no authority over Chinese personnel outside of the American training centers, and his instructions were that American personnel should only serve as instructors and advisors and in liaison roles. He was also adamant that the original mission guidance of the U.S. Army in China be strictly followed: "The official mission of the U.S. Army in China is to increase the combat efficiency of the Chinese Army—and nothing else," which meant that Y Force personnel would work through existing Chinese structures and leaders.[7] A notable exception was that because medical and engineering roles were completely lacking from Chinese units, Americans often filled these critical positions. The Nationalist army, for example, had only one doctor for every 2,000 to 3,000 soldiers, compared to one per 150 soldiers in the U.S. Army.[8] In Chinese medical and engineering units, the level of knowledge was often extremely low, and Americans would similarly take a more direct place in Chinese combat engineering operations and also operate field hospitals and portable surgical hospitals near the front lines.[9] Dorn, like Stilwell, had a difficult relationship with Chennault, and although Dorn would be able to collaborate with him, Chennault's style of leadership and personal habits ran against Dorn's military ethics, complicating American coordination in Yunnan.[10] Chennault not only saw Dorn as a close confidant of Stilwell but also adopted his familiar refrain that Dorn was "completely in the dark on airpower" when faced with any criticism of air operations.[11]

The primary American method for shaping Y Force tactics would be through short-term training programs, and in the field, small groups of American liaison teams would theoretically operate with Chinese units to provide advice and assistance. This decision, which was in some ways inevitable due to resource constraints and the political environment, meant that the training program in Yunnan would not change the organizational structure and culture of Chinese army units. American officers calculated that to equip ten Chinese divisions, even with a spartan equipment allocation, would require 2,500 tons to be transported over the Hump. Although this would require a major effort, it was much less than the tonnage allocated to Chennault's air operations.[12]

In the Y Force units, Chinese personnel would cycle through American training centers as individuals, not as a complete group, to learn critical skills, and they would then return to their units, where hopefully they would pass on their training. These courses, for example in artillery or communications, were brief, with most courses scheduled to last only four or six weeks, which was enough time to learn a specific skill but not enough to impact the culture or habits of Chinese personnel. This approach also required a large number of U.S. personnel to serve as training and liaison staff. In contrast, the CAI in northern Burma relied on limited number of American specialists to conduct training at Ramgarh that brought together all personnel in a unit and trained them as a cohesive group.[13] In addition, in Yunnan the larger scope of the program meant that even with a small liaison program, assigning American officers to each unit of the Chinese Expeditionary Force would require more than 1,800 officers and 4,000 enlisted personnel.[14] Furthermore, having U.S. personnel dispersed in small groups and interacting with Chinese personnel directly would require hundreds of interpreters. By 1944, American Y Force units had hired more than seven hundred Chinese interpreters, and while many were highly educated and committed to the war effort, translation barriers

Stilwell speaks to American soldiers in Burma. *National Archives and Records Administration*

Brig. Gen. Frank Dorn, Stilwell's longtime aide and commander of the American effort in Yunnan *National Archives and Records Administration*

Brig. Gen. Claire Chennault, Stilwell's long-time rival and advocate for airpower in the CBI theater *National Archives and Records Administration*

General George C. Marshall, Army Chief of Staff during World War II and a close ally of Stilwell throughout his tenure *Library of Congress*

Adm. Louis Mountbatten, Supreme Allied Commander of Southeast Asia Command (SEAC), speaks to American personnel in northeast India. *National Archives and Records Administration*

Senior Allied leaders meeting at Cairo in November 1943. Front row (*left to right*): Chiang Kai-shek, Franklin D. Roosevelt, Winston Churchill, Mei-ling Soong. Stilwell is standing behind Roosevelt, looking at camera; Mountbatten is standing behind and between Churchill and Soong. *Library of Congress*

A crew composed of Chinese and American soldiers from the 1st Provisional Tank Group takes a break during the Burma campaign. *National Archives and Records Administration*

American engineers work to complete a portion of the Burma Road, illustrating the rugged terrain and dense vegetation in Burma.
National Archives and Records Administration

Chinese soldiers in Yunnan preparing to advance westward into Burma *National Archives and Records Administration*

An American engineer unit assisting Chinese forces at a base camp overlooking the Salween river *National Archives and Records Administration*

Stilwell looks toward the frontlines during the fighting around Myitkyina in the summer of 1944. *National Archives and Records Administration*

The Myitkyina airfield shortly after being captured by Stilwell's forces *National Archives and Records Administration*

were a significant problem.[15] A final and vitally important area of American support was the establishment of three field hospitals and ten portable surgical hospitals, which dramatically improved the quality of medical care to Y Force soldiers.[16]

Even these limited goals were delayed by the fractious Chinese political environment. The Y Force infantry and artillery training schools officially opened on April 1, 1943, but disputes between Chiang Kai-shek and Yunnan governor Lung Yun delayed the actual beginning of operations because a compromise had to be reached over which leader would have authority over the soldiers at the schools.[17] In March 1943, a tentative compromise was reached for the thirty-division Y Force to included forces loyal to Chiang Kai-shek and local Yunnan forces loyal to Lung Yun.[18] While this political balancing act solved many of the general problems, it illustrated the stark political divisions within the Y Force, which would impact planning the campaign into Burma. Ambassador Walter E. Jenkins Jr., then a young American officer assigned to the Y Force, recalled that "it became quite clear that the Chinese government under Chiang Kai-shek was less interested in using them [Y Force divisions] to open the Burma Road than for keeping an eye on the provincial Yunnan forces under Warlord Governor Lung Yun. . . . So some of his best units were actually used for that purpose in our region of southwest China."[19] Moreover, although the framework of a force structure had been decided, many of the Chinese units assigned to the Y Force were not yet in Yunnan, and in August 1943, Colonel Dorn reported that only six divisions were fully engaged with American training and equipping programs.[20]

Initial training plans developed by Stilwell and Dorn soon proved to be wildly optimistic. By the late spring of 1943, fourteen KMT divisions had arrived in Yunnan far below strength, but Chinese commanders still wanted the total allocation of supplies and weapons. American officers suspected that this was a blatant ploy to gain access to additional American weapons, which would then be diverted to Chinese units surrounding Communist areas.[21] Stilwell attempted to get political support from leaders in Washington who could pressure Chiang Kai-shek, but in early 1943 he found it difficult to convince President Roosevelt. After the disastrous Trident Conference, Stilwell believed he had no support or authority, writing,

"It seems absolutely impossible to do anything. The President has undercut me and the Chinese resist manfully every attempt to help them fight."[22] Throughout the summer and fall of 1943, the Chinese forces in Yunnan continued to go through the motions of training and received steadily increasing amounts of American supplies, but no serious preparations for an offensive took place as a lack of personnel remained an insurmountable barrier to progress.[23] Lacking Chinese political support for an attack into Burma, little actual progress was made. At the Cairo Conference in November 1943, Chiang gave his hesitant approval for an expanded Y Force training program and approved an attack from Yunnan into northern Burma. The reason for this turnaround by Chiang was political maneuvering in Cairo and Stilwell's effort to use equipment transfers for political leverage. Specifically, Stilwell promised to expand the transfer of weapons and supplies to Y Force units, and by February 1944 new deliveries had allowed for the Y Force to equip fifteen divisions, and shipments of submachine guns, mortars, and small howitzers for offensive operations in mountainous terrain were also transferred to the Chinese troops.[24] These transfers helped Chinese forces in Yunnan standardize their equipment, which was often a mixture of French-, German-, and Chinese-produced weapons.[25]

Despite the approval by Chiang of an attack into Burma, repeated delays and continuing attempts by Chinese to link an offensive with increased aid led to an American political backlash. In December 1943, President Roosevelt sent a message to Chiang that military supplies were to support attacks on Japanese forces, not to support Chinese military forces in general. With no updates or acknowledgment, Roosevelt took an even stronger position on January 14, 1944, and suggested that supplies to Chinese forces would be curtailed if no action was taken: "If the Yunnan forces cannot be employed it would appear that we should avoid for the present the movement of critical supplies to them over the limited lines of communication and curtail the continuing build-up of stockpiles in India beyond that which will be brought to bear against the enemy."[26] Roosevelt's message, which was a sharp departure from his earlier policy of not linking aid to specific military action by the Chinese, took place in the context of a Chinese request for a $1 billion loan.[27] The enormous size of the loan and that it was requested before forces in Yunnan could go into action to support the forces already engaged in northern Burma, struck many Americans as de facto extortion. Roosevelt's strong transactional stance, which Stilwell had advocated for eighteen months, was also supported by Mountbatten, who supported a more aggressive negotiating position with Chiang.

While Chiang's stalling led to further American concerns, the Japanese launched a major offensive from western Burma against the British in India, Operation U-Go, and an attack from Yunnan became critically important to divert Japanese forces. On April 3, 1944, Roosevelt sent yet another terse message to Chiang, noting that "to me the time is ripe for elements of your Seventy-first Army group to advance without further delay and seize the Tengchong-Longling areas. A shell of a division opposes you on the Salween. Your advance to the west cannot help to succeed."[28] Backing up Roosevelt's message was a message from General Marshall to Stilwell that suggested that in light of "our failure to secure aggressive action by the Yunnan Force at this critical period of the campaign in Burma," supply deliveries flown over the Hump should be reallocated. This message was informally circulated to senior Chinese military leaders.[29]

Increasing the diplomatic pressure on Chiang, and hinting about withdrawing supplies, proved effective, and on April 14, 1944, Ho Ying-chin, minister of war and chief of staff of the Chinese army, gave his formal approval, with the face-saving addendum that the "decision to move part of [the] Y Force across [the] Salween was made on initiative of [the] Chinese without influence of outside pressure, and was based on the realization that China must contribute its share to [the] common war effort."[30] Ho also demanded assurances from Dorn personally that American air support would be provided throughout the campaign and ammunition would be supplied for units in combat, rather than used to train new units.[31] Plans for an offensive focused on seizing a portion of the Burma Road and opening a route to Allied forces driving toward Myitkyina. Japanese opposition in the area was centered on the 56th Division, which had taken part in the initial Japanese conquest of Burma and had remained in northeast Burma preparing defensive positions. The commander of the 56th Division was Lieutenant General Yuzo Matsuyama, who had more than thirty years of military service.[32] Japanese defensive plans made use of the rugged mountainous terrain to channel any Chinese attack into areas exposed to Japanese artillery and machine-gun fire. Japanese forces gained an unexpected advantage in February 1944, when a Chinese plane forced down near Tengchong included the Chinese Expeditionary Force order of battle as well as multiple code books.[33] Despite the Japanese combat experience, thorough preparations, and intelligence advantages, the 56th Division strength of roughly 11,000 soldiers would be vastly outnumbered by Chinese forces by a ratio of more than six to one along a nearly hundred-mile front.[34]

While designing the campaign, Chinese and American planners would rely heavily on U.S. Army engineering support and aerial resupply to overcome the geographic barriers they faced. From their staging areas, Chinese troops would need to cross the swift-flowing Salween River, which was 250 feet wide, using rafts and ferries.[35] Initial reconnaissance revealed that the Japanese were not prepared to defend the river line but had pulled back to the mountains several miles to the west. The small number of passes through the mountains meant that Chinese forces would have no alternative except to mount direct attacks on prepared positions. Even without Japanese defenses, these passes were all over nine thousand feet in elevation, which would restrict movement of supplies and heavy weapons, placing a great burden on infantry forces. Once through the mountains, the primary transportation hub in the area was the walled town of Tengchong. Occupation of Tengchong would open the possibility of reaching the Myitkyina area through a well-established trail network. South of Tengchong, the Japanese had heavily fortified Songshan, a large mountain that dominated the Burma Road and from which Japanese artillery emplacements could block all traffic. Fifteen miles down the road from Songshan the town of Longling was the largest community in the area and was heavily defended. Japanese forces were evenly split, with the 148th Regiment north of the Burma Road, with the bulk of their forces in Tengchong, while farther south, the 113th Regiment had forces in Songshan and Longling to control the Burma Road. The third regiment of the Japanese division was dispersed throughout the hundred-mile front in small garrisons and observation positions.

The Chinese forces marshaled for the offensive into Burma in the spring of 1944 consisted of 70,000 soldiers divided into two armies, and later reinforcements would provide more than 50,000 additional personnel. In overall command of the China Expeditionary Force was Chinese general Wei Li-Huang, who had joined the KMT in the 1920s and participated in many of the anticommunist campaigns in the 1930s. Dorn liked Wei and felt that he was well-educated, a realist, "pro-American," and "inclined to study both sides of any problem before reaching a decision."[36] In the northern part of the sector, the XXth Group Army was led by General Huo Kuei-chang, who had two Chinese armies to seize the passes of the Kaoli-kung (Gaoligong) mountains and drive on Tengchong.[37] Farther south, General Sung Hsi-lian (Song Xilian) commanded the XI Army, and he also had two armies to open the Burma Road and overcome the Japanese defenses around Longling.[38]

When the offensive began, American support had provided Chinese units with more than four hundred light 75-mm pack howitzers and 37-mm antitank guns, which would provide fire support and be moved through the difficult mountainous terrain. In most Chinese artillery battalions, small teams of American liaison personnel were assigned to provide technical support such as weapon maintenance and integrated fire control.[39] Chinese officers often took steps to keep American personnel separate from their units, preferring to use them as technical specialists rather than embed them with Chinese soldiers.[40] More than one thousand mortars and hundreds of rocket launchers would also prove to be incredibly valuable in reducing Japanese strongpoints and fortifications. More than five thousand Thompson submachine guns and hundreds of light machine guns also increased the firepower of Chinese infantry units, particularly at close range.[41] Generous American ammunition allotments would also give Chinese units the ability to expend large numbers of shells in supporting their attacks.[42] Dorn's guidance to his liaison personnel was to remain on good terms with their Chinese counterparts and that "Americans could recommend; they could persuade; they could cajole, but they were not to command the Chinese."[43] American training and recommendations to use flexibility to bypass Japanese formations and prepared defenses was counter to the Chinese tactical habit of attacking Japanese positions

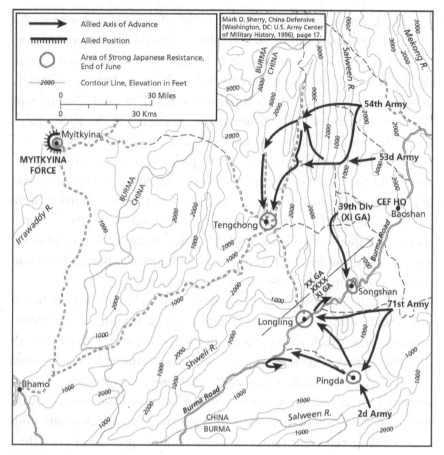

MAP 4. The North Burma Campaign

directly. Less controversial areas of American support, such as medical and veterinary care, communications teams, and engineer support, were easily integrated into the campaign plan.[44]

The operational plans, which had been developed with American advice, sought to utilize Chinese numerical advantages to isolate the scattered Japanese garrisons. An inherent challenge of the plan was that individual units, each fixed on a specific geographic target, would need to move in a coherent, coordinated advance, otherwise the Japanese could potentially redeploy their forces to defeat each column individually. The XXth Group Army would need to move swiftly to seize the mountain passes through the Kaoli-kung mountains before the Japanese could reinforce the defenders. The Mamian pass, less than five miles from the Salween River crossing, was the target of the 54th Army, and American liaison teams recommended that light infantry groups use mountain trails to move around Japanese defenses and avoid costly frontal assaults on well-prepared fortifications. Once through the mountains, these troops could then be supplied by airdrops. Seventeen miles south, the second major pass through the mountains, the Tatangtzu pass, was much more heavily defended, with an estimated full Japanese battalion ready to stop any movement through the pass.[45] This pass was the target of the Chinese 53rd Army, and if both passes were seized successfully and quickly, the Chinese would be in a position to move a force of six divisions against the critical town of Tengchong in a matter of weeks. Tengchong was a major garrison and patrol base that allowed Japanese forces to control trail networks throughout the region, and capture of the town would help open the path for land communications with forces in north Burma. Forty miles farther south along the Salween, two additional Chinese armies, the 71st and 2nd, would seek to block the Burma Road and drive on the town of Longling. By moving along unguarded trails and by seizing the important town of Pingda, this southern wing of the Chinese advance would be able to bypass the key Japanese fortifications along the Salween River and cut the Burma Road supply route.

Initial crossing operations on May 11 along the Salween River were uncontested, and the Japanese had withdrawn their forces because they would be easy targets for superior Chinese and American firepower.[46] In the initial two days of the attack the greatest challenge was constructing ferries that could manage the fast-moving river waters, and in Dorn's assessment the Chinese engineers performed superbly.[47] By the afternoon of May 12, Chinese troops from the 54th Army were already attacking the northernmost pass, Mamian, and after sharp fighting were able to drive the Japanese defenders back into a fortified village. American airdrops of more than thirty tons of food and ammunition enabled the Chinese forces to keep moving into the pass despite the difficult terrain.[48] Once the Japanese artillery positions were cleared from the eastern face of the mountains, American engineering teams began construction of a footbridge, constructed of wire rope and timber, that could support soldiers and pack animals but not artillery heavier than the 75-mm howitzer.[49] Without heavy artillery, Chinese forces relied on American close air support and frontal assaults to slowly wear down the Japanese defenders. It took the 54th Army a month, until June 13, to eliminate the Japanese forces from the pass, as they overcame staunch defenses and monsoon weather.

Chinese tactical decisions during the battle of the Mamian pass confirmed Americans' worst fears, that the Chinese forces would move slowly and seek to eliminate every Japanese position and thereby suffer heavy casualties, rather than maneuver around strongpoints. American liaison officers praised the courage of the Chinese soldiers for their "suicidal charges" and esprit de corps but noted that a lack of coordination led to excessive casualties.[50] The situation was repeated fifteen miles to the south, where the 53rd Army attempted to drive Japanese defenders from the Tatungtzu pass but also suffered heavy casualties for minimal gains.[51] American personnel again suggested movement to outflank the Japanese positions, but the standard Chinese tactical response remained to conduct frontal attacks on well-prepared Japanese defenses. Only in late May did the Japanese troops withdraw from their positions, allowing a Chinese advance, and by early June the 53rd Army had entered the Shweli Valley, at the cost of heavy casualties to one of its best divisions. Once clear of the mountains and into the Shweli Valley, the 53rd and 54th Armies were able to move more efficiently and better coordinate their movements. American airdrops of supplies were also more efficient when conducted in the flat valley terrain as opposed to forested hills. The fortified town of Chiang-chu, which had been the major Japanese base in the northern Shweli Valley, was captured on June 22, as Chinese pressure and American air support led to a Japanese withdrawal to their main base at Tengchong.

The crossing of the Salween, capture of the vital passes, and clearing of the northern part of the Shweli Valley had taken six weeks, and Chinese forces had suffered heavy casualties. Despite a numerical advantage of more than seven to one, complete air control, and access to the American equipment flown over the Hump, progress had been slow, and most Japanese forces had escaped to fight again. Some American officers believed that the XXth Group Army would now be more receptive to American tactics and advice, having seen the usefulness of improved firepower, air support, and infiltration tactics.[52] Chinese actions had also provided ample evidence that American weapons and training remained underutilized by Chinese commanders who reverted to their ingrained habits and procedures. In particular, the Chinese habit of stopping in the face of a Japanese position for days or even weeks while resources were slowly assembled for an attack left them exposed to Japanese counterattacks.[53] The low "return on investment" for Y Force training programs and expensive equipment, especially compared to the more efficient CAI units, was also clearly evident to American observers.

While the campaign to clear the Shweli Valley had reached a natural pause, as both Chinese and Japanese prepared for the inevitable battle at Tengchong, Chinese forces south of the Burma Road were also making steady, albeit slow progress. The XI Group Army had similarly launched its attack on May 11, and with the more open terrain in the lower Salween area, was able to make substantial progress in the initial days of the campaign. Rather than attack the heavily fortified mountain of Songshan, the XI Group Army attempted to cut the Burma Road at the key transportation hub of Longling. Capture of Longling would cut off the Japanese garrisons at Songshan and Tengchong, but like with the XXth Group Army operations, dispersing units across a large area would lead to command-and-control issues.

The XI Group Army was composed of two armies, each with three divisions, but Dorn was concerned about the poor quality of the senior leaders and doubted their competence in maneuvering a large force through difficult terrain.[54] The 2nd Army attacked on May 11, moving toward the fortified town of Pingda, which was held by one Japanese battalion, and a lack of coordination between the Chinese 88th and 76th Divisions led to a series of uncoordinated frontal assaults on well-prepared Japanese positions, which were defended by mortars and machine guns. Japanese counterattacks to seize key terrain also led to Chinese efforts becoming disorganized.[55] By late May the 2nd Army had moved most of its forces to support the drive on Longling, leaving only a regiment to contain the Japanese battalion in Pingda. By the end of May 1944, with Chinese forces slowly taking control of the mountain passes, and with Pingda isolated, the commander of the Chinese Expeditionary Force, General Wei

Li-huang, decided to gamble that the center of the Japanese defenses at Longling was vulnerable and ordered the 71st Army from General Song's XI Group Army to seize the town. American logistics advisors opposed the plan because opening another avenue of advance would further overwhelm the fragile Chinese logistics system, which relied on pack animals and porters, along with airdrops.[56] By the end of May, logistics units were already showing the strain of three weeks of operations with increasing rainfall as the monsoon season arrived.[57] Despite these difficulties, Stilwell embraced Wei's concept and encouraged Dorn to fully support a rapid advance, writing, "Impress on all concerned the vital importance of getting forward on your front," because it could relieve Japanese pressure on Myitkyina and potentially create a breakthrough to make contact with the north Burma forces.[58] Dorn frequently went forward to view the front lines, normally taking his G-2 intelligence officer, so that he could gain a better understanding of the situation without relying on incomplete or misleading official reports.[59]

General Wei's offensive started smoothly, and Chinese forces took less than a week to converge on Longling, with the 87th and 88th Divisions reaching the town walls by June 8. The total number of Japanese in Longling was estimated to be 1,500 personnel, giving the Chinese attackers a ten to one advantage, and a series of infantry attacks began on June 9, but a lack of supplies and poor weather hampered artillery and close air support. The two Chinese divisions also failed to fully envelope the town, allowing Japanese reinforcements to arrive and counterattack, and Dorn was highly critical of General Song's tactical command of the attack.[60] General Wei ordered his reserve division into the area, but without effective coordination with the two divisions in the area, both of which had been driven back by the Japanese, the attempt to capture Longling ground to an ignominious halt. American assessments of the attack were scathing, with advisors noting that the Chinese never utilized their full force at any one time, units inevitably failed to support each other, and a lack of aggressiveness meant that the Japanese were able to not only hold off attacks but push the Chinese back. American reports also noted systemic confusion within the Chinese chain of command, with different instructions issued by General Wei and the General Song, commander of the XI Army Group. Moreover, local Chinese commanders disregarded orders from higher headquarters and on occasion withdrew without coordinating with nearby units.[61] The poorly coordinated gamble to seize Longling meant that by late June, as the monsoon season began, operations in the area ground to a halt, and Longling would not be captured until November 3, 1944.[62]

By mid-June, in the northern sector of the Salween front, the XXth Group Army slowly approached Tengchong, which had 20,000 prewar inhabitants and solid Japanese defenses. After the missed opportunity in June to engage the Japanese in a war of maneuver, Chinese forces would be faced with breaching Tengchong's city walls, which were often more than thirty feet high and forty feet thick, making them impervious to the light 75-mm howitzers laboriously pulled over the mountains. The city walls also offered Japanese machine guns clear fields of fire, and although American air support would be valuable, breaching the walls with bombing attacks would require sustained bombardment. When the attack on Tengchong began on June 26, the Chinese XXth Group Army had five divisions around the city and were opposed by a hastily assembled force of 2,000 Japanese.[63] In anticipation of significant casualties, three American portable field hospitals were established in the area.[64] American air support was also vital, and P-40 fighters conducted strafing runs and B-25 medium bombers hit key targets.[65]

In the last week of July, Chinese forces captured a hill overlooking the Tengchong area, which had been occupied by Japanese artillery, and cleared several of the surrounding villages outside the wall. Despite Chinese engineers using TNT charges placed directly against the wall, progress was slow.[66] A week later, American bombers were able to successfully breach the wall, and Chinese infantry established a foothold within the town on August 3, but Chinese forces continued to be deployed in a piecemeal manner that allowed the badly outnumbered Japanese to slow the advance, frustrating American liaison officers.[67] Faced with continued Japanese resistance, the fight for Tengchong became an urban battle, with superior Chinese numbers slowly advancing through Japanese fortifications. Like at Myitkyina, the Japanese showed no inclination to withdraw, and the battle would continue into mid-September. When Tengchong fell on September 14, a force of more than 45,000 Chinese troops had been engaged to eliminate 2,000 Japanese.[68] While they achieved their objective, the cost in equipment and casualties had been extremely high.

In the southern portion of the Salween front, the chaotic Chinese withdrawal from Longling in June made the capture of Songshan, which blocked the Burma Road, essential because Chinese troops would need to be better supplied and coordinated for a second assault on Longling.[69] The main peak of Songshan rose to a height of over three thousand feet and gave a commanding view of the surrounding area. Chinese forces had attempted to bypass Songshan in May after probing attacks had revealed extensive Japanese fortifications. The Japanese on Songshan had dug a network of fortified artillery emplacements, tunnels, and concealed machine gun positions, all designed for mutual support. These positions included reinforced overhead cover, which reduced the value of bombing attacks and close air support.[70] Although the 1,200 men in the Songshan garrison were running low on food and ammunition, they showed little inclination to retreat.

Two divisions of the XI Group Army launched an attack on Songshan in early June, which seized outlying positions but made little progress.[71] Heavy Chinese casualties led General Wei to send elements of three additional divisions to the Songshan area, and an American advisory team, led by Col. Carlos G. Spahn, also arrived to coordinate combat engineering support.[72] It was hoped that American equipment and demolitions training would allow Chinese attackers to destroy the heavily fortified positions with flamethrowers, TNT, or shaped charges, but training specialized assault teams took time. Chinese troops continued to launch attacks during the day, but after taking casualties, and with supporting units often not coordinating a relief in place, Japanese nighttime counterattacks frequently retook the ground, leading to limited gains.[73] An American liaison officer noted that heavy losses often occurred due to "attempts to walk or rather climb up through interlocking bands of machine-gun fire. As a demonstration of sheer bravery the attacks were magnificent but sickeningly wasteful."[74]

In late July, the Chinese improved their artillery coordination, which provided direct fire support against Japanese positions, although these guns were left exposed to Japanese air and nighttime infiltration attacks.[75] Further improvements and training continued, and by the end of August specialized teams of combat engineers had been created to cut barbed wire defenses, and specialized demolition groups with flamethrowers and TNT had been formed to lead attacks.[76] With limited alternatives and faced with mounting losses to infantry units, American engineers advised the digging of mines under Japanese positions, but construction of the tunnels took more than a week.[77] The detonation of six thousand pounds of TNT in these mines caused heavy casualties among the Japanese and eliminated several key positions that had been blocking Chinese attacks, but it wasn't until September 7 that the last Japanese troops were cleared from the mountain and the Burma Road was open to traffic.[78] American liaison officers estimated that at Songshan, the Japanese force of 1,200 had cost the Chinese over 7,500 killed and many thousands more wounded.[79] While the Japanese garrison at Songshan could not have been effectively bypassed, taking the position absorbed the efforts of three Chinese divisions for nearly the entire summer of 1944.[80]

CONCLUSION

The Yunnan campaign struggled to overcome its combined military and political challenges with little direct assistance from Stilwell, which was part of his plan to have a "light footprint" and to stay out of political issues. Japanese plans developed in the spring of 1944 had been based on holding fortified positions for long periods of time and using mobile columns to counterattack Chinese positions. These had been highly effective in forcing the vastly numerically superior Chinese forces into an uncoordinated and uneven advance, and Chinese attacks had failed to build momentum.[81] Confronted with incessant political negotiating with Chinese military and political leaders, and with those who consented to aggressive action only with overwhelming superiority, many American liaison officers concluded that Chinese ground forces could never play a decisive role in the war against Japan. The Yunnan campaign revealed that short-term training and limited American efforts to improve Chinese forces through indirect roles, such as providing technical services, was ineffectual. Similar to American assessments of Chinese soldiers in north Burma, Frank Dorn remarked that the fighting "demonstrated the correctness of the basic assumption that properly trained, equipped, and led, Chinese soldiers are fully capable of beating back the Jap armies."[82] What was lacking was any improvement in the planning, organizational, and staff functions to enable brave, dedicated soldiers to make an impact as a unit.

The American advisory program was also a mixture of success and failure. American logistics support had kept Chinese forces supplied in difficult terrain, but Chinese commanders continued to regard supplies delivered to their units as unit property, rarely distributing it to other formations that might be in greater need. When supplies were airdropped, units on the ground had no system of property accountability, meaning that higher-level commanders had extraordinarily little visibility or leverage to resolve issues.[83] Another issue exposed by the reliance on small, decentralized liaison efforts was that it placed a heavy burden on interpreters, many of whom had received no basic military training.[84] Internal Chinese cultural tensions between interpreters, many of whom were from wealthy or educated backgrounds, and Chinese soldiers, who were often from a peasant background, further complicated coordination efforts, and these were noted by American liaison personnel.[85] Last, short-duration training programs had been unable to change deep-rooted military concepts among Chinese officers. The continued emphasis of Chinese officers on direct frontal assaults meant that the units of the Y Force often suffered heavy casualties, with some divisions having more than 50 percent of their strength killed or wounded.[86] British general William Slim noted that losses could also be attributed to the different organizational approach of the Y Force and that "their training, armament, and leadership, which were much below those of Stilwell's troops, made them no match for the Japanese."[87] These heavy losses meant that the training investment in these personnel could not be further developed and their experiences shared with the larger Chinese military.

In contrast to the campaign in northern Burma, where Americans had been much more directly involved in operational decisions, the Yunnan campaign highlights clear limits to the effectiveness of indirect training and advisory efforts. Heavy investments in equipment and highly trained personnel had been useful in developing temporary solutions to problems, but it was not decisive in making Chinese operations more effective.[88] In mid-June, for example, the Y Force included more than 3,300 U.S. Army personnel, a disproportionate number of whom were officers, engineers, medical specialists, and other highly skilled fields that were desperately needed in other organizations.[89] While Chinese forces in northern Burma had been systematically educated in American doctrine, concepts, and military behavior, forces in Yunnan were given targeting training on specific aspects of military operations. As a result, during the battle of Songshan for example, Chinese forces, although armed with new submachine guns and radios, continued to make frontal assaults that were familiar to their units and where the type of simple, direct operations the small cadre of experienced leaders could command and control. In contrast, Chinese troops in India had been given eighteen months to develop into a cohesive force, with unit-level training to allow officers to evaluate their understanding of American tactics and concepts. Overall, the heavy investment that Stilwell and the U.S. Army made to send hundreds of specialized and highly trained personnel, use expensive assets like aircraft, and attempt to train a large force was effective but not very efficient. The losses sustained meant that many of the soldiers that had received training would not remain in their units, and the allocation of significant American support to more than a dozen divisions minimized the ability to make a decisive impact and create a smaller but more elite force. Resolving enduring issues with Chinese army forces would require much deeper engagement at both a military and a political level to be effective in improving the capabilities of the Chinese army. Until Chiang was faced with an existential crisis to his power, and until Stilwell felt he had the support of American political leadership, there was little opportunity to refine the methods and programs that led to the flawed coordination of the Yunnan campaign.

★ **CHAPTER 6** ★

SUPPORTING LOCAL ALLIES

May–October 1944

**A brief experience with international politics
confirms me in my preference for
driving a garbage truck.**
—General Stilwell near the end of his tenure[1]

IN THE SPRING AND SUMMER of 1944, while Stilwell was commanding Chinese and American forces engaged in northern Burma, supervising the Salween offensive of the Y Force, and acting as Mountbatten's deputy, he was drawn deeper into Chinese political affairs due to renewed Japanese offensives. Stilwell's original mission statement in 1942 had called on him to work to make China a more effective and efficient military ally, but changing political trends had shifted his efforts away from this area of focus. The failure of Chinese forces to respond effectively to Japanese attacks also gave Stilwell an opportunity, because by the spring of 1944, American political leaders like President Roosevelt had cooled toward Chiang Kai-shek. As the difficulties of using China as an air base as envisioned in early 1943 mounted, and the Pacific island-hopping strategy gained steam, China's importance in fighting Japan had declined. At the same time, Stilwell's stature had risen, and the X Force, the Chinese Army in India, had demonstrated by the spring of 1944 that structural changes, retraining, and complete reequipping of Chinese units could lead to dramatic improvements in combat performance. The divergent experiences of the X Force, the Chinese Army in India, and the Y Force in Yunnan provided a stark contrast in the merits of an intensive, comprehensive advisory program versus a "light footprint" approach. The capture of Myitkyina was a particularly notable exclamation point for Stilwell's programs and the ability of Chinese forces to fight well in the right conditions.

In the fall of 1943 and the spring of 1944, as Stilwell focused his efforts on the north Burma campaign, the program to develop the capabilities and improve the efficiency of the Chinese army on a large-scale basis had been stalled by a lack of supplies and personnel. On January 1, 1944, a nascent "Z Force" (continuing the motif of an X Force in India, Y Force in Yunnan, and now Z Force in China) operational staff was established under the leadership of Brig. Gen. Malcolm F. Lindsay as chief of staff, although Stilwell remained the nominal commander.[2] The official mission of the Z Force was to build a force of thirty Chinese divisions with improved capabilities, although which abilities needed to be reformed or modified differed depending on Chinese or American assessments. While the X Force in northern Burma had integrated Chinese army units into a coalition force after complete retraining in American tactics, and the Y Force relied on a program of retraining in technical areas, weapons transfers, and large numbers of liaison personnel, the initial American plan for the Z Force would be restrictive in terms of personnel strength and roles. A total of only 1,500 American officers and 1,000 enlisted personnel would be spread thinly throughout thirty Chinese divisions.[3] This approach had the benefits of a light footprint, with few Americans exposed to combat, but with a vastly reduced ability to influence Chinese decision making. Like in Yunnan, the Z Force leadership had little ability to mandate organizational changes or intervene in decision making. Moreover, the smaller role for U.S. liaison and assistance efforts meant that logistics and technical support would be rudimentary. For example, while Chinese soldiers in northern Burma were cared for by American medical personnel, and on the Salween front American medics and doctors augmented Chinese medical units, in east China, Z Force medical teams ran training centers but were not directly engaged in supporting Chinese units.[4]

This light footprint approach to reforming the Chinese army was driven by Stilwell's failure to gain political support for his program in 1943, continued supply issues as tonnage over the Hump slowly increased, and, most important, Stilwell's desire to work through the Chinese army's existing national command structure. In the spring and summer of 1944, Stilwell would be increasingly drawn into Chinese political and military affairs over which he felt he had little leverage, influence, or authority. While Stilwell had clashed repeatedly with Chiang since he began his assignment in early 1942, he had always taken a strict hands-off policy regarding Chinese politics and refused to place a greater emphasis on supporting regional leaders. A more politically aware commander, who understood that Washington was increasingly skeptical of Chiang, could have pushed for more effective policies that utilized the shifting balance of power within the Allied command. For example, Stilwell took no action after receiving a detailed report from General Dorn that a group of senior military leaders, including Xue Yue in Hunan, Zhang Fakui, Hu Hanmou, and possibly Lung Yun, was coordinating to form an opposition coalition to Chiang.[5] In another situation, General Dorn reported that Ho Ying-chin was in a precarious position as chief of staff and hinted that American pressure might be able to push him to resign, but again no action was taken.[6]

Despite his near total lack of confidence in Chiang's leadership and the often incompetent generals surrounding Chiang, Stilwell maintained a strict determination to work through what he perceived as the legitimate national government structure. Stilwell's focus on supporting a national government overlooked the fact that the "national government" was essentially a KMT-controlled organization with limited power in much of China and that many regional leaders had repeatedly demonstrated their military skills and desire to oppose the Japanese with a more active military strategy. In the summer of 1944, these regional forces bore the brunt of Japanese attacks, while American aid and military assistance was misused by army forces loyal to Chiang. Rather than support regional forces, Stilwell took a bold and politically dangerous approach to seek command authority over Chinese army units. His gamble offered the possibility that in one bold move, he could gain a position to make drastic and critical changes, but it was politically unfeasible for China to place a foreign officer as the senior commander of their army. A more realistic and politically aware approach from Stilwell would have been to continue the successful training and advisory model he developed at Ramgarh and support regional forces that could contribute to the war against Japan.

DECLINING FAITH IN CHIANG AND AN OPPORTUNITY TO CHANGE STRATEGY

While Chinese forces in Burma were forging a reputation for bravery, by the spring of 1944 the situation of the Chinese army as a whole was largely unchanged since the retreat from the Yangtze River Valley in 1937 and 1938, and Ambassador Gauss had sent increasingly pessimistic reports to Washington that highlighted significant difficulties trying to "impel China's leaders and soldiers to put forth materially greater effort in the war against Japan."[7] In addition, Gauss reported to the secretary of state in January 1944 that Chinese military forces were deteriorating, and commonly,

> draftees, from 18 to 45 years of age, receive three weeks' basic training which includes political indoctrination of questionable quality, following which they may be sent into actual combat service or used as required for replacements in battle-trained units. Weapons and ammunition are insufficient, and poor communications and difficulty of obtaining replenishment supplies frequently result in Chinese units running short of ammunition during battle. An important factor causing poor morale among Chinese troops is the knowledge that they will not be likely to be treated for wounds they may receive.[8]

Four days later, Gauss provided a strategic assessment: "The Chinese strategy is entirely defensive in character; in spirit and morale the Chinese soldier is absolutely defense-minded without any conception of offensive operations; in training, equipment, physical condition and medical care the Chinese soldier suffers such serious deficiencies that from an offensive standpoint he has no value."[9] Stilwell's political advisor, John P. Davies, was also in contact with presidential aide Harry Hopkins and provided additional scathing reports that highlighted Chiang's role in the dysfunction in the theater:

> The Generalissimo seeks to dominate because he has no appreciation of what genuine democracy means. His philosophy is the unintegrated product of his limited intelligence, his Japanese military education, his former close contact with German military advisors, his alliance with the usurious banker-landlord class, and his reversion to the sterile moralisms of the Chinese classics. The primitive power complex which was his original motivation has developed into a bigoted conviction that China can realize its destiny only under his preceptorship.

These assessments were slowly beginning to have an effect on President Roosevelt, who had previously been a steadfast supporter of Chiang and Chennault. On January 14, 1944, Roosevelt hinted that Chinese military activity was needed to justify further supply shipments.[10] Chiang's haughty tone in an exasperating dispute over a massive loan, which he demanded in January 1944, appeared to confirm to many American observers that the KMT prioritized extracting American aid over fighting Japan.[11] Even the American public, which had been inundated with pro-Chiang reports since 1941, was becoming increasing skeptical of the long-term and postwar importance of China, and the British embassy in Washington reported that Americans "are beginning to doubt whether China will be a friendly democracy protecting American interests in the Pacific and whether the China market will be so lucrative after all."[12]

With declining support for Chiang and his KMT-dominated "national government" in Washington, an alternative strategy to build and develop greater influence in China was to support regional military leaders. Although Chiang Kai-shek had nominal authority over the Republic of China, regional military leaders, such as Lung Yun in Yunnan and, more importantly, the Chinese Communists led by Mao Zedong, operated largely free of orders from Chungking (Chongqing) and maintained military forces that could include several hundred thousand soldiers. This situation offered American military officers the ability to provide access to supplies, training, and air support in return for specific military actions, such as rescuing downed American pilots or defending a key supply route. Using a more "transactional" approach to military aid at the regional level would have made coordination of larger offensives difficult, but in their particular area these units were often highly effective and well-motivated.

A likely candidate for a regional military assistance program was General Xue Yue, commander of the 9th Military Region.[13] Xue commanded forces in Hunan and Guangdong, and although he was a member of the KMT and had graduated from the KMT military training school, the Whampoa Academy, he acted largely outside the authority of Chungking. Within his regional power base, Xue oversaw recruitment, collected his own supplies, and appointed subordinates loyal to him. Since 1937, he had defended his area with remarkable success, and multiple Japanese drives on his main city of Changsha had been defeated. Despite these victories, regional forces like Xue's could not rely on support from the KMT-led government in Chungking, and his troops suffered severely from supply problems, a lack of modern weapons, and a lack of professional military training.[14] Xue also had to be careful in assessing which orders from Chiang to follow, because Chiang often ordered regional forces to take the lead in military operations while preserving his loyal troops safely behind the front lines.[15] A State Department assessment of Xue in May 1944 described him as "in excellent health and spirits" and that he "enjoys a reputation among Chinese as an implacable and successful anti-Japanese warrior."[16]

Another option for the United States to build alternative military support in China was to establish connections with Chinese Communist forces in north China. The KMT had half-heartedly attempted to form a united front with the Chinese Communists in the late 1930s, but this effort had broken down in January 1941 with renewed fighting between the KMT troops and the Communist Red Army. Throughout the war, Chiang had kept many of his most loyal, well-equipped troops and capable military officers in a cordon around the Chinese Communist base in Yenan.[17] Stilwell's political advisor, John P. Davies, had suggested military engagement with the Communists in June 1943, and in January 1944 he had refined his proposal to emphasize the need to gather information on the north China area, where the KMT had little intelligence. President Roosevelt supported the proposal and sent a message to Chiang Kai-shek on February

9 requesting that an American military mission be allowed into north China. Chiang adamantly refused and condescendingly informed Stilwell that "the President does not understand the conditions and the sinister intentions of the Communists.[18] After repeated delays, Chiang reluctantly agreed after a personal plea by U.S. vice president Henry Wallace during his visit to Chungking in late June 1944, but Chiang continued to reject the idea that the Chinese Communists would be trustworthy and maintained his opposition to the plan.[19]

Despite the shifting political context of U.S. military operations in China, Stilwell's relationship with Mountbatten was showing signs of strain. Stilwell had been cautious in his dealing with Mountbatten during the fall of 1943, waiting to see how the commander of SEAC would support his plans for a north Burma offensive. After the campaign began, Stilwell viewed any British attempt to minimize the investment of troops and supplies for Stilwell's forces as an underhanded attempt to stifle his forward movement. Stilwell's prickly disposition had led to continuing British complaints about Stilwell's behavior and demeanor, but George C. Marshall maintained his steadfast support of Stilwell and lobbied Mountbatten to form a more effective partnership. In a private message to Mountbatten in late January 1944, Marshall acknowledged that Stilwell was not always easy to work with, but he was only "intolerant of slow motion, excessive caution and cut-and-dried procedure." While Stilwell could have used more tact and careful language in his methods, Marshall encouraged Mountbatten to understand that "he will provide tremendous energy, courage and unlimited ingenuity and imagination to any aggressive proposals or operations. His mind is far more alert than almost any of our generals and his training and understanding are on an unusually high level."[20]

The ink was barely dry on Marshall's message when Stilwell and Mountbatten's relationship suffered in irreparable rift over the support of the north Burma offensive. In February 1944, Mountbatten dispatched senior members of the SEAC staff, led by Maj. Gen. Albert Wedemeyer, to London and Washington, with plans to sharply reduce operations in north Burma because of Chiang Kai-shek's continued failure to order the Chinese forces in Yunnan to attack and his miserly support of the Chinese army in India. Instead, Mountbatten and his staff believed that an amphibious assault on the west coast of Sumatra would isolate Japanese forces in Burma and provide a staging area for an assault on Singapore. Mountbatten's plan would require air and naval resources that would likely not be available until Germany was defeated, so in effect, the plan, codenamed Culverin, would pause offensive operations in the SEAC for at least six months and possibly a year.[21] Stilwell heard of the mission and dispatched Brig. Gen. Hayden Boatner, who had been commanding the Chinese Army in India, to Washington to argue against Mountbatten's plan. Stilwell believed that as the commanding general of U.S. forces in the CBI theater, he was acting within his authority to send a delegation to brief U.S. military officials on his objections to the proposed plan. But Stilwell failed to inform Mountbatten, his direct superior in the SEAC chain of command, that he was sending a delegation with instructions to oppose Mountbatten's plans. Boatner was able to brief senior U.S. military officials and meet with President Roosevelt, who generally agreed with Stilwell's assertions that delaying a Burma campaign was unnecessary given the balance of forces and progress being made in north Burma.[22]

Even thirty years after this episode, Wedemeyer recalled this tremendous breach of protocol with anger.

> They [Stilwell's team] arrived before my group from SEAC. . . . They talked to the War Department Plans Group, my old policy planning group, and convinced them that the SEAC plan would fall flat. Davies went over to the State Department and generated opposition there, and between the two, they convinced the U.S. officials that the British had influenced me to support their views concerning plans for Burma and India and that I was completely in their pocket.[23]

Despite Stilwell's success in maintaining American support for his plans, Mountbatten interpreted the dispatch of Boatner to Washington as a deliberate and provocative undermining of his authority.

The U.S. Joint Chiefs of Staff tried to mend the rift and sent a message to their British counterparts that neither Mountbatten's nor Stilwell's briefing teams had changed the already established policy, so the competing delegations had not had an impact on strategy, with neither general gaining or losing support.[24] In addition, General Marshall wrote an "Eyes Only" message to Stilwell on March 1, 1944, to inform him that the British were concerned about what they perceived as disloyalty by an American officer to a British commander. In blunt language, Marshall scolded Stilwell for his negligence in developing a good working relationship and that "you do not appear to have made an effort to establish a smooth-working relation with Mountbatten and his staff regardless of whether or not you agree with the final decisions." Marshall continued that Stilwell needed to address this situation quickly and thoroughly and he instructed him to meet personally with Mountbatten and "talk over the whole matter frankly and at length repeat at length, and see if you can reach a working accord which is essential between two officials in the positions he and you occupy."[25] At the meeting Stilwell apologized for not informing Mountbatten about dispatching a team to Washington, and he radioed Marshall that "I have eaten crow for my bungle in not informing him of our mission to Washington," and his mea culpa mended fences within the SEAC headquarters for the time being.[26]

Stilwell's coordination with Gauss and the U.S. embassy in Chungking was difficult. Gauss felt that "General Stilwell is, of course, frequently absent from Chungking for long periods of time, and the Headquarters does not appear to have an appreciation of the necessity of cooperation and liaison in political matters—and military matters having political aspect—with the Embassy as the representative political agency of the Government." Moreover, despite the attachment of several State Department officers to Stilwell's command, Gauss felt that in the military headquarters, "there is apparently no intelligent recognition of the political aspect of problems which come to them as military matters."[27]

These personality and policy differences within the Allies serve to highlight that despite the massive increase in American military and economic engagement in the CBI theater, and Chiang's declining prestige, Stilwell continued to have problems developing an integrated strategic approach. During his visit to Washington as part of General Boatner's delegation, John P. Davies had stated that United States policy in the CBI theater was "badly handicapped in our overall policy by a lack of coordination in our military, political and economic programs," which resulted in greater internal friction and wasted time.[28] It also meant that due to Stilwell's poor political awareness he would be unable to gain allies for his programs to increase his command authority in China.

ICHI-GO AND INCREASING AMERICAN LEVERAGE

In February and March 1944, intelligence reports from Japanese-occupied areas, aerial reconnaissance, and intercepted communications all revealed Japanese preparations for a major offensive, code-named Ichi-Go, scheduled to begin in April. The Japanese objective was to seize a land route running continuously from north China, through the Yangtze River Valley, and then south to Hong Kong.[29] This plan would mean attacking into Hunan and Guangxi Provinces, which were not only important agricultural regions but also included numerous American air bases.[30] For the Japanese, opening a land route was a priority because of significant attacks on Japanese shipping as American advances in the Pacific began to restrict shipping routes. In a March 17 message to President Roosevelt, Chiang had noted Japanese preparations for an attack in south China, but he had given greater prominence to clashes between the KMT and Soviets in Xinjiang and a possible Chinese Communist attack on Xian.[31] In fact, in early 1944, while Chiang had stalled the Salween offensive, he had quickly dispatched roughly 120,000 loyal troops to Xinjiang, gaining greater control over the vast central Asian region during a dispute with the Soviet Union.[32] There was also no indication that Chiang was sufficiently alarmed to redeploy the 500,000 capable and well-armed troops he had assigned to blockade Chinese Communist base areas.[33]

As Japanese forces continued to mass for a late spring offensive, General Chennault made appeals to both Chiang Kai-shek and President Roosevelt for greater support and also to preemptively blame Stilwell for any future problems. Chennault's request to Stilwell for additional supplies was denied on the grounds that the major supply bases in Assam, India, were under direct threat of a Japanese U-Go offensive.[34] On April 15, Chennault sent an assessment to Chiang Kai-shek that emphasized Chinese weaknesses in east China and directly blamed the diversion of forces to support the Salween campaign for increased vulnerability to a Japanese attack. Despite Stilwell's direct instructions to Chennault not to provide

Chiang with independent and uncoordinated military advice, Chennault argued for an expanded air effort in east China at the expense of other programs.[35] Furthermore, in a personal message to President Roosevelt, Chennault wrote on April 19 that "owing to the present concentration of our resources on the fighting in Burma, little has been done to strengthen the Chinese Armies in the interior, and for the same reason the Fourteenth and Chinese Air Forces are still operating on a shoestring. If we were even a little stronger, I should not be worried."[36] Chennault failed to mentioned that in April 1943, in the lead-up to the Trident Conference where Chennault had won support for an expanded air campaign, Chinese representatives had passed along Chiang Kai-shek's "personal assurance that in the event the enemy attempts to interrupt the air offensive by a ground advance on the air bases, the advance can be halted by the existing Chinese forces."[37] The result of Chennault's continued entreaties for more support from Washington was that on the eve of the Japanese offensive, deliveries of supplies for air forces received priority over supplies for ground forces, further weakening ground forces shortly before they would be severely tested in combat.[38]

On April 19, 1944, Japanese forces began operation Ichi-Go, and while Chennault's Fourteenth Air Force was able to target key bridges and railway junctions, his bombing attacks slowed but did not halt the Japanese advance in north China as Chinese troops put up only a token resistance before fleeing.[39] By this point in the war, Chinese units—after years of inactivity, endemic corruption, and a high rate of desertions—had little combat power.[40] Within weeks, a Japanese force of roughly 60,000 soldiers shattered a Chinese force roughly five times as large.[41] The rapid collapse of Chinese forces startled Americans, who had become accustomed to Chiang's grandiose propaganda speeches.[42] In response to continued Japanese attacks, Chiang requested further increases in American military aid, but observers noted that he had a poor grasp of the situation and his staff shielded him from negative reports.[43] Chiang continued to emphasize airpower, requesting that Chennault's Fourteenth Air Force "be strengthened," that supplies for B-29 bomber units be redistributed to frontline operations, and that further aid be given to Chinese air force units. Chiang also strangely made a specific request for eight thousand rocket launchers, the M1 bazooka, which had been rushed into production. But this weapon was designed to provide extremely short-range antitank capability, a battlefield situation that rarely occurred in China.[44] Under his own authority over the Hump airlift, Stilwell was able to divert increasing resources to Chennault, and in June 1944, the Fourteenth Air Force received more than 12,500 tons of supplies, while other organizations saw their allocations reduced.[45]

Despite these efforts, getting supplies to Chinese forces and Chennault in east China was constrained by logistics within China as well as the Hump airlift capacity. After supplies landed in Kunming, they still had to be loaded into a meter gauge railway, to be moved one hundred miles farther east before being transferred to trucks for a four-hundred-mile drive over dirt roads. Finally, at Tushan, supplies were reloaded onto railcars for delivery to airfields. The entire process took roughly one month, from the time supplies were loaded onto an airplane in India to reaching forward bases in east China.[46] American Services of Supply officers and a small number of mechanics and quartermaster troops had attempted to improve the capacity of this route, but by 1944 most Chinese trucks were worn out after years of use, and railways had suffered from a lack of maintenance.[47] Even if supplies were available, Chennault again attempted to shift blame for the situation and identified bad weather in China during May and June 1944 as the reason his air forces could not stop the Japanese ground forces.[48]

Stilwell was not above a degree of schadenfreude in Chennault's failures and noted that "he [Chennault] has not caused any Jap withdrawals. On the contrary, our preparations have done exactly what I prophesied, i.e., drawn a Jap reaction, which he now acknowledges the ground forces can't handle, even with the total air support he asked for and got."[49] Without a way to stop the Japanese advance, Stilwell's staff estimated that the destruction of the east China airfields would mean a six-to-nine-month setback, as new facilities and infrastructure would need to be developed farther west.[50] Politically, by late May, Chennault and Chiang were increasingly seen as responsible for a major strategic failure due to their flawed plans and poor management.

While Chiang and Chennault suffered from the fallout of their defeats, in the late spring of 1944, Stilwell received new instructions from the U.S.

Joint Chiefs of Staff that would increase his ability to reshape his mission objectives. As the advance in the south and central Pacific both moved steadily closer to Japan, the role of American forces in China was redefined to focus on providing air support for Allied operations against Taiwan (Formosa), the Philippines, and the Ryukyus. In late May, Marshall elaborated that offensive operations and a major ground campaign in the China theater were now seen as unnecessary in Washington and that "your paramount mission in the China theater for the immediate future is to conduct such military operations as will most effectively support the main effort directed against the enemy by forces in the Pacific."[51]

With a new, more limited mission that did not call for China to play a key role in the defeat of Japan, Stilwell pressed for a "transactional" approach to dealing with Chiang Kai-shek. In a May 24 message to Marshall, Stilwell noted that to achieve his mission, "I have never had any means of exerting pressure. I am continuing to work on the problem as I have from the beginning,—by personal acquaintance and influence, by argument and demonstration." Stilwell sharply criticized Chiang's mercenary approach to Allied operations: "CKS will squeeze out of us everything he can get to make us pay for the privilege of getting at Japan through China. He will do nothing to help unless forced into it."[52] Marshall did not reply to Stilwell's suggestion of a more assertive approach to dealing with Chiang but did reiterate on May 27 that the China theater was to support the "main operation" as best it could.[53]

STILWELL'S REGIONAL MILITARY OPTION

By June 1944, the effects of the Ichi-Go offensive were clearly being felt in Chungking, as the Japanese advances exposed Chiang's empty rhetoric and the effect of atrophy on KMT military capabilities. Ambassador Gauss reported that "there is covert and fearful criticism by officials, intellectuals and others of Generalissimo Chiang; of his complete concentration of all power and authority in his own hands; of his engrossment with a heavy volume of petty details of administration; . . . of his unwillingness to repose any confidence, authority, or trust in anyone or to consult or seek or consider any advice or intelligent opinion."[54] American military officials reported similar concerns by important officials who were "stunned" by the military defeats and who "criticize government bitterly for not making effort to inflict losses on the Japanese."[55] During the offensive, strategic planners on the Combined Chiefs of Staff and the U.S. Joint Chiefs of Staff were continuing to limit the mission parameters of the CBI theater. In a June 3 directive sent to Mountbatten by the CCS, the role of SEAC, and particularly Stilwell, was to place priority on developing air links and continue efforts to develop an overland link but with the already assigned resources.[56] With Allied plans being revised, Mountbatten also took the opportunity to request through his British chain of command that Stilwell be taken out of the SEAC area due to continued frictions and replaced with either Wedemeyer or Maj. Gen. Dan Sultan.[57]

One potential solution for the growing skepticism of further American support to China, and belated recognition of Stilwell's accomplishments in Burma, was to expand his authority and status so that he could take a more direct role in shaping Chinese military policy. On June 30, 1944, the Army staff proposed that Stilwell be promoted to the rank of full general (four stars) in recognition of his accomplishments.[58] This promotion would also provide Stilwell with increased status in dealing with the status-conscious Chinese. The U.S. Joint Chiefs of Staff also reappraised their estimates of the situation in China, in light of Chinese defeats, and noted that the reliance on airpower had been proven to be a failure and noted Stilwell's repeated attempts to improve the capabilities of Chinese ground troops. In a memorandum for the president, it was noted that "had his [Stilwell's] advice been followed, it is now apparent that we would have cleared the Japanese from northeast Burma before the monsoon and opened the way to effective action in China proper. Had his advice been followed the Chinese ground forces east of the Hump would have been far better equipped and prepared to resist or at least delay the Japanese advances."[59] These assessments had the strong support of General Marshall, who had become exasperated in his dealing with the Chinese and continued to give Stilwell his full trust and confidence.[60] American military assessments also showed optimism about Stilwell's programs, particularly the training model developed at Ramgarh. U.S. Army studies concluded that by June 1944, 15,000 Chinese officers had received training, alongside 78,000 soldiers in India and 190,000 in China, and the X Force of five divisions in Burma (14th,

22nd, 30th, 38th, and 50th) had now proven themselves.[61] Stilwell's programs, although slow to develop due to resource constraints and political decisions, were finally reaching a critical mass where they could begin to achieve the original mission goals established in 1942.

Faced with united American military support for a more direct role in reforming the Chinese army and growing questions about Chiang's integrity and leadership, President Roosevelt sent China a message on July 6, 1944, requesting that Stilwell be appointed "directly under you in command of all Chinese and American forces, and that you charge him with the full responsibility and authority for coordination and direction of the operations required to stem the tide of the enemy's advances."[62] While Chiang Kai-shek understood his declining leverage in dealing with Roosevelt, he agreed on July 8 only "in principle" and requested that there be a "preparatory period" before General Stilwell could take command of Chinese forces.[63] At this time Chiang was also dealing with a domestic political crisis due to widespread discussion of the birth of his illegitimate child with his longtime mistress and rumors of a possible split between Chiang and his famous wife, Mei-ling Soong.[64] In addition to this obvious delaying tactic, Chiang asked that an "influential personal representative" be sent to China by Roosevelt so that these new political and military arrangements can be implemented to "adjust the relations between me and General Stilwell," prior to his taking command.[65]

While Roosevelt's message was being digested in Chungking, Marshall took the opportunity to caution Stilwell to make a greater political effort if the reorganization of the command resulted in Stilwell's elevation to command forces in China. In a July 7 message, he wrote to Stilwell that political niceties required greater attention because of "the offense you have given, usually in small affairs, both to the Generalissimo and to the President. Had you yourself, or at least someone on your staff, devoted a little attention to promoting harmonious relations, I think the above proposal of the President, at least insofar as his backing you and your recommendations, would have been made long ago." In the near future, Marshall urged Stilwell to "win over to your side anyone who can help in the battle which will result from the violent hostility of those Chinese who will lose face by your appointment."[66]

While diplomatic and political maneuvers continued, on May 27 the second phase of the Ichi-Go offensive began, and the Japanese targeted Xue Yue's ninth war zone both as a vital transportation route and a major food-producing region and also because of the numerous American airbases.[67] Xue received some American air support and limited supplies through informal arrangements with Chennault, in return for protecting the bases, but these transfers were strictly "off the record" because Stilwell had forbidden arming local military leaders without going through the national government.[68] A small supply of weapons collected by the Z Force for training was delivered to Hengyang in mid-June, and American liaison teams were attached to the headquarters of the IX and IV war zones. Additional liaison teams were formed and attached to roughly half a dozen group armies and armies, and Chennault's Fourteenth Air Force also established forward air controller teams to improve air support.[69] These efforts were helpful, but the overwhelming majority of Chinese troops continued to mount little resistance to Japanese advances, and Changsha, the capital of Hunan Province, fell on June 18, 1944.[70]

The next target of the Japanese drive was the town of Hengyang, in southern Hunan, but faced with strong resistance by Xue Yue's 10th Army, led by the capable Major General Fong Hsien-chueh, and more difficult terrain, Japanese attacks faltered.[71] Airstrikes on Japanese supply lines stalled a full attack on the city, and Fourteenth Air Force bombing and strafing helped keep the battle lines in place, keeping Hengyang in Allied hands through August 8.[72] Despite continuing success at Hengyang, ingrained habits of poor coordination and mistrust between Chinese army commanders continued to inhibit a unified defense. Brigadier General Lindsey, in charge of the Z Force and the senior American officer in east China, reported that both General Xue Yue and Bai Chongxi, another senior commander in southeast China, were unwilling to request supplies from Chungking because they did not believe their requests would be given any attention.

They were likely correct, and Chiang Kai-shek took little action to support these local forces, although he did pledge in his diary to order the baptism of the Tenth Army if they were able to successfully defend Hengyang.[73] Even Chiang Kai-shek's sympathetic biographer, Jay Taylor, concedes that despite the Japanese advance, "Chiang showed that concern over disloyalty among his general was more important to him than the successful defense of these cities."[74] Instead, Bai Chongxi, in conjunction with Zhang Fakui, asked Lindsey directly for six sets of U.S. division equipment so that he could defend Guangxi.[75] A day later, General Xue Yue made a similar request for U.S. military equipment for his 4th Army, again bypassing the central government, which had not provided any equipment despite the ongoing heavy fighting.[76] The response from Stilwell to these requests for supplies and a greater American engagement with regional forces came in a terse message on July 24: "Boss [Stilwell] does not repeat not approve."[77]

After his meetings with senior regional Chinese military leaders, Lindsey also reported that he had information from reliable sources that a majority of the senior commanders in southern China, including Generals Xue Yue in Hunan and Lung Yun in Yunnan, were discussing the formation of an autonomous government outside of Chiang Kai-shek's authority.[78] Opposition to Chiang's government had been growing in south China, and as early as November 1943, clandestine meetings by prestigious military and political figures hinted of a possible anti-Chiang coalition being formed.[79] This nascent opposition group included prominent military leaders as well as non-KMT political groups, such as the League of Democratic Parties, that sought to form a national coalition government that would not be dominated by Chiang or the KMT.[80] In July, Chinese military officers approached the American consulate in Kweilin and outlined a plan to form an autonomous "Southwestern Government of Joint Defense."[81] Stilwell was apprised of these efforts and advised the Americans in China to listen but not take action: "Our policy is to lay off the internal affairs of China but we now have a big stake in this business and must keep ourselves informed. Listen to any propositions that may be made, but do not make any commitments nor even express any opinion. Just say you will forward any messages proposed."[82]

General Hearn, the senior American officer in China while Stilwell was in Burma, reiterated Stilwell's guidance and wrote to Lindsey on August 10 that "our concern in political factions is limited to the manner and degree in which they affect our mission in China, viz., to promote the war against Japan."[83] Stilwell dispatched Brig. Gen. Thomas Timberman, an experienced "China Hand" who had served with Stilwell at the American embassy and who spoke fluent Chinese, to meet with General Bai Chongxi to gain more information. Stilwell had worked with Bai in 1943 to establish several military schools in China and had found him to be hardworking and genuinely interested in systemic Army reforms, and he saw him as "perhaps the best man in China."[84] General Bai and his close military ally Li Tsung-jen had both gained a reputation as capable military leaders under the challenges of civilian government, and they would be needed for any regional government to have legitimacy and a prospect of success, but Timberman reported that Bai did not appear to be part of the effort.[85]

While these political maneuvers among Chinese military commanders were underway, Stilwell was loath to inflame the situation and supply weapons directly to leaders such as Xue Yue, and he continued to deliver military supplies only to the Chungking government organizations. At the same time, Stilwell noted that if Bai joined the dissidents, he had "character and ability as well as common sense and has always been most cooperative with us. In case this matter reaches a more serious stage, I strongly recommend that he be kept in mind as the one man best fitted to take over."[86] In a follow-up message, Stilwell reported to General Marshall on August 16 that although there was "widespread dissatisfaction and already the effects of agitation are apparent," the regional leaders were not making an active effort and were "fishing for information on the attitude of the U.S." before making a move.[87] Despite these possible avenues to influence and improve Chinese ground forces, Stilwell maintained the same policies of noninterference in political issues and kept the focus on national government forces, cabling a reminder to his staff in China, "Our policy is to lay off the internal affairs of China. . . . Do not repeat not make any commitments or even express any opinion" regardless of recent events.[88] This decision was true to form for Stilwell; in December 1943 he had similarly refused to be drawn into a movement by young officers, dissatisfied by KMT corruption and incompetence, to replace many of Chiang's most incompetent officials. That movement collapsed, and more than a dozen general officers were executed by Dai Li's agents.[89]

Possibly in response to plans to form a regional government, the American consul in Kweilin reported in late August that troops loyal to the Chungking government were arriving in south China but, rather than fighting the Japanese, had assumed garrison positions near Xue Yue's remaining forces, possibly to intimidate and stifle criticism.[90] While news of the opposition to Chiang was transmitted to President Roosevelt, with the assessment that the movement could be useful and "bring home to Chiang Kai-shek the necessity for broadening the base of his present government to include influential non-Kuomintang elements," there is no indication Roosevelt provided any guidance or instructions.[91] While in China during the summer of 1944, Vice President Henry Wallace had frequent contact with one of Stilwell's political advisors, John Stewart Service, who outlined to the visiting politician the opportunity for a new policy in China, based on more direct bargaining for aid and cultivating ties to non-KMT leaders. Service also advocated that the United States should reduce contact with the most disreputable parts of Chiang's government, such as Dai Li, and support a more even-handed media reporting on China so that the American public could form a more realistic assessment.[92] Wallace in turn reported to Roosevelt that shifting some degree of American support to a new, more progressive and democratic coalition might achieve a more proactive war policy and better align a postwar China with the United States. Wallace even noted that "the emergence of such a coalition could be aided by the manner of allocating both American military and economic aid," although he did not mention a specific leader of a non-KMT coalition.[93]

SHIFTING ALLIED PRIORITIES: STILWELL'S WINDOW OF OPPORTUNITY CLOSES

President Roosevelt's messages in early July had sent a clear signal to Chiang and Americans in the CBI theater that Washington appeared to finally be willing to make major changes in the command structure and utilize American military leverage. The continuing impact of the Ichi-Go offensive removed any remaining American military support for Chiang, and while he retained supporters in the State Department and among influential Americans, he could only hope to stall, rather than directly veto, American desires for changes.[94] Chiang's agreement to Stilwell being given command of Chinese forces "in principle" in early July was modified by a July 23 message, which raised three provisions that were required before a new command arrangement could be made. First, Chiang stated that the Chinese Communist forces, to whom the United States had dispatched a liaison group in July, could only fall under Stilwell if they also recognized the authority of the Chinese central government. Second, Stilwell's command role would need to be clearly defined in terms of functions, authority, title, and organizational relationships. Last, the Chinese government should assume control over all Lend-Lease supplies and have full authority over their use.[95] These stipulations, while sensible on paper, were carefully designed to reduce Stilwell's potential authority, and requiring agreement with the Chinese Communists to recognize the KMT-dominated central government, which had been pursuing them for years, was extremely unlikely.

While Chiang's message was circulating in Washington, Secretary of War Stimson and General Marshall worked with Maj. Gen. Patrick Hurley to assume the role of the personal representative Chiang had requested. Hurley had served as secretary of war during the Hoover administration, had demonstrated savvy negotiation and political skills as a corporate lawyer, and had visited China in 1943. Roosevelt approved of Hurley's appointment as his personal representative but did not directly address the stipulations that Chiang had raised in late July. In his personal instruction to Hurley, Roosevelt stated that "your principal mission is to promote efficient and harmonious relations between the Generalissimo and General Stilwell to facilitate General Stilwell's exercise of command over the Chinese Armies placed under his direction."[96] In a message to Chiang Kai-shek, Roosevelt went a step further and stated that Hurley's role was to "coordinate the whole military picture under you [Chiang]."[97] In a later message to Chiang, Roosevelt reiterated his desire for a rapid transition to Stilwell's command but gave no definitive statement on a title, Lend-Lease authority, or the Chinese Communist role.[98] Stilwell took a largely passive role in the discussion in July and August, being informed of the exchange of messages but with much of his attention focused on the conclusion of the battle of Myitkyina, which fell on August 3, 1944, and the Salween campaign. In Washington, Stilwell's State Department political advisor worked to dampen enthusiasm that a changed command relationship would lead to rapid improvement, noting that "in India and Burma we had far more control over Chinese units than we have had or will have in China."⁹⁹ Stilwell's lack of involvement in critical discussions during July and August echoed his failures in 1942 and 1943 to be aware of political opportunities and take proactive steps to shape his assignment.

On September 6, 1944, Stilwell and Hurley arrived in Chungking for initial meetings with Chiang and to begin preliminary discussion of a revised command relationship. Chiang noted that as commander of Chinese forces, Stilwell should receive orders from the National Military Council, which Chiang Kai-shek chaired and which included a large number of staff organizations and field commands.¹⁰⁰ In contrast, Hurley conveyed Roosevelt's impression that Stilwell would fill a role similar to Eisenhower in Europe, with Stilwell acting as the supreme commander of Allied forces in the China theater.¹⁰¹ The British representative in Chungking, Lieutenant General Carton de Wiart, lent quiet support to the American plan and in his personal conversations with Chiang Kai-shek highlighted how a similar Allied command structure had worked well in North Africa and France.¹⁰² Stilwell noted on September 13 that to effectively command the Chinese army, he needed to operate between Chiang and the National Military Council rather than under it and that a commander required the authority to relieve or appoint military personnel as required.¹⁰³

While this discussion of command authority was continuing in Chungking, by mid-September the Japanese advances in east China had now reached the vicinity of Kweilin, a major city and location of numerous air bases for the Fourteenth Air Force.¹⁰⁴ Chiang requested forces be withdrawn from Burma to bolster the defenses in east China, a position that was not supported by any American commander, and he also sent a personal letter to Roosevelt that placed the blame for Chinese defeats on poor American support: "The military reverses which China has suffered in recent months are accounted for by the lack of supplies in materiel. . . . The Chinese people have held on throughout the severest trials to wait for the day when the arsenal of democracy, which has hitherto abundantly supplied other allied powers, can equally furnish China with the necessary weapons."¹⁰⁵ This letter seems to have had the opposite effect, and in September 1944 Stilwell received the most direct and total support from President Roosevelt than at any time in the CBI theater. Roosevelt, writing from Quebec, where he was attending the Octagon Conference, was by this point clearly exasperated with Chiang. On September 16, Roosevelt bluntly stated that Chiang's plan to redeploy forces was misguided: "Any pause in your attack across the Salween or suggestion of withdrawal is exactly what the Jap has been striving to cause you to do by his operations in Eastern China." Roosevelt urged Chiang to "reinforce your Salween armies immediately and press their offensive, while at once placing General Stilwell in unrestricted command of all your forces."[106] Chiang's response to Roosevelt's unvarnished critique of Chiang's judgments and commitments was to pause further discussion and search for an alternative approach to the negotiations, as well as find an outlet for his anger.

Ironically, President Roosevelt's desire to change Stilwell's role had the effect of putting him directly in the crosshairs of the discussion of the importance of the China theater. At a September 24 meeting with Patrick Hurley, Chiang made it clear that Stilwell's continued role in the China theater was unacceptable because it would cause "grave dissensions in the new command" due to his contentious personal relationships with many Chinese military leaders.[107] The combined impact of a decreasing importance of China to the overall Allied strategy against Japan and the hard line adopted by Chiang presented Roosevelt with a difficult choice of how much political capital and energy he wanted to invest for a potentially negligible military payoff. While Stilwell's support in Washington eroded, Chiang doubled down on his criticism of Stilwell, and on October 9 Chiang gave Patrick Hurley a message for President Roosevelt that stated that

> I am willing and indeed anxious to meet your wishes, whether by the appointment of an American officer to command all Chinese Forces, or one to command only those in Yunnan and Burma. I am likewise agreeable to your other proposals. The officer chosen, however, must be one in whom I can repose confidence, and must be capable of frank and sincere cooperation. You will, I am sure, agree with me that these are indispensable qualifications. . . . General Stilwell has shown himself conspicuously lacking in these all-essential qualifications and you will understand that I cannot maintain in authority such an officer.[108]

Chiang's message skillfully widened the wedge between American policy and the personal role of Stilwell, who had become Chiang's harshest critic, and it placed Roosevelt in a position where he could move forward with Stilwell only by ignoring Chiang's messages, which could be used by American supporters of the KMT if events did not work out for Stilwell. Hurley also exacerbated the issue with his own separate message that stated bluntly that it was either Chiang or Stilwell: "You are now confronted by a choice between the two."[109] Hurley's comments further boxed Stilwell into a corner, and despite his instructions to resolve differences, Hurley magnified and highlighted problems. Stilwell could also no longer count on British support, which had been instrumental in saving Stilwell's position in the fall of 1943. Stilwell's bypassing of Mountbatten in sending Boatner to Washington, his clear anti-British prejudices, and his poor handling of British forces in the Burma campaign had all eroded whatever confidence Stilwell had earned over the years.[110] During the fall of 1944, Stilwell had also failed to forge a close partnership with Hurley, although Hurley's erratic behavior struck many Americans as indicative of both unfamiliarity with the key issues and personal problems. Foreign service officer John F. Melby stated in a postwar interview that "Hurley was crazy. I think he was beginning to get a little senile."[111] After more than a week of deliberation, on October 18, 1944, President Roosevelt made the decision to recall Stilwell.[112] A week later, the Joint Chiefs of Staff abolished the China-Burma-India theater and divided the area into a separate Burma-India theater and China theater, each with a three-star general in command.[113]

CONCLUSION

The decision to recall Stilwell was quickly followed by a diplomatic change of personnel, and after submitting his resignation in late October, Ambassador Gauss left China on November 14, 1944.[114] Roosevelt's sudden decision to acquiesce to Chiang's demand and recall Stilwell was a major turning point in the U.S. Army's role in the CBI theater and U.S. relations in China. Historian Michael Schaller concludes that Roosevelt's willingness to "walk-back" his demands after raising a seemingly vital issue "could only affirm Chiang's conviction that America could not abandon him."[115]

Stilwell's desire to form an effective national army is a long-standing preoccupation with American Army officers, but it overlooks the valuable role that regional forces can play in military conflicts. Since the American Revolutionary War, when officers of the standing Continental Army complained about poorly trained and poorly disciplined militia forces, American Army officers have generally viewed regional forces as a poor substitute for a standing national army. This bias overlooks the fact that local forces are often highly motivated, can more quickly be trained due to their smaller size, and can serve a valuable role in tying down enemy forces. The American military system only moved decisively in the direction of a dominant national army, compared to volunteer units or state national guard or militia formations, after the Spanish-American War revealed issues with coordination, logistics, and training during overseas deployments. This overlooks the fact that in many areas where the United States has provided military assistance, such as in South Vietnam or Afghanistan, the primary focus is defensive, and deployments outside the local or national area are not envisioned. When U.S. military leaders do decide to supply local forces to achieve a specific goal, particularly if the goal is maintaining control over a defined area, the results can be very impressive. In Iraq, for example, the "Anbar Awakening" involved the U.S. military providing weapons, training, and support to local tribal forces after the national government in Baghdad had proven unwilling and incapable of providing security in the province. In Anbar Province, local forces with U.S. military support were able to quickly mobilize local defense efforts and successfully destroyed the insurgents in the province. While Stilwell likely would have paid a political cost to support regional forces with arms and military support, it likely would have alleviated issues of low morale, corruption, and mismanagement demonstrated by the Chinese national army. Stilwell's decision to channel American assistance through the national government, which was neither national in character nor a functioning government, was a critical strategic mistake.

CONCLUSION

STILWELL'S OVERALL PERFORMANCE as the commander of the CBI theater was clearly a mixture of success and failure, with many of the failures being due to self-inflicted wounds caused by his lack of political awareness. Stilwell was able to achieve notable victories, often with only limited political and military support, and effectively made the north Burma campaign a success through sheer force of his character. The development of the Ramgarh training center in India led Stilwell to solve the problem of creating capable and reliable allies and improving the Chinese army, but his other main problem, his ambiguous mission, was never resolved. Despite his battlefield effectiveness, Stilwell was continually hampered by a lack of political awareness that was partly due to his specific personality but is also indicative of larger trends within the military profession. Throughout his tenure he displayed an unwillingness to understand political leaders and their motivations, and he displayed a disdain for "Washington." Stilwell, like many other military leaders since 1945, was convinced that many of his difficulties were due to his voice "not being heard" and that if only senior leaders listened to his military advice, problems would be solved. Stilwell clearly should have included political advisors on his staff far earlier as well as more diverse perspectives among his military staff. He also should have made more of an effort to engage with the American media and Congress, not as part of an effort to "spin" public opinion but as part of a mutual engagement and where he could learn about nonmilitary attitudes.

Despite these personal failings, the challenges he faced in dealing with the British and Chinese from a position as a negotiator, coordinator, and manager, rather than as a commander of U.S. combat forces, would become increasingly normal in American military affairs. In Iraq, Afghanistan, South Vietnam, and Korea, American commanders were forced to navigate unfamiliar political terrain to achieve their military objectives, and not only were several relieved outright, but many others were reassigned or quietly retired, suggesting that Stilwell was only the beginning of a long-term trend, rather than a unique case. Military commanders at the highest levels need to have political antennae that can differentiate short-term political campaigning or grandstanding from long-term substantive attitudes and goals.

In a postwar interview in 1956, Marshall recognized that the role of Stilwell in the CBI theater had been a difficult and highly personalized situation, where political influence had often been more important than command relationships. Marshall praised Stilwell's dedication to training Chinese troops and noted that this process required great diligence because the Chinese would backslide without U.S. pressure. Marshall noted that if only Stilwell's "tactlessness" could be removed, he would have been brilliant even in this difficult role. He also maintained that Stilwell had also been hindered by the political and media maneuvers of Chennault and his staff officer, Alsop.[1] American officers in the CBI theater expressed similar views.

> He [Stilwell] didn't like it in China, and he didn't like what he had to do in China which was entirely one of coordination, of trying to better relations and to find out some way to compromise and deal with Chiang Kai-shek whom he, you know, thought very little of. . . . We [Army officers] used to make an unkind remark about Stilwell staying in Burma. We said that when he got even a little frustrated in China, he'd go back to Burma where he would sit under a bush and command a squad.[2]

Stilwell's replacement, Gen. Albert C. Wedemeyer, shared a similar view that Stilwell was easily frustrated with administrative and political issues: "I think General Stilwell must have been a self-centered man with extreme likes and dislikes and very quick to anger.... There is so much evidence that he had little or no tact, no concept of diplomacy, and was self-centered."[3]

UNRELIABLE ALLIES AND AMBIGUOUS MISSIONS
One of the major themes of this book, unreliable allies, was clearly a factor throughout the CBI theater, with both the British and Chinese having divergent policies on many key issues, and the policies developed by Stilwell from early 1942 through late 1944 suggest two possible solutions to this enduring dilemma.

One solution to this problem was to scale down the goals so that they could be accomplished with the personnel and equipment in the time available. Rather than attempt to reshape the Chinese army as a whole, Stilwell determined that systemic reforms to a small element, starting from an initial force at Ramgarh, were the only way to move forward. Smaller forces can be more easily managed and controlled, and it is also easier to retain trained personnel, which ensures that critically trained personnel are not lost to injuries and desertion. Compartmentalizing a small force is also possible in a way that is not viable for an entire army, and increasing American influence over personnel decisions was a vital part of making the Chinese Army in India more aligned with U.S. tactics, doctrine, and operational behaviors. In the postwar assessment of the CBI theater conducted at Fort Leavenworth, the programs developed by Stilwell to train, coordinate, and improve the performance of the Chinese military was given high marks: "For the first time in [its] history, the United States, in CBI, exploited the manpower and resources of other nations against a common enemy at relatively minor cost to itself."[4]

Stilwell's development of a training program at Ramgarh in northeastern India enabled Chinese forces to become competent and motivated to take the offensive in northern Burma. More importantly, Stilwell's program largely insulated Chinese units from their own chain of command and provided a reliable basis for pay, medical care, and equipment. An additional, and significant, benefit of Stilwell's Ramgarh model was that it limited desertion and retained trained personnel within the Chinese army. Most units in China regularly lost roughly 10 percent of their personnel every month to desertion, and even elite units could have more than half their personnel leave the unit every year, to be replaced by untrained conscripts.[5]

Since World War II, this approach, focusing on small, capable units rather than a larger but unreformable force, was applied successfully in Iraq, where the Iraqi Counter Terrorism Service, a brigade-sized element, was given extensive training and support, becoming the spearhead of many operations and trusted by American partners. In contrast, the larger Iraqi army, like the Chinese army, was a flawed institution that was too big to change, with fundamentally broken organizational processes that led to endemic corruption, inept logistics, and poor leadership.[6] A particularly challenging issue for the Chinese and the Iraqi armies was the problem of widespread desertion, which Stilwell largely solved. Desertion, and retention more broadly, was a recurring issue in Iraq, Afghanistan, and South Vietnam, and the U.S. military often found itself training regular army units over and over again because of the high turnover, which kept indigenous forces from becoming skilled and proficient soldiers. In Afghanistan, even after sustained efforts to retain trained soldiers, roughly 25 percent of personnel deserted every year, leading to continual challenges in fielding trained units.[7] Building small, coherent organizations that were insulated from the problems of the larger army allowed the development of reliable allies that could both fight capably and maintain their strength over time.

The second military solution to the challenge of uncertain allies is to break down the goals of the theater into smaller pieces and then find more capable local, regional, or organizational allies. Chapter 6 highlighted that while Chiang Kai-shek's forces were both unwilling and incapable of defending key airfields in east China, local regional leaders offered to help and sought U.S. assistance. In Iraq, looking at security from a more regional and local perspective allowed U.S. military forces to overcome the problems in the national Iraqi army and target key tribal groups for aid and assistance, such as in the Anbar Awakening. In another case, the Montagnards in Vietnam had almost a limited relationship with the Vietnamese government yet were very highly effective military partners when provided U.S. military assistance.

At the political level, the collapse of U.S.-supported forces in Iraq and Afghanistan has energized new research that suggests Stilwell's (and

Marshall's) desire to make aid contingent on specific policies is likely more effective than attempting to pursue reforms after declaring unwavering support for an ally. Walter Ladwig, King's College London, in conjunction with a team of historians and political scientists, found that detailed studies of U.S. support for countries such as South Vietnam, El Salvador, and the Philippines showed that a "conditionality strategy," where U.S. aid and military support was linked to specific objectives and policies, was more effective than unilateral grants of support that were delivered regardless of implementation.[8] Stilwell's desire to make aid to Chinese, and to a lesser extent British, forces contingent was repeatedly vetoed by Roosevelt, denying him the ability to use American logistics advantages to shape policy in the CBI theater. Ladwig's research also suggests that despite Stilwell's dislike of engaging with opponents of the allied government, cultivating ties to other parties is important not just to give U.S. policymakers a broader range of options but because it can prevent the relationship from becoming "personalized" around one individual, such as Chiang Kai-shek, Ngo Dinh-Diem, or Hamid Karzai.[9] A similar study of cases of American military relationships with allies conducted by a group led by Eli Berman and David Lake similarly concluded that transactional policies work because "agents do respond to incentives." The study also criticized the pattern of providing unilateral aid, like Roosevelt ordered, because "the United States too often assumes that its interests are closely aligned with those of its proxy, and funnels unconditional aid and support to the proxy's leader—ostensibly to build greater capacity—and failing to use the levers it possesses to induce appropriate effort."[10] Roosevelt's dismissal of Stilwell and Marshall's proposals would unfortunately be replicated by numerous American political leaders after 1945, with crippling consequences to American foreign policy.

Unreliability was also evident in the CBI theater at the political level, and there is no easy lesson that can be drawn from Stilwell's experience. Stilwell's difficulty with Chiang has been replicated again and again since 1945: in Korea with Gen. Matthew Ridgway and Syngman Rhee; in Vietnam with General Creighton Abrams and Nguyen van Thieu; in Iraq with Gen. David Petraeus and Nouri al-Maliki; or in Afghanistan with General McChrystal and Hamid Karzai. British and Chinese political figures were not the only source of political problems; a key irritation for Stilwell was the reoccurrence throughout the war of American special envoys, both military and political. As early as 1942, Chiang had perfected a carefully scripted "dog and pony show," where prestigious and travel-lagged Americans were given a "special" personal meeting with Chiang, briefings that highlighted the benefits of further American aid, all followed by a banquet capped off with heavy drinking. Chiang and other Chinese officials also worked to ensure that visiting Americans had little contact with embassy officials or military personnel working in China, who might have a more negative view of Chinese capabilities.[11] The effect of this scripted performance made many Americans lose their objectivity. Mountbatten was equally difficult to manage because he could rely on his own chain of command to London and his aristocratic connections to ensure that his views were given a warm reception among senior British policymakers. Despite the close U.S.-U.K. military relationship since 1941, British forces, even when under American commanders' authority, have continued to use their own chain of command to review orders before taking action. A notable example was British general Michael Jackson's refusal to obey American general Wesley Clark's order to block airport access to Russian soldiers in 1999 during the Kosovo conflict. General Clark was subsequently reassigned, and Jackson was promoted to chief of the British General Staff. The incident highlighted the limits of Clark's authority in a political context where the formal military chain of command was subordinate to unwritten political codes of conduct.

The shifting by political decision makers of Stilwell's already ambiguous assignment, which he was able to refine at times, led to a lack of policy consistency, and this has been another enduring trend in American military affairs since 1945. In March 1943, John P. Davies had identified the particular difficulties that Stilwell's personality and military-centric approach to his mission were causing to the overall success of the mission. Davies noted,

> [In] addition to his professional military task, he [Stilwell] is involved, whether he likes it or not, in Chinese domestic politics. He is a major force in Chinese politics. By instinct, temperament and convictions, he

seeks to avoid involvement in Chinese domestic politics. But the fact that he commands a military force in China, is empowered to issue orders in the Generalissimo's name and has under his control lend-lease material for distribution in China makes him, despite all of his wishes to the contrary, a Chinese political factor. While he endeavors to avoid playing domestic politics, he cannot prevent politics being played on him.[12]

Postwar analysis has concurred with this assessment, with an assessment in the Army War College journal *Parameters* noting, "Despite Stilwell's disappointment for politicians and politicians, he was up to his neck in high-level political battles requiring negotiation, compromise, and coalition-building."[13] Tang Tsou, author of the seminal work *America's Failure in China*, concluded that even when he had effective policies, Stilwell's personality often led to setbacks, noting that "Stilwell's quid quo pro policy inevitably entailed a contest of will between the Nationalist government and the United States. . . . More important, Stilwell's lack of tact tended to confuse the issue of the proper method of dealing with the Nationalist government. Many who rightly condemned Stilwell's personal shortcoming consequently tended to disapprove the correct policy Stilwell advocated."[14] Dean Rusk, a staff officer in the CBI theater and future secretary of state, concurred that Stilwell "was not particularly interested in or talented in the command where the relationships are at least 50 percent political and 50 percent military."[15] As a result of this lack of interest in politics, even Stilwell's close aides lamented that "he neglected to develop a strong coterie of powerful American backers to counteract his natural enemies when he had opportunities right in his lap."[16] The problem of ambiguous missions and a lack of interest by the military in shaping the political context of their role has been clearly seen in Afghanistan, where successive commanders worked with changing authority, modified timelines, and even specific targeting guidance coming from the White House.[17]

It should be noted that Stilwell faced an unusually disengaged president, whose policies in Asia have been the subject of lengthy analysis and widespread criticism. Historian Warren Cohen contends that Roosevelt's desire to build an enduring relationship with China, and Chiang in particular, was based on deeply flawed assumptions: "Had Roosevelt read Chiang's *China's Destiny* or understood the Chinese Communist movement, he would have understood that neither major force in China excepted the United States from the hostility directed against the imperialists."[18] Chinese historian Tao Wenzhao concurs and finds that Roosevelt's desire to build a lasting partnership with China and his effort to present Chiang Kai-shek as a global leader limited American policy and undercut the efforts of Marshall and Stilwell to shape policy.[19] Sally Burt found Roosevelt's lack of strategic clarity to be a major issue in the CBI theater. "President Roosevelt did not enunciate a clear military strategy for U.S. Army officials in China, nor did he articulate a coherent diplomatic policy on China for the State Department."[20] Secretary of War Henry Stimson noted in his memoirs that "more than any other American theater commander in the war, Stilwell required the constant and vigorous political support of his government, and less than any other commander did he get it."[21]

Historian Eric Larrabee suggests that a more politically savvy senior officer, like Eisenhower, might have been able to overcome political differences in the CBI theater, but this ignores the important fact that Eisenhower was dealing with long-standing allies with close shared culture and traditions.[22] While Eisenhower might have avoided some of the difficulties caused by Stilwell's personality, the experience in the European theater was a vastly different context from which to judge leadership of coalition warfare. Eisenhower's role as commander of the Supreme Allied Expeditionary Force was rooted in a shared language, cultural traditions, and close coordination between British and American forces. Other cases, such as Gen. Norman Schwarzkopf's command of coalition forces in the Persian Gulf in 1990 and 1991, are equally difficult. Schwarzkopf's command was based on a preponderant role of American forces, with U.S. personnel constituting more than 60 percent of the force, and the short duration of the campaign. In situations where the U.S. military is operating as a relatively small percentage of the overall coalition strength, or in campaigns that last for more than two years, the result is often more complicated, with frequent military and political negotiation and renegotiation of strategies and objectives.

IMPLICATIONS FOR FUTURE MILITARY OPERATIONS

Stilwell's stark separation of military and political spheres employed in World War II has become increasingly common, and in the 1950s the dominant professional ethos of the U.S. military was the concept of objective civilian control developed by Samuel Huntington.[23] This concept was developed at a time when military officers were much more closely linked to political, economic, and social elites, and Huntington feared the impact the Cold War might have on maintaining civilian control.[24] Over the past fifty years, Huntington's concept has increasingly hardened into dogma that allows the U.S. military to disengage from potentially messy issues and in effect say "that's not my job" for many tasks. Taken to extremes, concepts of objective civilian control can produce a highly insulated military, disconnected from the massive social, cultural, and economic changes of the past fifty years.

Since 9/11, the disconnect between military operations and national strategy has led to renewed discussion of civil-military relations, and while many military commentators, such as William Rapp, have made the conventional case for a louder, more strident military voice in policy discussions, a more nuanced and articulate assessment has highlighted the poor political understanding of American military officers.[25] In 2020, Risa Brooks, writing in the journal *International Security*, argued that "officers need to be political aware, so that they can distinguish negative and partisan behaviors that are contrary to civilian control from those that are essential to achieving strategic success and ensuring a healthy civil-military partnership."[26] There are also scattered indications that officers within the military are questioning the lack of political understanding and limited awareness in light of recent military failures. Maj. Brian Babcock-Lumish, in an unusually strident article in *Military Review*, the professional journal of the Army's Command and General Staff College, noted that the desire for the military to be politically uninvolved "has meant that those in uniform who express political understanding are suspect in the eyes of their peers (and, often also, their civilian masters). . . . The lack of nuance when lumped together under the catch-all term has catastrophic potential in all three spheres: domestic, multinational, and host nation."[27] He further argues that "political understanding" among officers needs to be improved, with programs to ensure that Army officers can appreciate the political process.[28]

Unfortunately, looking at the social and political context of American military operations, the disconnect that occurred between Stilwell and senior policymakers in Washington seems to be becoming even more salient, and by the 2020s the American military, particularly the Army, is becoming a niche career field, removed from mainstream American political life. A Council on Foreign Relations report on civil-military relations found that "career military personnel now exist in a world apart from 99.5 percent of American society: they go to different schools, live and work in a specialized system of promotions and deployments, and often belong to successive generations of the same families."[29] After the end of conscription in 1973, military service in the United States has drawn members of a decreasing percentage of the American public, and by the mid-2010s, the overwhelming majority of new military personnel had a family member that had previously served, and for nearly 30 percent, this was a parent or guardian.[30] Gen. James C. McConville, who served as chief of staff of the Army from 2019 to 2023, is a notable example of this trend because all three of his children became officers in the U.S. Army.[31]

Another challenge for political awareness in the military is that increased educational opportunities for Americans has also led to fewer elite students deciding to become military officers. A 2016 article in the National Defense University *Joint Forces Quarterly* highlights that since the 1980s, average test scores for officers have been declining, and for an increasingly complex military and political battlefield for modern warfare, the military is "not getting the leaders it needs."[32] This is a stark contrast to the early twentieth century, when military schools like the United States Military Academy (West Point) were considered elite institutions, where cadets required political support to gain admission. An Army War College report concurs and finds that as complexity in warfare has grown, the intellectual standards of military officers have declined, and perhaps more importantly for political awareness, military officers are increasingly less likely to be part of national economic and political life.[33]

There's further evidence of a shift from an officer corps that often studied broad subjects such as political science, history, and economics.

By 2021 the most common major for ROTC cadets was criminal justice, a major that develops physical fitness and familiarity with firearms but does not seem like it would prepare students for complex civil-military affairs.[34] In 2013, former Army War College commandant Maj. Gen. Bob Scales lamented that these changes in Army education and culture over the past sixty years had increasingly lauded plain-spoken commanders with technical skills but limited ability to think outside of the military institutional structure, lamenting that the military needed "officers with the ability to think in time, who are able to express themselves with elegance, clarity, and conviction, and intellect, *and yes, navigate the swamp of political-military policymaking*" (emphasis added).[35] By the late 2010s even key figures within the military, such as General McChrystal, had become concerned that the force had become "a little insular and caste-like," which suggests that challenges in aligning military tactics and operations with strategy driven by broader American political, economic, and social currents will remain a problem for the foreseeable future.

While the senior officers that gathered at Fort Leavenworth in the late spring of 1946 to review the lessons of the CBI theater likely could have not imagined the challenges faced by modern military commanders, the core elements of their findings remain valid. In the CBI theater, Stilwell was able to forge a powerful and reliable military force that relied on non-U.S. personnel, but a severe disconnect between military actions and American national strategy meant that the imaginative, grueling, and dangerous work was often a wasted effort. Military officers in the CBI, and particularly General Stilwell, failed to properly understand the political context of their assignment and did not situate their operational and tactical policies in line with larger objectives. Since 1945, American military operations have continued to be hindered by similar dynamics within the military, and the conclusion of the study in 1946, that military victory was only important if it secures "economic and political advantages for the United States," suggests that the lessons of the CBI theater and General Stilwell remain relevant today.

NOTES

INTRODUCTION

1. Col. A. J. Kinney, *Lessons from the CBI Theater*, Second Command Class, June 21, 1946, Appendix B, Command and General Staff School, Fort Leavenworth, Ike Skelton Combined Arms Research Library.
2. Kinney, *Lessons from the CBI Theater*.
3. Kinney, *Lessons from the CBI Theater*.
4. The Ambassador in China (Gauss) to the Secretary of State, February 9, 1944. *Foreign Relations of the United States*, vol. 5, *China*, 1944, https://history.state.gov/historicaldocuments/frus1944v06/d17. .
5. Kinney, *Lessons from the CBI Theater*.
6. Charles Romanus and Riley Sunderland, *Stilwell's Mission to China* (Washington, D.C.: U.S. Army Center of Military History, 1953), 74.
7. Romanus and Sunderland, *Stilwell's Mission to China*, 73.
8. Morris Janowitz, *The Professional Soldier: A Social and Political Portrait* (New York: The Free Press, 1960), 234.
9. Gallup Organization. Gallup Poll (AIPO), Feb. 1940 [survey question]. USGALLUP.40-185.QK04. Gallup Organization [producer]. Cornell University, Ithaca, NY: Roper Center for Public Opinion Research, iPOLL [distributor], accessed September 9, 2019.
10. Gallup Organization. Gallup Poll, Sep. 1943 [survey question]; National Opinion Research Center, University of Chicago. Foreign Affairs Survey, Aug. 1945 [survey question]. USNORC.450133.R02G. National Opinion Research Center, University of Chicago [producer]. Cornell University, Ithaca, NY: Roper Center for Public Opinion Research, iPOLL [distributor], accessed September 9, 2019.
11. Fred Eldridge, *Wrath in Burma: The Uncensored Story of General Stilwell and International Maneuvers in the Far East* (New York: Doubleday and Company, 1946).
12. Gordon S. Seagrave Jr., *Burma Surgeon Returns* (New York: W. W. Norton and Co., 1946).
13. Joseph W. Stilwell, *The Stilwell Papers*, edited by Theodore H. White (New Work: William Sloane Associates, 1948).
14. Donald Lohbeck, *Patrick J. Hurley* (Chicago: Henry Regnery Co., 1956), 305.
15. Albert C. Wedemeyer, *Wedemeyer Reports!: An Objective, Dispassionate Examination of World War II, Postwar Policies, and Grand Strategy* (New York: Henry Holt and Co., 1958).

16. Claire L. Chennault, *Way of a Fighter: The Memoirs of Claire Lee Chennault* (New York: G. P. Putnam, 1949).
17. F. F. Liu, *A Military History of Modern China, 1924–1949* (Princeton, N.J.: Princeton University Press, 1956), 208–22.
18. Herbert Feis, *The China Tangle: The American Effort in China from Pearl Harbor to the Marshall Mission* (Princeton, N.J.: Princeton University Press, 1953), 429–30.
19. Romanus and Sunderland, *Stilwell's Mission to China*; Charles Romanus and Riley Sunderland, *Stilwell's Command Problems* (Washington, D.C.: U.S. Center for Military History, 1956); Charles Romanus and Riley Sunderland, *Time Runs Out in CBI* (Washington, D.C.: U.S. Army Center for Military History, 1958).
20. Tang Tsou, *America's Failure in China, 1941–1950* (Chicago: University of Chicago Press, 1963), 87.
21. Barbara Tuchman, *Stilwell and the American Experience in China, 1911–1945* (New York: Macmillan Publishers, 1970), 531.
22. John P. Davies, *Dragon by the Tail: American, British, Japanese, and Russian Encounters with China and One Another* (New York: W. W. Norton and Co., 1972), 258–59.
23. Frank Dorn, *Walkout: With Stilwell in Burma* (New York: Thomas Y. Crowell Co., 1971), 242.
24. Jingbin Wang, "No Lost Chance in China: The False Realism of American Foreign Service Officers, 1943–1945," *Journal of American-East Asian Relations* 17, no. 2 (2010): 119.
25. Lloyd Eastman, *Seeds of Destruction: Nationalist China in War and Revolution, 1937–1945* (Stanford, Calif.: Stanford University Press, 1984), 225.
26. Michael Schaller, *The U.S. Crusade in China, 1938–1945* (New York: Columbia University Press, 1979).
27. Michael Schaller, "The Command Crisis in China, 1944: A Road Not Taken," *Diplomatic History* 4, no. 3 (Summer 1980): 329.
28. John K. Fairbank, "Dangerous Acquaintances," *New York Times Book Review*, May 17, 1979.
29. Chen Jian, "The Myth of America's 'Lost Chance' in China: A Chinese Perspective in Light of New Evidence," *Diplomatic History* 21, no. 1 (Winter 1997): 77–86.
30. William R. Peers and Dean Brelis, *Behind the Burma Road* (Boston: Little Brown and Co., 1963).
31. Richard Dunlop, *Behind Japanese Lines: With the OSS in Burma* (New York: Rand McNally and Co., 1979).
32. David W. Hogan, *U.S. Army Special Operations in World War II* (Washington D.C.: Government Printing Office, 1992); Troy J. Sacquety, *The OSS in Burma: Jungle War Against the Japanese* (Lawrence: University Press of Kansas, 2013); Maochun Yu, *OSS in China: Prelude to Cold War* (Annapolis, Md.: Naval Institute Press, 1996).
33. Rana Mitter, *Forgotten Ally: China's World War II, 1937–1945* (Boston: Houghton Mifflin, 2013); Keith Schoppa, *In a Sea of Bitterness: Refugees During the Sino-Japanese*

War (Cambridge, Mass.: Harvard University Press, 2011); Parks Coble, *China's War Reporters: The Legacy of Resistance against Japan* (Cambridge, Mass.: Harvard University Press, 2015); Micah Muscalino, *The Ecology of War in China: Henan Province, the Yellow River, and Beyond, 1938–1950* (Cambridge: Cambridge University Press, 2016); Diana Lary and Stephen MacKinnon, *Scars of War: The Impact of Warfare on Modern China* (Vancouver: University of British Columbia Press, 2001); Hsi-cheng Chi, *Nationalist China at War: Military Defeats and Political Collapse, 1937–1945* (Ann Arbor: University of Michigan Press, 1982); James Hsiung and Steven Levine, *China's Bitter Victory: The War with Japan, 1937–1945* (Armonk, N.Y.: M. E. Sharpe and Co., 1992).
34. Riley Sunderland and Charles F. Romanus, eds., *Stilwell's Personal File: China-Burma-India, 1942–1944* (Wilmington, Del.: Scholarly Resources, 1976), xvii.

CHAPTER 1. MISSION OBJECTIVES AND MILITARY AUTHORITY

1. Grace Person Hayes, *The History of the Joint Chiefs of Staff in World War II: The War against Japan* (Annapolis, Md.: Naval Institute Press, 1982), 220.
2. Warren I. Cohen, *America's Response to China: A History of Sino-American Relations* (New York: Columbia University Press, 2010), 132.
3. Eric Larrabee, *Commander in Chief: Franklin Delano Roosevelt, His Lieutenants, and Their War* (New York: Simon & Schuster, 1987), 520.
4. John W. Garver, "China's Wartime Diplomacy," in *China's Bitter Victory: The War with Japan 1937–1945*, ed. James C. Hsiung and Steven I. Levine (Armonk, N.Y.: M. E. Sharpe, Inc., 1992), 11; Jonathon Fenby, *Chiang Kai-shek: China's Generalissimo and the Nation He Lost* (London: Free Press, 2003), 321.
5. Marc Gallicchio, "The Other China Hands: U.S. Army Officers and America's Failure in China, 1941–1950," *Journal of American-East Asian Relations* 4, no. 1 (1995): 50.
6. Barbara Tuchman, *Stilwell and the American Experience in China, 1911–1945* (New York: Macmillan Publishers, 1970), 180–87.
7. Mark Skinner Watson, *Chief of Staff: Prewar Plans and Preparations* (Washington, D.C.: Government Printing Office, 2003), 113.
8. Frank Kluckhorn, "U.S. Army Mission to Assist China," *New York Times*, August 27, 1941; Watson, *Chief of Staff*, 328; Maurice Matloff and Edwin M. Snell, *Strategic Planning for Coalition Warfare: 1941–1942* (Washington, D.C.: Government Printing Office, 1999), 63; Maochun Yu, *OSS in China: Prelude to Cold War* (Annapolis, Md.: Naval Institute Press, 1996), 27.
9. Charles Romanus and Riley Sunderland, *Stilwell's Mission to China* (Washington, D.C.: U.S. Army Center of Military History, 1953), 36.
10. John Paton Davies Jr., *China Hand: An Autobiography* (Philadelphia: University of Pennsylvania Press, 2012), 40.
11. The Military Mission in China to the War Department, February 10, 1942, in *Foreign Relations of the United States, 1942*, vol. 5, *China* (Washington, D.C.: Government Printing Office, 1956), 13–15; file on China and India infantry weapons, 020

HIA-Goodfellow-4-A-4-6-7, February 2, 1942, Millard Preston Goodfellow Papers, Hoover Institution Library & Archives, 14–15. https://digitalcollections.hoover.org/objects/65276/file-on-china-and-india-infantry-weapons.
12. "Defense Aid Program for China," Memorandum for the President by Lauchlin Currie, September 22, 1941, Franklin D. Roosevelt Presidential Library, PSFA 0272, box 28; Judd Kinzley, "The Power of the 'Stockpile': American Aid and China's Wartime Everyday," *Journal of Modern Chinese History* 13, no. 1 (2019): 174–75.
13. D. Clayton James, American and Japanese Strategies in the Pacific War," in *Makers of Modern Strategy: From Machiavelli to the Nuclear Age*, ed. Peter Paret (Princeton, N.J.: Princeton University Press, 1986), 721.
14. F. F. Liu, *A Military History of Modern China* (Princeton, N.J.: Princeton University Press, 1956), 209; Romanus and Sunderland, *Stilwell's Mission to China*, 63.
15. Ronald H. Spector, *Eagle against the Sun: The American War with Japan* (New York: Random House, 1985), 327.
16. Peiji Tang, *Kangzhan shiqi de duiwai guanxi* [Foreign relations during the Sino-Japanese War] (Beijing: Beijing Yanshan chubanshe, 1997), 255–57; Louis Morton, *Strategy and Command: The First Two Years* (Washington, D.C.: Government Printing Office, 2014), 155.
17. Larrabee, *Commander in Chief*, 512.
18. Romanus and Sunderland, *Stilwell's Mission to China*, 66.
19. Hayes, *The History of the Joint Chiefs of Staff in World War II*, 77.
20. Ed Cray, *General of the Army: George C. Marshall, Soldier and Statesman* (New York: W. W. Norton and Co., 1990), 281.
21. *The Papers of George Catlett Marshall*, ed. Larry I. Bland and Sharon Ritenour Stevens (Lexington, Va.: The George C. Marshall Foundation, 1981–). Electronic version based on *The Papers of George Catlett Marshall*, vol. 3, *"The Right Man for the Job," December 7, 1941–May 31, 1943* (Baltimore: The Johns Hopkins University Press, 1991) (hereafter Marshall, vol. 3), 55–56.
22. Marshall, vol. 3, 57–59.
23. Tuchman, *Stilwell and the American Experience in China, 1911–1945*, 232–33, 243; Joseph Stilwell, *The Stilwell Papers*, ed. Theodore H. White (New York: Sloane and Associates, 1948), 25–26.
24. Cray, *General of the Army*, 100.
25. Edward M. Coffman, "The American 15th Infantry Regiment in China, 1912–1938: A Vignette in Social History," *Journal of Military History* 58, no. 1 (1994): 67–68.
26. Paul Kesaris, *U.S. Military Intelligence Reports: China 1911–1941* (Frederick, Md.: University Publications of America, 1983).
27. Jonathan Templin Ritter, *Stilwell and Mountbatten in Burma: Allies at War, 1943–1944* (Denton: University of North Texas Press, 2017), 197.
28. Marshall, vol. 3, 140–41.

29. Paul L. Freeman, Senior Officers Debriefing Program, U.S. Army Military History Research Institute, Carlisle Barracks, 1974, 60.
30. Organizational Developments of the Joint Chiefs of Staff, 1942–2013, Joint Chiefs of Staff History Office, 2013, 2.
31. The Assistant Chief of Staff (Gerow) to the Department's Liaison Officer (Wilson), February 5, 1942, *Foreign Relations of the United States*, vol. 5, *China*, 1942, 12; Davies, *China Hand*, 46.
32. Romanus and Sunderland, *Stilwell's Mission to China*, 74.
33. Romanus and Sunderland, *Stilwell's Mission to China*, 74.
34. Steven L. Rearden, *Council of War: A History of the Joint Chiefs of Staff, 1942–1991* (Washington, D.C.: Joint Chiefs of Staff History Office, 2012), 34.
35. Joint Planning Committee Report to the Chiefs of Staff, January 10, 1942, Immediate Assistance to China, 1, Joint Chiefs of Staff History Office, the Arcadia Conference, December 24, 1941–January 14, 1942.
36. The Military Mission in China to the War Department, February 10, 1942, *Foreign Relations of the United States*, vol. 5, *China*, 1942, 15.
37. Tuchman, *Stilwell and the American Experience in China; 1911–1945*, 262.
38. Cohen, *America's Response to China*, 141.
39. The Ambassador in China (Gauss) to the Secretary of State, March 7, 1942, *Foreign Relations of the United States*, vol. 5, *China*, 1942, 27.
40. Wenzhao Tao, *Kangri zhanzheng shiqi Zhongguo duiwai guanxi* [Foreign relations during the Sino-Japanese War era] (Beijing: Zhongguo shehui kexue chubanshe, 2009), 286–88; Tuchman, *Stilwell and the American Experience in China: 1911–1945*, 253–54.
41. Joseph E. Persico, *Roosevelt's Centurions: FDR and the Commanders He Led to Victory in World War II* (New York: Random House, 2013), 147–49; Stilwell, *The Stilwell Papers*, 15–16.
42. Stilwell, *The Stilwell Papers*, 36.
43. Radio Message, March 4, 1942, Washington to Chungking, "Eyes Alone" Correspondence of General Joseph W. Stilwell, National Archives and Records Administration, Microfilm Publication M1419, reel 1.
44. Riley Sunderland and Charles F. Romanus, eds., *Stilwell's Personal File: China-Burma-India, 1942–1944* (Wilmington, Del.: Scholarly Resources, 1976), 208.
45. Frank McLynn, *The Burma Campaign: Disaster into Triumph, 1942–1945* (New Haven, Conn.: Yale University Press, 2011), 23–25.
46. Romanus and Sunderland, *Stilwell's Mission to China*, 86.
47. Frank Dorn, *Walkout: With Stilwell in Burma* (New York: Thomas Y. Crowell Co., 1971), 40–42.
48. Richard M. Young, Oral History Interview, September 21, 2003, National Museum of the Pacific War.
49. "The Campaign in Burma, Report to the War Department," General Joseph Stilwell, May 2, 1943, ProQuest History Vault, Folder: 003249-001-0660, Records of the

War Department's Operations Division, 1942–1945, Part 1. World War II Operations, Series B, Pacific Theater, 1.
50. Memorandum, March 21, 1942, ProQuest History Vault, Folder: 003249-001-0198, Records of the War Department's Operations Division, 1942–1945, Part 1. World War II Operations, Series B, Pacific Theater.
51. "The Campaign in Burma," September 1, 1943, Entry for March 8, 1942, ProQuest History Vault, Folder 003249-002-0001, Records of the War Department's Operations Division, 1942–1945, Part 1. World War II Operations, Series B, Pacific Theater, 8.
52. Sam Kleiner, *The Flying Tigers: The Untold Story of the American Pilots Who Waged a Secret War against Japan* (New York: Penguin Books, 2019), 175–76.
53. "Message to Generalissimo Chiang Kai-Shek," President Franklin D. Roosevelt, March 11, 1942, Franklin D. Roosevelt Presidential Library, Presidential Secretary Files 0266, box 27.
54. Li Chen, "The Chinese Army in the First Burma Campaign," *Journal of Chinese Military History* 2 (2013): 45; Hu Pu-Yu, *A Brief History of the Sino-Japanese War, 1937–1945* (Taipei: Chung Wu Publishing, 1974), 205; Kazutaka Kikuchi, *Chūgoku kōnichi gunjishi: 1937–1945* [A history of China's war against Japan: 1937–1945] (Tokyo: Yushisha, 2009), 145–46.
55. Chang Jui-Te, "The Nationalist Army on the Eve of the War," in *The Battle for China: Essays on the Military History of the Sino-Japanese War of 1937–1945*, ed. Mark Peattie, Edward J. Drea, and Hans van de Ven (Stanford, Calif.: Stanford University Press, 2011), 88–94.
56. Romanus and Sunderland, *Stilwell's Mission to China*, 103.
57. He Husheng, *Banian kangzhan Zhong de jiang jieshi, 1937-1945* [Chiang Kai-shek and the Eight Year War against Japan] (Taipei: Fengyun shidai, 2013), 349–51.
58. Li Chen, "The Chinese Army in the First Burma Campaign," 52–53; Larrabee, *Commander in Chief*, 529.
59. *Notes on Duties with the Chinese Expeditionary Force*, Brig. Gen. John Bowerman, n.d. N16436, "Analysis of Boatner Materials," Fort Leavenworth Research Library Collection, 9.
60. Fenby, *Chiang Kai-shek*, 375.
61. Richard M. Young, Oral History Interview, September 21, 2003, National Museum of the Pacific War.
62. S. Woodburn Kirby, *The War against Japan, Vol. II: India's Most Dangerous Hour* (London: Her Majesty's Stationery Office, 1958), 156.
63. Winston S. Churchill, *The Second World War: The Hinge of Fate* (Boston: Houghton Mifflin Co., 1950), 168.
64. Radio Message, April 1, 1942, Stilwell to Stimson and Marshall, "Eyes Alone" Correspondence of General Joseph W. Stilwell, National Archives and Records Administration, Microfilm Publication M1419, reel 1.

65. Hsi-sheng Chi, "The Military Dimension, 1942–1945," in *China's Bitter Victory: The War with Japan 1937–1945*, ed. James C. Hsiung and Steven I. Levine (Armonk, N.Y.: M. E. Sharpe, Inc., 1992), 167–68.
66. Romanus and Sunderland, *Stilwell's Mission to China*, 157.
67. Harold Tanner, *Where Chiang Kai-shek Lost China: The Liao-Shen Campaign, 1948* (Bloomington: Indiana University Press, 2015); Harold Tanner, *The Battle for Manchuria and the Fate of China: Siping, 1946* (Bloomington: Indiana University Press, 2013); Chang Jui-Te, "Chiang Kai-shek's Coordination by Personal Directives," in *China at War: Regions of China, 1937–1945*, ed. Stephen R. MacKinnon (Stanford, Calif.: Stanford University Press, 2007), chap. 4; Stephen R. MacKinnon, "The Sino-Japanese Conflict, 1931–1945," in *A Military History of China*, ed. David A Graff and Robin Higham (Lexington: University of Kentucky Press, 2002), 218; Philip D. Sprouse, Oral History Interview, February 11, 1974, Harry S. Truman Presidential Library, https://www.trumanlibrary.gov/library/oral-histories/sprousep.
68. Stilwell, *The Stilwell Papers*, 70–72.
69. "The Campaign in Burma," September 1, 1943, ProQuest History Vault, Folder 003249-002-0001, Records of the War Department's Operations Division, 1942–1945, Part 1. World War II Operations, Series B, Pacific Theater, 22; Alan K. Lathrop, "The Employment of Chinese Nationalist Troops in the First Burma Campaign," *Journal of Southeast Asian Studies* 12, no. 2 (Sept. 1981): 413; Dorn, *Walkout*, 50–51; Sunderland and Romanus, *Stilwell's Personal File*, 218.
70. Li Chen, "The Chinese Army in the First Burma Campaign," 55–56.
71. "The Campaign in Burma," September 1, 1943, ProQuest History Vault, Folder 003249-002-0001, Records of the War Department's Operations Division, 1942–1945, Part 1. World War II Operations, Series B, Pacific Theater, 49–50; Liu, *A Military History of Modern China*, 212.
72. Zheng Jinju, *Yi dai zhanshen: Sun Liren* [A generation's war hero: Sun Liren] (Taipei: Shuiniu chuban youxian gongsi, 2004), 87–89.
73. Recommendation by Supreme Allied Commander, Louis Mountbatten, n.d. War Office, Lieutenant General, Chinese Army, Sun Li-jen. United Kingdom, National Archives, Reference WO 373/145/1.
74. William Slim, *Defeat into Victory* (New York: David McKay Company, Inc., 1961), 47.
75. Kirby, *The War against Japan, Vol. II*, 168.
76. "The Campaign in Burma," September 1, 1943, ProQuest History Vault, Folder 003249-002-0001, Records of the War Department's Operations Division, 1942–1945, Part 1. World War II Operations, Series B, Pacific Theater, 62; Gordon S. Seagrave, *Burma Surgeon Returns* (New York: W. W. Norton and Co., 1946), 40; Dorn, *Walkout*, 86.
77. Maj. Gen. H. L. Boatner, A Statement of the Record by Maj. Gen. H. L. Boatner, Boatner Papers, Hoover Archives, box 2, 5.
78. Rana Mitter, "Identities and Alliances: China's Place in World War II, 1941–1945," in *Beyond Pearl Harbor: A Pacific History*, ed. Beth Bailey and David Farber (Lawrence:

University Press of Kansas, 2019), 115; Sunderland and Romanus, *Stilwell's Personal File*, 215.
79. Hoover Institution Archives, The World War II Diaries of Joseph W. Stilwell, 1942, 44–45; McLynn, *The Burma Campaign*, 62.
80. Lathrop, "The Employment of Chinese Nationalist Troops in the First Burma Campaign," 429.
81. Hans Van de Ven, "Stilwell in the Stocks: The Chinese Nationalists and the Allied Powers in the Second World War," *Asian Affairs* 34, no. 3 (2003); "The Campaign in Burma," September 1, 1943, ProQuest History Vault, Folder 003249-002-0001, Records of the War Department's Operations Division, 1942–1945, Part 1. World War II Operations, Series B, Pacific Theater, 79–82; Dorn, *Walkout*, 125.
82. Henrietta Thompson, "Walk a Little Faster: Escape from Burma with General Stilwell in 1942" (Master's thesis, University of Maine, 1992), 84–85.
83. Richard M. Young, Oral History Interview, September 21, 2003, National Museum of the Pacific War.
84. Hoover Institution Archives, The World War II Diaries of Joseph W, Stilwell, 56; Dorn, *Walkout*, 243.
85. "New Delhi to AGWAR," May 25, 1942, Franklin D. Roosevelt Presidential Library, Map Room 300, box 80; Maurice Matloff and Edwin M. Snell, *Strategic Planning for Coalition Warfare: 1941–1942* (Washington, D.C.: Government Printing Office, 1999), 228.
86. Memorandum, Subject: Keeping China in the War, ProQuest History Vault, George Marshall Correspondence on China and India, January 1942 through December 1942, May 28, 1942.
87. Memorandum, Subject: Withdrawal of Chinese Forces, April 30, 1942, Proquest History Vault, Folder: 003249-001-0198, Records of the War Department's Operations Division, 1942–1945, Part 1. World War II Operations, Series B, Pacific Theater.
88. Romanus and Sunderland, *Stilwell's Mission to China*, 153–54.
89. Tao, *Kangri zhanzheng shiqi Zhongguo duiwai guanxi*, 299–300.
90. Han Yongli, *Zhanshi Meiguo dazhan lüeyu Zhongguo kangri zhanzheng (1941–1945 nian)* [The United States wartime grand strategy and China's anti-Japanese theater, 1941–1945] (Wuhang: Wuhan daxue chubanshe, 2003), 128; Romanus and Sunderland, *Stilwell's Mission to China*, 172; Hayes, *The History of the Joint Chiefs of Staff in World War II*, 216.
91. Stilwell, *The Stilwell Papers*, 121.
92. Henry L. Stimson and McGeorge Bundy, *On Active Service: In Peace and War* (New York: Harper and Bros., 1948), 533.
93. Radio Message, June 17, 1942, Stimson to Stilwell, "Eyes Alone" Correspondence of General Joseph W. Stilwell, National Archives and Records Administration, Microfilm Publication M1419, reel 1.

94. "Chiang Discusses War with Gandhi," *The New York Times*, February 19, 1942; Jay Taylor, *The Generalissimo: Chiang Kai-shek and the Struggle for Modern China* (Cambridge, Mass.: Belknap Press, 2009), 195.
95. The Ambassador in China (Gauss) to the Secretary of State, April 28, 1942, *Foreign Relations of the United States*, 1942, vol. 5, *China*, 35.
96. Zhibingtang bianjibu, *1942-1945 Zhongguo yuan zheng jun Miandian zhan ji, 1942-1945* [A Record of the China Expeditionary Army in Burma, 1942–1945] (Taipei: Zhibingtang wenhua chuanmei youxian gongsi, 2014), 10.
97. Romanus and Sunderland, *Stilwell's Mission to China*, 179.
98. Stimson and Bundy, *On Active Service*, 536; Sally Burt, "The Ambassador, the General, and the President: FDR's Mismanagement of Interdepartmental Relations in Wartime China," *Journal of American-East Asian Relations* 19, no. 3–4 (2012): 298.
99. Hoover Institution Archives, The World War II Diaries of General Joseph W. Stilwell, 1942, 67.
100. Tang Tsou, *America's Failure in China, 1941–50* (Chicago: University of Chicago Press, 1963), 97.
101. "The Campaign in Burma," September 1, 1943, ProQuest History Vault, Folder 003249-002-0001, Records of the War Department's Operations Division, 1942–1945, Part 1. World War II Operations, Series B, Pacific Theater, 25–26.
102. War Cabinet, W.P. 42 (449), October 7, 1942, United Kingdom, National Archives, Reference # CAB 66/29/29.
103. Yin Cao, "Establishing the Ramgarh Training Center: The Burma Campaign, the Colonial Internment Camp, and the Wartime Sino-British Relations," *TRaNS: Trans-Regional and -National Studies of Southeast Asia* 9 (2021): 4.
104. "Memorandum for the President," General George C. Marshall, April 29, 1942, Franklin D. Roosevelt Presidential Library, PSFA 0015, box 2.
105. Stilwell, *The Stilwell Papers*, 172.
106. Tang, *kangzhan shiqi de duiwai guanxi*, 267; Romanus and Sunderland, *Stilwell's Mission to China*, 179; Yuming Du and Song Xilan, *Yuanzheng yinmian kangzhan* [The Burma Expeditionary Army's Campaign] (Beijing: Zhongguo wenshi chubanshe, 2015), 116.
107. Rosters and other documents, 1942/1944, Joseph Warren Stilwell Papers, 002-HIA-R-Stilwell-Joseph-W-3B-1-527-0, Hoover Institution Archives, 6, https://digitalcollections.hoover.org/objects/62848/rosters-and-other-documents.
108. Philip Jowett, *Soldiers of the White Sun: The Chinese Army at War, 1931–1949* (Atglen, Pa.: Schiffer Military History, 2011), 120–24.
109. Man Luo, *Lanying bingtuan: Zhongguo yuanzheng jun mian yin xie zhan ji* [The Blue Eagles: China's Expeditionary Force in Burma and India] (Taipei: Xing Guang Publishers, 1991), 96–101; Liaison Memorandum Number 5, Col. Clarence W. Bennett, Chief, Liaison Group, 38th Division, October 1, National Archives and Records Administration, College Park, Records Group 493, box 6.

110. Liaison Training Memorandum No. 1, Chinese Army in India, February 10, 1943, National Archives and Records Administration, College Park, Records Group 493, box 17.
111. Memorandum for Record: Payment of Gratuities in Case of Death, March 16, 1944. N16436, "Analysis of Boatner Materials," Fort Leavenworth Research Library Collection, 93.
112. Maj. Gen. H. L. Boatner, A Statement of the Record by Maj. Gen. H. L. Boatner, Boatner Papers, Hoover Archives, box 2, 4; Gallicchio, "The Other China Hands," 52.
113. Letter for General Stilwell, Colonel H. L. Boatner, November 13, 1942, National Archives Microfilm Publications, M1419, "Eyes Alone" Correspondence of General Joseph W. Stilwell, January 1942–October 1944, reel 5.
114. Spector, *Eagle against the Sun*, 334.
115. Gallicchio, "The Other China Hands," 52.
116. Memorandum for General Sibert, August 5, 1942, N16436, "Analysis of Boatner Materials," Fort Leavenworth Research Library Collection, 5.
117. "The Campaign in Burma," September 1, 1943, ProQuest History Vault, Folder 003249-002-0001, Records of the War Department's Operations Division, 1942–1945, Part 1. World War II Operations, Series B, Pacific Theater, 94; Daniel Jackson, *Famine, Sword, and Fire: The Liberation of Southwest China in World War II* (Atglen, Pa.: Schiffer Publishing, 2015), 78.
118. "Liaison Memorandum Number Five," October 1, 1943, National Archives and Record Administration, Record Group 493, stack 290, box 6.
119. Slim, *Defeat into Victory*, 144.
120. Li Chen, "The Chinese Army in the First Burma Campaign," 48; General Paul L. Freeman, Senior Officers Debriefing Program, U.S. Army Military History Research Institute, Carlisle, Pa., 1974, 55.
121. "Yunnan: Low Morale of the Chinese 5th Army," December 1, 1942, War Office 106/3547, The National Archives (London), cited in Yin Cao, "The Return of Chen Ching Lin: Chinese Deserters and Chinatowns in the British Raj, 1943–1946," *Journal of South Asian Studies* 44, no. 5 (2021): 892.
122. "Instructions for Liaison Officers from This Headquarters to Chinese Units," October 14, 1943, National Archives and Records Administration, Record Group 493, stack 290, box 6.
123. Romanus and Sunderland, *Stilwell's Mission to China*, 194.
124. Romanus and Sunderland, *Stilwell's Mission to China*, 223.
125. The Chief of Staff (Marshall) to President Roosevelt, October 6, 1942, *Foreign Relations of the United States, 1942*, vol. 5, *China*, 159.
126. Memorandum for Mr. Currie from General Stilwell," August 1, 1942, ProQuest History Vault, Folder: 003249-001-0381, Records of the War Department's Operations Division, 1942–1945, Part 1. World War II Operations, Series B, Pacific Theater.

127. "Memorandum for General Marshall," Franklin D. Roosevelt, October 3, 1942, Franklin D. Roosevelt Presidential Library, Personal Secretary Files, 0266, box 27; "Memorandum for the President, Re: General Stilwell," Lauchlin Currie, October 1, 1942, Franklin D. Roosevelt Presidential Library, Personal Secretary Files, 0266, box 27; "Memorandum for the President," Gen. George C. Marshall, October 6, 1942, Franklin D. Roosevelt Presidential Library, Personal Secretary Files, 0266, box 27; Elliott Roosevelt, ed., *The Roosevelt Letters: Being the Personal Correspondence of Franklin Delano Roosevelt, Vol. III* (London: George G. Harrap and Co., 1952), 440.
128. Dayna Barnes, "Plans and Expectations: The American News Media and Postwar Japan," *Japanese Studies* 34, no. 3 (2014): 13.
129. Louis Morton, "Army and Marines on the China Station: A Study in Military and Political Rivalry," *Pacific Historical Review* 29, no. 1 (1960): 68–69.
130. Tuchman, *Stilwell and the American Experience in China; 1911–1945*, 322.
131. Memorandum by the Chief of the Division of Far Eastern Affairs (Hamilton), June 17, 1942, *Foreign Relations of the United States*, vol. 5, *China*, 1942, 72–73.
132. The Ambassador in China (Gauss) to the Secretary of State, July 3, 1942, *Foreign Relations of the United States*, vol. 5, *China*, 1942, 93.
133. Michael J. Green, *By More than Providence: Grand Strategy and American Power in the Asia Pacific since 1783* (New York: Columbia University Press, 2017), 213.
134. Hayes, *The History of the Joint Chiefs of Staff in World War II*, 223–24; Memorandum for Chiang Kai-shek, October 12, 1942, "Eyes Alone" Correspondence of General Joseph W. Stilwell, National Archives and Records Administration, Microfilm Publication M1419, reel 1.
135. Marshall, vol. 3, 319–20.
136. The Ambassador in China (Gauss) to the Secretary of State, August 12, 1942, *Foreign Relations of the United States*, vol. 5, *China*, 1942, 127.
137. Kirby, *The War against Japan, Vol. II*, 154.
138. Marshall, vol. 3, 384–85.
139. Kirby, *The War against Japan, Vol. II*, 291.
140. Romanus and Sunderland, *Stilwell's Mission to China*, 227.
141. Slim, *Defeat into Victory*, 249.
142. Kirby, *The War against Japan, Vol. II*, 292; Leslie Anders, *The Ledo Road: General Joseph W. Stilwell's Highway to China* (Norman: University of Oklahoma Press, 1965), 16.
143. Retaking of Burma, ProQuest History Vault, Folder: 003183-012-0704, Records of the Joint Chiefs of Staff, Part 1: 1942–1945, The Pacific Theater, C.C.S. 104/1, August 29, 1942, 18.
144. Hayes, *The History of the Joint Chiefs of Staff in World War II*, 241; Maurice Matloff and Edwin M. Snell, *Strategic Planning for Coalition Warfare: 1941–1942* (Washington, D.C.: Government Printing Office, 1999), 372–73; Stilwell, *The Stilwell Papers*, 175.
145. Matloff and Snell, *Strategic Planning for Coalition Warfare*, 372–73.
146. Slim, *Defeat into Victory*, 144.

147. Marshall, vol. 3, 474–75.
148. Memorandum for Record: Strength of Chinese Units at Camp Ramgarh, November 13, 1942, N16436, "Analysis of Boatner Materials," Fort Leavenworth Research Library Collection, 35.
149. Memorandum of Conversation, by Ambassador in China (Gauss), July 11, 1942, *Foreign Relations of the United States*, vol. 5, *China*, 1942, 111.
150. Davies, *China Hand*, 50.
151. "Memorandum for the Joint Chiefs of Staff, Subject: General Stilwell," December 21, 1942, ProQuest History Vault, Folder: 003249-001-0660, Records of the War Department's Operations Division, 1942–1945, Part 1. World War II Operations, Series B, Pacific Theater.
152. MacKinnon, "The Sino-Japanese Conflict, 1931–1945," 216.
153. T'ien-wei Wu, "Contending Political Forces," in *China's Bitter Victory: The War with Japan 1937–1945*, ed. James C. Hsiung and Steven I. Levine (Armonk, N.Y.: M. E. Sharpe, Inc., 1992), 60–61.
154. Tuchman, *Stilwell and the American Experience in China; 1911–1945*, 316.
155. Fenby, *Chiang Kai-shek*, 116–17.
156. Albert C. Wedemeyer, *Wedemeyer Reports!: An Objective, Dispassionate Examination of World War II, Postwar Policies, and Grand Strategy* (New York: Henry Holt and Co., 1958), 202.
157. "The Campaign in Burma, Report to the War Department," General Joseph Stilwell, May 2, 1943, ProQuest History Vault, Folder: 003249-001-0660, Records of the War Department's Operations Division, 1942–1945, Part 1. World War II Operations, Series B, Pacific Theater, 3.
158. Radio Message, Stilwell to Marshall, September 1, 1942, "Eyes Alone" Correspondence of General Joseph W. Stilwell, National Archives and Records Administration, Microfilm Publication M1419, reel 1.
159. Burt, "The Ambassador, the General, and the President," 288.
160. Mitter, "Identities and Alliances," 105–6; Robert Dallek, *Franklin D. Roosevelt and American Foreign Policy, 1932–1945* (New York: Oxford University Press, 1979), 29.
161. Eisenhower National Historic Site, https://www.nps.gov/museum/exhibits/eise/allied.html.
162. Joel D. Rayburn and Frank K. Sobchak, *The U.S. Army in the Iraq War*, vol. 1: *Invasion—Insurgency—Civil War, 2003–2006* (Carlisle, PA: U.S. Army War College Press, 2019), 32, https://press.armywarcollege.edu/monographs/386.

CHAPTER 2. AIRPOWER

1. Henry L. Stimson and McGeorge Bundy, *On Active Service: In Peace and War* (New York: Harper and Bros., 1948), 530.
2. Barbara Tuchman, *Stilwell and the American Experience in China, 1911–1945* (New York: Macmillan Publishers, 1970), 217; Sam Kleiner, *The Flying Tigers: The Untold*

Story of the American Pilots Who Waged a Secret War against Japan (New York: Penguin Books, 2019), 20–21.

3. Xu Guangqiu, "Americans and Chinese Nationalist Military Aviation, 1929–1949," *Journal of Asian History* 31, no. 2 (1997): 170–71; Charles Romanus and Riley Sunderland, *Stilwell's Mission to China* (Washington, D.C.: U.S. Army Center of Military History, 1953), 10–11.
4. Romanus and Sunderland, *Stilwell's Mission to China*, 18–19.
5. Maurice Matloff and Edwin M. Snell, *Strategic Planning for Coalition Warfare: 1941–1942* (Washington, D.C.: Government Printing Office, 1999), 140–41; Romanus and Sunderland, *Stilwell's Mission to China*, 78–79.
6. Claire Lee Chennault, *Way of a Fighter: The Memoirs of Claire Lee Chennault* (New York: G. P. Putnam, 1949), 201.
7. Kleiner, *The Flying Tigers*, 9–11.
8. Frank McLynn, *The Burma Campaign: Disaster into Triumph, 1942–1945* (New Haven, Conn.: Yale University Press, 2011), 115–16.
9. Radio Message, October 19, 1942, Stilwell to Marshall, "Eyes Alone" Correspondence of General Joseph W. Stilwell, National Archives and Records Administration, Microfilm Publication M1419, reel 1.
10. Dillard Marion Eubank, Midwest China Oral History Interviews, Luther Seminary, June 10, 1980, 37–38; Radio Message, June 28, 1943, Dorn to Stilwell, "Eyes Alone" Correspondence of General Joseph W. Stilwell, National Archives and Records Administration, Microfilm Publication M1419, reel 2.
11. Chennault, *Way of a Fighter*, 142; Maochun Yu, *The Dragon's War: Allied Operations and the Fate of China, 1937–1947* (Annapolis, Md.: Naval Institute Press, 2013), 241.
12. Robert L. Scott, *Flying Tiger: Chennault of China* (New York: Doubleday, 1959), 73.
13. Scott, *Flying Tiger*, 211.
14. H. H. Arnold, *Global Mission* (New York: Harper and Brothers, 1949), 419.
15. William D. Leahy, *I Was There* (New York: Whittlesey House, 1950), 157.
16. Wesley F. Craven and James L. Cate, eds., *The Army Air Forces in World War II: Volume 1: Plans and Early Operations: January 1939 to August 1942* (Washington, D.C.: Office of Air Force History, 1983), 512.
17. Matloff and Snell, *Strategic Planning for Coalition Warfare: 1941–1942*, 311.
18. Romanus and Sunderland, *Stilwell's Mission to China*, 188–89.
19. Romanus and Sunderland, *Stilwell's Mission to China*, 199.
20. Chennault, *Way of a Fighter*, 161.
21. Ronald H. Spector, *Eagle against the Sun: The American War with Japan* (New York: Random House, 1985), 340; Romanus and Sunderland, *Stilwell's Mission to China*, 251.
22. Wesley F. Craven and James L. Cate, eds., *The Army Air Forces in World War II: Volume 4: The Pacific: Guadalcanal to Saipan, August 1942 to July 1944* (Washington, D.C.: Office of Air Force History, 1983), 424.

23. Tuchman, *Stilwell and the American Experience in China, 1911–1944*, 337; Romanus and Sunderland, *Stilwell's Mission to China*, 253; John Paton Davies Jr., *China Hand: An Autobiography* (Philadelphia: University of Pennsylvania Press, 2012), 96–98; Kleiner, *The Flying Tigers*, 215.
24. Chennault, *Way of a Fighter*, 212.
25. *The Papers of George Catlett Marshall*, ed. Larry I. Bland and Sharon Ritenour Stevens (Lexington, Va.: The George C. Marshall Foundation, 1981–). Electronic version based on *The Papers of George Catlett Marshall*, vol. 3, *"The Right Man for the Job," December 7, 1941–May 31, 1943* (Baltimore: The Johns Hopkins University Press, 1991) (hereafter Marshall, vol. 3), 481–83.
26. Hoover Institution Archives, The World War II Diaries of General Joseph W. Stilwell, 95.
27. Marshall, vol. 3, 584–86.
28. Marshall, vol. 3, 502–3.
29. Radio Message, January 6, 1943, "Eyes Alone" Correspondence of General Joseph W. Stilwell, National Archives and Records Administration, Microfilm Publication M1419, reel 1.
30. George Marshall Correspondence on China and India, Jan. 1, 1943, through August 31, 1943, ProQuest History Vault, Folder: 003255-008-0292, Radio Message to General J. W. Stilwell, January 5, 1943.
31. Romanus and Sunderland, *Stilwell's Mission to China*, 260.
32. Combined Chiefs of Staff: Report to the President and Prime Minister, January 22, 1943, Joint Chiefs of Staff History Office, Casablanca Conference, 107; Grace Person Hayes, *The History of the Joint Chiefs of Staff in World War II: The War against Japan* (Annapolis, Md.: Naval Institute Press, 1982), 292; War Cabinet, Weekly Resume, No. 43, April 29, 1943, United Kingdom National Archives, Reference #CAB 65/38/4.
33. Minutes of Meeting held at Anfa Camp, January 18, 1943, Joint Chiefs of Staff History Office, Casablanca Conference, 145.
34. Minutes of Meeting held at Anfa Camp, January 23, 1943, Joint Chiefs of Staff History Office, Casablanca Conference, 167–68.
35. Minutes of Meeting held at Anfa Camp, January 17, 1943, Joint Chiefs of Staff History Office, Casablanca Conference, 228.
36. President Roosevelt and Prime Minister Churchill to Generalissimo Chiang Kai-Shek, January 25, 1943, in *Foreign Relations of the United States, 1943*, vol. 5, *China* (Washington, D.C.: Government Printing Office, 1956).
37. Romanus and Sunderland, *Stilwell's Mission to China*, 277.
38. Forrest C. Pogue, *George C. Marshall: Ordeal and Hope* (New York: Viking Press, 1965), 369.
39. Marshall, vol. 3, 475–77.
40. Romanus and Sunderland, *Stilwell's Mission to China*, 280–82; Marshall, vol. 3, 586–89.

41. Maurice Matloff, *Strategic Planning for Coalition Warfare, 1943–1944* (Washington, D.C.: Government Printing Office, 1999), 529.
42. Memorandum by the Chief of the Division of Far Eastern Affairs (Hamilton), March 5, 1943, *Foreign Relations of the United States*, vol. 5, *China*.
43. The Charge in China (Vincent) to the Secretary of State, March 19, 1943, *Foreign Relations of the United States*, vol. 5, *China*.
44. Memorandum by the Second Secretary of Embassy in China (Davies) to the Ambassador in China (Gauss), March 9, 1943, *Foreign Relations of the United States*, vol. 5, *China*.
45. Davies, *China Hand*, 107.
46. Albert C. Wedemeyer, *Wedemeyer Reports!: An Objective, Dispassionate Examination of World War II, Postwar Policies, and Grand Strategy* (New York: Henry Holt and Co., 1958), 201.
47. Matloff, *Strategic Planning for Coalition Warfare, 1943–1944*, 78; Riley Sunderland and Charles F. Romanus, eds., *Stilwell's Personal File: China-Burma-India, 1942–1944* (Wilmington, Del.: Scholarly Resources, 1976), 454.
48. Chinese American-British Conference, Chungking, Combined Chiefs of Staff, ProQuest History Vault, Folder: 003183-012-1035, February 1943.
49. Hayes, *The History of the Joint Chiefs of Staff in World War II*, 339.
50. Arnold, *Global Mission*, 416.
51. Romanus and Sunderland, *Stilwell's Mission to China*, 284.
52. Romanus and Sunderland, *Stilwell's Mission to China*, 286; Hayes, *The History of the Joint Chiefs of Staff in World War II*, 347.
53. Hayes, *The History of the Joint Chiefs of Staff in World War II*, 343; Arnold, *Global Mission*, 418.
54. Wesley F. Craven and James L. Cate, *The Army Air Forces in World War II: Volume VII: Services around the World* (Washington, D.C.: Office of Air Force History, 1983), 124.
55. John P. Davies, *Dragon by the Tail: American, British, Japanese, and Russian Encounters with China and One Another* (New York: W. W. Norton and Co., 1972), 264.
56. Romanus and Sunderland, *Stilwell's Mission to China*, 321.
57. Hayes, *The History of the Joint Chiefs of Staff in World War II*, 380.
58. Joseph G. Taylor, *Air Interdiction in China in World War II*, USAF Historical Studies No. 132 (Montgomery, Ala.: Air University, 1956), 4.
59. Romanus and Sunderland, *Stilwell's Mission to China*, 322.
60. Marshall, vol. 3, 674–75.
61. Matloff, *Strategic Planning for Coalition Warfare, 1943–1944*, 143.
62. Davies, *Dragon by the Tail*, 267.
63. Wedemeyer, *Wedemeyer Reports!*, 202–3.
64. Ed Cray, *General of the Army: George C. Marshall, Soldier and Stateman* (New York: W. W. Norton and Co., 1990), 391–93.
65. Claire L. Chennault's Plan for Air Force Operations in China, ProQuest History Vault, Folder: 003248-004-0797, War Department General Staff, May 9, 1943.

66. Leahy, *I Was There*, 157; Yongli Han, *Zhanshi Meiguo dazhan lüeyu Zhongguo kangri zhanzheng (1941–1945 nian)* [The United States wartime grand strategy and China's anti-Japanese theater, 1941–1945] (Wuhang: Wuhan daxue chubanshe, 2003), 201.
67. Combined Chiefs of Staff, Minutes, 1st Meeting, The White House, May 12, 1943 (Trident Conference, Joint Chiefs of Staff History Office), 259–60.
68. Hayes, *The History of the Joint Chiefs of Staff in World War II*, 394.
69. Winston S. Churchill, *The Second World War: The Hinge of Fate* (Boston: Houghton Mifflin Co., 1950), 785–86; War Cabinet, W.P. 42(236), June 3, 1942, United Kingdom, National Archives, Reference # CAB 66/25/16, 1–4.
70. Chennault, *Way of a Fighter*, 220.
71. Stimson and Bundy, *On Active Service in Peace and War*, 540.
72. Tuchman, *Stilwell and the American Experience in China, 1911–1944*, 367–68.
73. Joseph Stilwell, *The Stilwell Papers*, ed. Theodore H. White (New York: Sloane and Associates, 1948), 205–6.
74. "Memorandum for George Marshall," from the President of the United States, March 8, 1943, Franklin D. Roosevelt Presidential Library, Map Room 0847, box 165.
75. Marshall, vol. 3, 675–76.
76. Stilwell, *The Stilwell Papers*, 204.
77. Romanus and Sunderland, *Stilwell's Mission to China*, 325.
78. Craven and Cate, *The Army Air Forces in World War II: Volume VII*, 125; Matloff, *Strategic Planning for Coalition Warfare, 1943–1944*, 141.
79. Stilwell, *The Stilwell Papers*, 205.
80. Memorandum by the U.S. Chiefs of Staff, Enclosure: Conduct of the War, 1943–1944, May 14, 1943 (Trident Conference, Joint Chiefs of Staff History Office), 28.
81. Romanus and Sunderland, *Stilwell's Mission to China*, 332.
82. Taylor, *Air Interdiction in China in World War II*, 23.
83. *The Fourteenth Air Force to 1 October 1943*, Assistant Chief of Air Staff, Historical Division, July 1945, Air Force Historical Research Agency, 97–102; Craven and Cate, *The Army Air Forces in World War II: Volume IV*, 526–27.
84. Taylor, *Air Interdiction in China in World War II*, 82.
85. Romanus and Sunderland, *Stilwell's Mission to China*, 338.
86. Charles N. Hunter, *Galahad* (San Antonio: Naylor Co., 1963), 156.
87. Tuchman, *Stilwell and the American Experience in China; 1911–1945*, 421.
88. Maj. Gen. H. L. Boatner, A Statement of the Record by Maj. Gen. H. L. Boatner, Hoover Archives, box 2, 14.
89. Ian Fellowes-Gordon, *The Battle for Naw Seng's Kingdom: General Stilwell's North Burma Campaign and Its Aftermath* (London: Leo Cooper Press, 1971), 50; McLynn, *The Burma Campaign*, 408.
90. Radio Message, November 7, 1943, Ferris to Stilwell, "Eyes Alone" Correspondence of General Joseph W. Stilwell, National Archives and Records Administration, Microfilm Publication M1419, reel 2.

91. Michael Hastings, "The Runaway General: The Profile that Brought Down McChrystal," *Rolling Stone*, June 22, 2010. https://www.rollingstone.com/politics/politics-news/the-runaway-general-the-profile-that-brought-down-mcchrystal-192609/.

CHAPTER 3. GLOBAL ALLIES

1. Radio Message, November 14, 1943, Marshall to Stilwell, "Eyes Alone" Correspondence of General Joseph W. Stilwell, National Archives and Records Administration, Microfilm Publication M1419, reel 2.
2. Winston S. Churchill, *Closing the Ring* (Boston: Houghton Mifflin Co., 1951), 329; Joseph E. Persico, *Roosevelt's Centurions: FDR and the Commanders He Led to Victory in World War II* (New York: Random House, 2013), 325; John P. Davies, *Dragon by the Tail: American, British, Japanese, and Russian Encounters with China and One Another* (New York: W. W. Norton and Co., 1972), 280; Michael J. Green, *By More than Providence: Grand Strategy and American Power in the Asia Pacific since 1783* (New York: Columbia University Press, 2017), 210.
3. Chinese Army in India, "Outline of Education," June 10, 1943, National Archives and Records Administration, College Park, Records Group 493, box 17.
4. William Slim, *Defeat into Victory* (New York: David McKay Company, Inc., 1961), 144.
5. Maj. Gen. H. L. Boatner, A Statement of the Record by Maj. Gen. H. L. Boatner, Hoover Institution Archives, box 2, 12.
6. Charles Romanus and Riley Sunderland, *Stilwell's Mission to China* (Washington, D.C.: U.S. Army Center of Military History, 1953), 300.
7. Romanus and Sunderland, *Stilwell's Mission to China*, 296.
8. Romanus and Sunderland, *Stilwell's Mission to China*, 352–53.
9. "Instructions for Liaison Officers from This Headquarters to Chinese Units," October 14, 1943, National Archives and Records Administration, College Park, Record Group 493, stack 290, box 6.
10. "Instructions for Liaison Officers from This Headquarters to Chinese Units," October 14, 1943, H. L. Boatner, National Archives and Records Administration, College Park, Record Group 493, box 6.
11. Combined Chiefs of Staff, Minutes of Meeting Held on August 17, 1943, at 1430, Quadrant Conference, Joint History Office, 449.
12. Churchill, *Closing the Ring*, 87; Combined Chiefs of Staff, Minutes, 2nd Meeting, The White House, May 14, 1943, Trident Conference, Joint History Office, 265.
13. Combined Chiefs of Staff, Minutes, 84th Meeting, May 14, 1943, Trident Conference, Joint History Office, 359.
14. Combined Chiefs of Staff: Specific Operations in the Pacific and Far East (C.C.C. 301/3), August 27, 1943, Quadrant Conference, Joint History Office, 65, 68; Combined Chiefs of Staff: Appreciation and Plan for the Defeat of Japan (C.C.C. 313) August 18, 1943, Quadrant Conference, Joint History Office, 160.

15. Philip Ziegler, *Mountbatten* (New York: Harper & Row, 1986), 216–21; Jonathan Templin Ritter, *Stilwell and Mountbatten in Burma: Allies at War, 1943–1944* (Denton: University of North Texas Press, 2017), 31–33.
16. Combined Chiefs of Staff: Southeast Asia Command (C.C.S. 308/3), August 21, 1943, Quadrant Conference, Joint History Office, 124.
17. Churchill, *Closing the Ring*, 89.
18. George Marshall Correspondence on China and India, Jan. 1, 1943, through August 31, 1943, ProQuest History Vault, Folder: 003255-008-0292. Radio Message to General J. W. Stilwell, August 26, 1943.
19. *The Papers of George Catlett Marshall*, ed. Larry I. Bland and Sharon Ritenour Stevens (Lexington, Va.: The George C. Marshall Foundation, 1981–). Electronic version based on *The Papers of George Catlett Marshall*, vol. 4, *"Aggressive and Determined Leadership," June 1, 1943–December 31, 1944* (Baltimore: The Johns Hopkins University Press, 1996) (hereafter Marshall, vol. 4), 95–97.
20. John D. Millett, *The Organization and Role of the Army Service Forces* (Washington, D.C.: Office of the Chief of Military History, Department of the Army, 1954), 391–94.
21. Combined Chiefs of Staff: Effect of Indian Floods on Burma Campaign (C.C.S. 305), August 14, 1943, Quadrant Conference, Joint History Office, 109; Robert W. Coakley and Richard Leighton, *Global Logistics and Strategy, 1943–1945* (Washington, D.C.: U.S. Army Center of Military History, 1989), 506.
22. Vice Admiral Mountbatten the Earl of Burma, *Report to the Combined Chiefs of Staff by the Supreme Allied Commander, Southeast Asia: 1943–1945* (London: His Majesty's Stationery Office, 1951), 12–13; Romanus and Sunderland, *Stilwell's Mission to China*, 360.
23. Letter to Maj. Gen. R. A. Wheeler from Lt. Gen. Brehon Somervell, August 24, 1943, National Archives Microfilm Publications, M1419, "Eyes Alone" Correspondence of General Joseph W. Stilwell, January 1942–October 1944, reel 5.
24. Combined Chiefs of Staff, Minutes of Meeting Held on Tuesday, August 24, at 1030, Quadrant Conference, Joint History Office, 492.
25. Combined Chiefs of Staff: Supply Routes in Northeast India (C.C.S. 25), August 21, 1943, Quadrant Conference, Joint History Office, 308.
26. Romanus and Sunderland, *Stilwell's Mission to China*, 362.
27. Combined Chiefs of Staff: Pipeline from India to China (C.C.S. 312), August 8, 1943, Quadrant Conference, Joint History Office, 146–49; Charles F. Romanus and Riley Sunderland, *Stilwell's Command Problems* (Washington, D.C.: U.S. Government Printing Office, 1955), 11.
28. Coakley and Leighton, *Global Logistics and Strategy, 1943–1945*, 510.
29. Maurice Matloff, *Strategic Planning for Coalition Warfare, 1943–1944* (Washington, D.C.: Government Printing Office, 1999), 323–24.
30. Romanus and Sunderland, *Stilwell's Mission to China*, 383.
31. Romanus and Sunderland, *Stilwell's Command Problems*, 10.

32. Ziegler, *Mountbatten*, 242.
33. Marshall, vol. 4, 95–97.
34. Romanus and Sunderland, *Stilwell's Mission to China*, 364.
35. The Secretary of War (Stimson) to the Secretary of State, June 29, 1943, *Foreign Relations of the United States*, vol. 5, *China*, 1943, 68.
36. The Secretary of State to the Secretary of War (Stimson), August 17, 1943, *Foreign Relations of the United States*, vol. 5, *China*, 1943, 91.
37. Romanus and Sunderland, *Stilwell's Command Problems*, 54–55.
38. Combined Chiefs of Staff: Specific Operations for the Defeat of Japan, 1944 (C.C.S. 397), 3 December 3, 1943, Sextant Conference, Joint History Office, 70.
39. Romanus and Sunderland, *Stilwell's Command Problems*, 64–65.
40. Davies, *Dragon by the Tail*, 277.
41. John Paton Davies Jr., *China Hand: An Autobiography* (Philadelphia: University of Pennsylvania Press, 2012), 144.
42. Combined Chiefs of Staff: Role of China in Defeat of Japan (C.C.S. 405), November 22, 1943, Sextant Conference: Joint History Office, 211–13.
43. Romanus and Sunderland, *Stilwell's Command Problems*, 64.
44. Joseph Stilwell, *The Stilwell Papers*, ed. Theodore H. White (New York: Sloane and Associates, 1948), 255; Barbara Tuchman, *Stilwell and the American Experience in China, 1911–1945* (New York: Macmillan Publishers, 1970), 403.
45. Alan Brooke's Diary, November 24, 1943, cited in Ronald I. Heiferman, "The Cairo Conference: A Turning Point in Sino-American Relations" (PhD diss., New York University, 1990), 172.
46. H. H. Arnold, *Global Mission* (New York: Harper and Brothers, 1949), 427.
47. The World War II Diaries of Joseph W. Stilwell, 1943, Hoover Institution Archives, transcribed 2005, 160.
48. Eric Larrabee, *Commander in Chief: Franklin Delano Roosevelt, His Lieutenants, and Their War* (New York: Simon & Schuster, 1987), 553; Jay Taylor, *The Generalissimo: Chiang Kai-shek and the Struggle for Modern China* (Cambridge, Mass.: Belknap, 2011), 245–46.
49. Memorandum by the Advisor on Political Relations (Hornbeck), October 26, 1943, *Foreign Relations of the United States*, vol. 5, *China*, 1943, 153; Davies, *Dragon by the Tail*, 220.
50. Tuchman, *Stilwell and the American Experience in China, 1911–1944*, 387.
51. OSS report on China's Destiny: A Political Bible for the New China, by Chiang Kai-shek, July 15, 1943, 019-HIA-Richardson-4-A-1-2-9, Alvin Franklin Richardson Papers, Hoover Institution Library and Archives, https://digitalcollections.hoover.org/objects/67028/oss-report-on-chinas-destiny-a-political-bible-for-the-new; Sally K. Burt, *At the President's Pleasure: FDR's Leadership of Wartime Sino-American Relations* (Boston: Brill, 2015), 183; Larrabee, *Commander in Chief*, 541.
52. Jonathon Fenby, *Chiang Kai-shek: China's Generalissimo and the Nation He Lost* (London: Free Press, 2003), 400–401.

53. Christopher Thorne, *Allies of a Kind: The United States, Britain, and the War against Japan, 1941–1945* (New York: Oxford University Press, 1978), 310.
54. Henry L. Stimson and McGeorge Bundy, *On Active Service: In Peace and War* (New York: Harper and Bros., 1948), 539.
55. Combined Chiefs of Staff: Estimate of the Enemy Situation, 1944-Pacific-Far East (C.C.S. 300/2), November 18, 1943, Sextant Conference, Joint History Office, 19.
56. Chang Jui-Te, "Nationalist Army Officers during the Sino-Japanese War, 1937–1945," *Modern Asian Studies* 30, no. 4 (1996): 1038.
57. Wang Chaoguang, "The Dark Side of the War: Corruption in the Guomindang Government during World War II," *Journal of Modern Chinese History* 11, no. 2 (2017): 257.
58. Davies, *China Hand*, 144.
59. Heiferman, "The Cairo Conference," 127.
60. Minutes of Meeting Held on Tuesday, November 23 at 1430, Sextant Conference, Joint History Office, 420.
61. Heiferman, "The Cairo Conference, 151.
62. Arnold, *Global Mission*, 464–65.
63. Minutes of Meeting Held on November 23 at 1430, Sextant Conference, Joint History Office, 381.
64. Combined Chiefs of Staff: Minutes of Meeting Held on Wednesday, November 24, 1943, at 1430, Sextant Conference, Joint History Office, 428.
65. Tuchman, *Stilwell and the American Experience in China, 1911–1944*, 413; Matloff, *Strategic Planning for Coalition Warfare*, 449–50.
66. Assistant Chief of Air Staff, Intelligence, Historical Division, *The Fourteenth Air Force to 1 October 1943* (Army Air Forces Historical Office, July 1945), 130–33.
67. Tuchman, *Stilwell and the American Experience in China, 1911–1944*, 377–78.
68. Grace Person Hayes, *The History of the Joint Chiefs of Staff in World War II: The War against Japan* (Annapolis, Md.: Naval Institute Press, 1982), 513–14.
69. Marshall, vol. 4, 124–25.
70. Memorandum of Conversation, by the Ambassador in China (Gauss), September 25, 1943, *Foreign Relations of the United States*, vol. 5, *China*, 1943, 131.
71. Larry I. Bland, ed., *George C. Marshall Interviews and Reminiscences for Forrest C. Pogue* (Lexington, Va.: George C. Marshall Foundation, 1996), October 29, 1956, 605.
72. Romanus and Sunderland, *Stilwell's Command Problems*, 81–82.
73. Marshall, vol. 4, 191–96.

CHAPTER 4. LEADING ALLIES IN BURMA

1. Fred Eldridge, *Wrath in Burma: The Uncensored Story of General Stilwell and International Maneuvers in the Far East* (New York: Doubleday, 1946), 140.
2. George A. McGee, *The History of the 2nd Battalion, Merrill's Marauders* (self-published, 1987), 19; Gen. Paul L. Freeman, Senior Officers Debriefing Program, U.S. Army Military History Research Institute, Carlisle Barracks, 1974, 57.

3. David W. Hogan, *U.S. Army Special Operations in World War II* (Washington, D.C.: Government Printing Office, 1992), 108.
4. Army Regulation 34-1, Interoperability, U.S. Army Training and Doctrine Command, April 9, 2020.
5. Chen Ju-hwa, *China's Role in the Recapture of Burma*, Ft. Leavenworth, Command and General Staff College, 1947, 3–4; Joseph Stilwell, *The Stilwell Papers*, ed. Theodore H. White (New York: Sloane and Associates, 1948), 264.
6. Zhibingtang bianjibu, *1942–1945 Zhongguo yuan zheng jun Miandian zhan ji, 1942–1945* [A record of the China Expeditionary Army in Burma, 1942–1945] (Taipei: Zhibingtang wenhua chuanmei youxian gongsi, 2014), 99–100.
7. *A Report Summarizing the Activities of U.S. Army Medical Department Units Assigned to Northern Combat Area Command during the Northern and Central Burma Campaigns*, Fort Leavenworth Research Library Collection, N-11207 A.
8. Charles F. Romanus and Riley Sunderland, *Stilwell's Command Problems* (Washington, D.C.: U.S. Government Printing Office, 1955), 32.
9. Hsu Long-hsuen and Chang Ming-kai, *History of the Sino-Japanese War* (Taipei: Chung Wu Publishing, 1971), 398.
10. "Memorandum for the President, from George C. Marshall," August 13, 1943, Franklin D. Roosevelt Presidential Library, Map Room 300, box 80.
11. Hoover Institution Archives, The World War II Diaries of Joseph W. Stilwell, 1943, transcribed 2005, 167; Stilwell, *The Stilwell Papers*, 266.
12. Raymond E. Bell Jr., "A Combined Efforts: Chinese and American Tanks in Burma, 1944–1945," *On Point* 17, no. 3 (Winter 2012): 34.
13. George Marshall correspondence on China and India, Message Marshall to Stilwell, September 1, 1943, ProQuest History Vault, Folder: 003255-008-0320 Date: Sept. 1, 1943–Dec. 31, 1943, Papers of George C. Marshall: Selected World War II Correspondence.
14. Combined Chiefs of Staff, Minutes of Meeting on Saturday, August 14, at 1630, Quadrant Conference, Joint History Office, 428.
15. Grace Person Hayes, *The History of the Joint Chiefs of Staff in World War II: The War against Japan* (Annapolis, Md.: Naval Institute Press, 1982), 451.
16. *The Papers of George Catlett Marshall*, ed. Larry I. Bland and Sharon Ritenour Stevens (Lexington, Va.: The George C. Marshall Foundation, 1981–). Electronic version based on *The Papers of George Catlett Marshall*, vol. 4, *"Aggressive and Determined Leadership," June 1, 1943–December 31, 1944* (Baltimore: The Johns Hopkins University Press, 1996) (hereafter Marshall, vol. 4), 110–12.
17. U.S. Army Center of Military History, *Merrill's Marauders* (Washington, D.C., Government Printing Office, 1990), 11–16.
18. *Merrill's Marauders* (February–May 1944), Military Intelligence Division, U.S. War Department, 1945, 8–9; War Department Operations Division, Outgoing Message to CINC SWPA and CG SPA," August 31, 1943, Franklin D. Roosevelt Presidential

Library, Map Room 0605, box 103; Radio Message, September 4, 1943, Marshall to Stilwell, "Eyes Alone" Correspondence of General Joseph W. Stilwell, National Archives and Records Administration, Microfilm Publication M1419, reel 2.
19. James E. T. Hopkins, Henry G. Stelling, and Tracy S. Voorhees, "The Marauders and the Microbes," in *Crisis Fleeting: Original Reports on Military Medicine in India and Burma in the Second World War* (Washington, D.C.: Office of the Surgeon General, 1969), 310–10; Barbara Tuchman, *Stilwell and the American Experience in China, 1911–1945* (New York: Macmillan Publishers, 1970), 433; Frank McLynn, *The Burma Campaign: Disaster into Triumph, 1942–1945* (New Haven, Conn.: Yale University Press, 2011), 328–29.
20. Scott R. McMichael, *A Historical Perspective on Light Infantry*, Combat Studies Institute, Fort Leavenworth, 1987, 14.
21. *Merrill's Marauders* (February–May 1944), Military Intelligence Division, U.S. War Department, 1945, 14; Romanus and Sunderland, *Stilwell's Command Problems*, 35.
22. *Development of Joint Air Ground Operations in North Burma*, Headquarters, 10th Air Force, Fort Leavenworth Research Library Collection, N-8226, 5.
23. Grant Hirabayashi, interview, Library of Congress, Veterans History Project, June 29, 2005. https://memory.loc.gov/diglib/vhp-stories/loc.natlib.afc2001001.28498/transcript?ID=mv0001.
24. Grant Hirabayashi, interview.
25. Charles N. Hunter, *Galahad* (San Antonio: Naylor Co., 1963), 3.
26. *History of the India-Burma Theater, Vol. I*, December 6, 1945, Combined Arms Research Library, Fort Leavenworth Research Library Collection, WWII Operational Documents, No. 4709, 38.
27. Vice Admiral Mountbatten, Earl of Burma, *Report to the Combined Chiefs of Staff by the Supreme Allied Commander, Southeast Asia: 1943–1945* (London: His Majesty's Stationery Office, 1951), 4.
28. Wesley F. Craven and James L. Cate, *The Army Air Forces in World War II: Volume IV: The Pacific: Guadalcanal to Saipan, August 1942 to July 1944* (Washington, D.C.: Office of Air Force History, 1983), 503–4; McMichael, *A Historical Perspective on Light Infantry*, 15.
29. Tuchman, *Stilwell and the American Experience in China, 1911–1944*, 418.
30. Memorandum for Record, Subject: Planning for Air Ground Coordination, H. L. Boatner, May 16, 1943, National Archives and Records Administration, College Park, Records Group 493, box 5.
31. Hopkins, Stelling, and Voorhees, "The Marauders and the Microbes"; Romanus and Sunderland, *Stilwell's Command Problems*, 91.
32. Romanus and Sunderland, *Stilwell's Command Problems*, 105.
33. *Burma Operations Record: 18th Division Operations in the Hukawng Area*, Japanese Monograph 131, 1949, U.S. Army Center of Military History, Fort McNair, Washington, D.C., 34.
34. *Stilwell Road Report*, Col. A. C. Welling, Theater Engineer, August 14, 1945, Fort Leavenworth Research Library Collection, R-10889, 14.

35. Karl C. Dod, *The Corps of Engineers in the War against Japan* (Washington, D.C.: U.S. Army Center of Military History, 1987), 433.
36. Leslie Anders, *The Ledo Road: General Joseph W. Stilwell's Highway to China* (Norman: University of Oklahoma Press, 1965), 37–40, 48–49; *Stilwell Road Report*, Col. A. C. Welling, Theater Engineer, August 14, 1945, Fort Leavenworth Research Library Collection, R-10889, 30–33.
37. *Cost Estimate, Ledo Road*, Office Chief of Engineers, January 1946, Fort Leavenworth Research Library Collection, 27.
38. George R. Thompson and Dixie R. Harris, *The Signal Corps: The Outcome* (Washington, D.C.: U.S. Army Center of Military History, 1991), 177.
39. Alexander Michnewich, Military Oral History Project, February 27, 2008, 9, Virginia Military Institute.
40. George Marshall correspondence on China and India, Message Stilwell to Marshall, July 1, 1944, ProQuest History Vault, Folder: 003255-008-0364 Date: July 1, 1944–Aug. 31, 1944, Papers of George C. Marshall: Selected World War II Correspondence.
41. Office of the Chief of Military History, History of the Northern Combat Area Command, China-Burma-India Theater and India-Burma Theater, 1943–1945, appendix 8, detachment 1010, October 1943–June 1945, U.S. Army Center of Military History, Fort McNair, Washington, D.C., Photo section.
42. William R. Peers and Dean Brelis, *Behind the Burma Road* (Boston: Little Brown and Co., 1963), 26–27.
43. Alan K. Lathrop, "The Employment of Chinese Nationalist Troops in the First Burma Campaign," *Journal of Southeast Asian Studies* 12, no. 2 (Sept. 1981): 426–27; Troy J. Sacquety, *The OSS in Burma: Jungle War against the Japanese* (Lawrence: University Press of Kansas, 2013), 125; Richard Dunlop, *Behind Japanese Lines: With the OSS in Burma* (New York: Rand McNally and Co., 1979), 333.
44. *Burma Operations Record: 18th Division Operations in the Hukawng Area*, Japanese Monograph 131, 1949, U.S. Army Center of Military History, Fort McNair, Washington, D.C., 10–11.
45. *Burma Operations Record: 15th Army Operations in Imphal Area and Withdrawal to Northern Burma*, Japanese Monograph 134. Headquarters, United States Army, Japan, 60.
46. *Maj. Gen. Haydon Boatner Historical Material*, Combined Arms Research Library, Fort Leavenworth Research Library Collection, WWII Operational Documents, No. 16436, 33.
47. Anders, *The Ledo Road*, 125, 136.
48. Romanus and Sunderland, *Stilwell's Command Problems*, 38.
49. *Burma Operations Record: 15th Army Operations in Imphal Area and Withdrawal to Northern Burma*, Japanese Monograph 134. Headquarters, United States Army, Japan, 60–61.
50. Hu Pu-Yu, *A Brief History of the Sino-Japanese War, 1937–1945* (Taipei: Chung Wu Publishing, 1974), 214.
51. Romanus and Sunderland, *Stilwell's Command Problems*, 44.

52. Hoover Institution Archives, The World War II Diaries of Joseph W. Stilwell, 1943, transcribed 2005, 168–69; Romanus and Sunderland, *Stilwell's Command Problems*, 125.
53. Gordon S. Seagrave, *Burma Surgeon Returns* (New York: W. W. Norton and Co., 1946), 94.
54. Hu, *A Brief History of the Sino-Japanese War*, 214; Romanus and Sunderland, *Stilwell's Command Problems*, 128.
55. "Memorandum for the President, Subject: Fighting Potential of Chinese Ground Forces," January 29, 1944, ProQuest History Vault, Folder: 003249-002-0360, Records of the War Department's Operations Division, 1942–1945, Part 1. World War II Operations, Series B, Pacific Theater.
56. Romanus and Sunderland, *Stilwell's Command Problems*, 128.
57. Memorandum for Record, Training Memorandum Number 6, November 1943, National Archives and Records Administration, Records Group 493, box 17, page 1–2.
58. Minutes of Third Conference with Officers, February 10, 1944, U.S. Army Center of Military History, Geographic Files; Tuchman, *Stilwell and the American Experience in China, 1911–1944*, 419; Marc Gallicchio, "The Other China Hands: U.S. Army Officers and America's Failure in China, 1941–1950," *Journal of American-East Asian Relations* 4, no. 1 (1995): 55.
59. Romanus and Sunderland, *Stilwell's Command Problems*, 33.
60. Walter S. Jones, "Chinese Liaison Detail," in *Crisis Fleeting: Original Reports on Military Medicine in India and Burma in the Second World War*, Office of the Surgeon General, 1969, 91.
61. Dod, *The Corps of Engineers in the War against Japan*, 444.
62. Romanus and Sunderland, *Stilwell's Command Problems*, 138.
63. Memorandum for Lt. Gen. Stilwell from Brig. Gen. H. L. Boatner, Subject: Explanations from General Liao, January 13, 1944, National Archives Microfilm Publications, M1419, "Eyes Alone" Correspondence of General Joseph W. Stilwell, January 1942–October 1944, reel 5; Shelford Bidwell, *The Chindit War: Stilwell, Wingate, and the Campaign in Burma: 1944* (New York: Macmillan, 1979), 261; McLynn, *The Burma Campaign*, 353.
64. David W. Hogan Jr., "MacArthur, Stilwell, and Special Operations in the War against Japan," *Parameters* XXV, no. 1 (Spring 1995): 108.
65. Joseph Stilwell diary transcript (37), 1944, Joseph Warren Stilwell Papers, Hoover Institution Library and Archives, 24, https://digitalcollections.hoover.org/objects/56332/joseph-stilwell-diary-transcript-37.
66. Hsu and Chang, *History of the Sino-Japanese War*, 400.
67. *Tactics and Strategy of the Japanese Army in the Burma Campaign from November 1943 to September 1944*, Joint Intelligence Collection Agency, Fort Leavenworth Research Library Collection, China-Burma-India, October 23, 1944, N-3748, 34.
68. Joseph Stilwell diary transcript (37), 1944, Joseph Warren Stilwell Papers, Hoover Institution Library and Archives, 28. https://digitalcollections.hoover.org/objects/

56332/joseph-stilwell-diary-transcript-37; Romanus and Sunderland, *Stilwell's Command Problems*, 148.
69. Bell, "A Combined Efforts," 38.
70. Dod, *The Corps of Engineers in the War against Japan*, 444.
71. Peers and Brelis, *Behind the Burma Road*, 121.
72. *Merrill's Marauders* (February–May 1944), Military Intelligence Division, U.S. War Department, 1945, 32.
73. *Burma Operations Record: 18th Division Operations in the Hukawng Area*, Japanese Monograph 131, 1949, U.S. Army Center of Military History, Fort McNair, Washington, D.C., 45–46.
74. Notes on Merrill Expedition, 1944, Joint Intelligence Coordination Agency, China-Burma-India, September 27, 1944, Fort Leavenworth Research Library Collection, N-3405, 11; *Merrill's Marauders* (February–May 1944), Military Intelligence Division, U.S. War Department, 1945, 41.
75. *Burma Operations Record: 15th Army Operations in Imphal Area and Withdrawal to Northern Burma*, Japanese Monograph 134. Headquarters, United States Army, Japan, 66; Peers and Brelis, *Behind the Burma Road*, 122–23.
76. Hsu and Chang, *History of the Sino-Japanese War*, 400.
77. Thompson and Harris, *The Signal Corps*, 194.
78. Hunter, *Galahad*, 127.
79. Romanus and Sunderland, *Stilwell's Command Problems*, 176.
80. *Merrill's Marauders* (February–May 1944), Military Intelligence Division, U.S. War Department, 1945, 49, 59.
81. Hopkins, Stelling, and Voorhees, "The Marauders and the Microbes," 307–27.
82. Hu, *A Brief History of the Sino-Japanese War*, 216.
83. Joseph Stilwell diary transcript (37), 1944, Joseph Warren Stilwell Papers, Hoover Institution Library and Archives, 34. https://digitalcollections.hoover.org/objects/56332/joseph-stilwell-diary-transcript-37.
84. Bell, "A Combined Efforts," 39; Romanus and Sunderland, *Stilwell's Command Problems*, 187.
85. Romanus and Sunderland, *Stilwell's Command Problems*, 181–82.
86. Hunter, *Galahad*, 73.
87. Mary E. Condon-Rall and Albert E. Cowdery, *Medical Service in the War against Japan* (Washington, D.C.: U.S. Army Center of Military History, 1998), 306.
88. Romanus and Sunderland, *Stilwell's Command Problems*, 191.
89. "Memorandum for the President," Gen. George C. Marshall, April 17, 1944, Franklin D. Roosevelt Presidential Library, Map Room, box 80; Radio Message from USAF Chungking to NCAC, 22 April 1944, "Eyes Alone" Correspondence of General Joseph W. Stilwell, National Archives and Records Administration, Microfilm Publication M1419, reel 3.
90. Romanus and Sunderland, *Stilwell's Command Problems*, 208.

91. Joseph Stilwell diary transcript (37), 1944, Joseph Warren Stilwell Papers, Hoover Institution Library and Archives, 57. https://digitalcollections.hoover.org/objects/56332/joseph-stilwell-diary-transcript-37.
92. Hu, *A Brief History of the Sino-Japanese War*, 216; Romanus and Sunderland, *Stilwell's Command Problems*, 215.
93. "SAC Southeast Asia to War Office," June 11, 1944, Franklin D. Roosevelt Presidential Library, Roosevelt Map Room Files, Map Room 0487, box 81, 2.
94. Mountbatten, *Report to the Combined Chiefs of Staff by the Supreme Allied Commander*, 36; McMichael, *A Historical Perspective on Light Infantry*, 4.
95. Joseph Stilwell diary transcript (37), 1944, Joseph Warren Stilwell Papers, Hoover Institution Library and Archives, 59. https://digitalcollections.hoover.org/objects/56332/joseph-stilwell-diary-transcript-37.
96. William Slim, *Defeat into Victory* (New York: David McKay Company, Inc., 1961), 275; Romanus and Sunderland, *Stilwell's Command Problems*, 221.
97. Michael Calvert, *Prisoners of Hope* (Havertown, Pa.: Pen and Sword, 2004), 250–51.
98. Mountbatten, *Report to the Combined Chiefs of Staff by the Supreme Allied Commander*, 63; Slim, *Defeat into Victory*, 279; Philip Ziegler, *Mountbatten* (New York: Harper & Row, 1986), 284.
99. Bidwell, *The Chindit War*, 266–68.
100. Calvert, *Prisoners of Hope*, 220–24; Joseph Stilwell diary transcript (37), 1944, Joseph Warren Stilwell Papers, Hoover Institution Library and Archives, 66. https://digitalcollections.hoover.org/objects/56332/joseph-stilwell-diary-transcript-37; Bidwell, *The Chindit War*, 270; Hu, *A Brief History of the Sino-Japanese War*, 216.
101. Luo, Man, *Lanying bingtuan: Zhongguo yuanzheng jun mian yin xie zhan ji* [The Blue Eagles: China's Expeditionary Force in Burma and India] (Taipei: Xing Guang Publishers, 1991), 187; *Merrill's Marauders* (February–May 1944), Military Intelligence Division, U.S. War Department, 1945, 94–97.
102. Office of the Chief of Military History, History of the Northern Combat Area Command, China-Burma-India Theater and India-Burma Theater, 1943–1945, appendix 8, detachment 101, October 1943–June 1945, U.S. Army Center of Military History, Fort McNair, Washington, D.C., 2.
103. Hunter, *Galahad*, 97.
104. *Merrill's Marauders* (February–May 1944), Military Intelligence Division, U.S. War Department, 1945, 109.
105. "CG U.S. Army China Burma India to War Department," May 22, 1944, Franklin D. Roosevelt Presidential Library, Map Room 0486, box 81.
106. Romanus and Sunderland, *Stilwell's Command Problems*, 237.
107. Romanus and Sunderland, *Stilwell's Command Problems*, 244.
108. Joseph Stilwell diary transcript (37), 1944, Joseph Warren Stilwell Papers, Hoover Institution Library and Archives, 62. https://digitalcollections.hoover.org/objects/56332/joseph-stilwell-diary-transcript-37.

109. Romanus and Sunderland, *Stilwell's Command Problems*, 250.
110. Dod, *The Corps of Engineers in the War against Japan*, 455.
111. Nathan N. Prefer, *Vinegar Joe's War: Stilwell's Campaigns for Burma* (Novato, Calif.: Presidio Press, 2000), 175–77.
112. Romanus and Sunderland, *Stilwell's Command Problems*, 250.
113. Romanus and Sunderland, *Stilwell's Command Problems*, 240.
114. *Development of Joint Air Ground Operations in North Burma*, Headquarters, 10th Air Force, Fort Leavenworth Research Library Collection, N-8226, 11.
115. "Main 11 Army Group SEA to War Department," August 5, 1944, Franklin D. Roosevelt Presidential Library, Roosevelt Map Room Files, Map Room 0490, box 82, 2; *Maj. Gen. Haydon Boatner Historical Material*, Combined Arms Research Library, Fort Leavenworth Research Library Collection, WWII Operational Documents, No. 16436, 49; Hoover Institution Archives, The World War II Diaries of Joseph W. Stilwell, 1944, transcribed 2005, 239.
116. Romanus and Sunderland, *Stilwell's Command Problems*, 253.
117. Christopher Thorne, *Allies of a Kind: The United States, Britain, and the War against Japan, 1941–1945* (New York: Oxford University Press, 1978), 453; McMichael, *A Historical Perspective on Light Infantry*, 233.
118. Condon-Rall and Cowdery, *Medical Service in the War against Japan*, 310–11.
119. Hopkins, Stelling, and Voorhees, "The Marauders and the Microbes," 307–8.
120. Thompson and Harris, *The Signal Corps*, 196.
121. Maj. Gen. W. J. Officer, "With Wingate's Chindits," in *Crisis Fleeting: Original Reports on Military Medicine in India and Burma in the Second World War*, Office of the Surgeon General, 1969, 212.
122. Hunter, *Galahad*, 146.
123. Bidwell, *The Chindit War*, 20–24.
124. Maj. Gen. H. L. Boatner, A Statement of the Record by Maj. Gen. H. L. Boatner, Hoover Archives, box 2, 35–36.
125. *Stilwell Road Report*, Col. A. C. Welling, Theater Engineer, August 14, 1945, Fort Leavenworth Research Library Collection, R-10889, 14–19.
126. *Maj. Gen. Haydon Boatner Historical Material*, Combined Arms Research Library, Fort Leavenworth Research Library Collection, WWII Operational Documents, No. 16436, 135.
127. Seagrave, *Burma Surgeon Returns*, 89.
128. *A Report Summarizing the Activities of U.S. Army Medical Department Units Assigned to Northern Combat Area Command during the Northern and Central Burma Campaigns*, Fort Leavenworth Research Library Collection, N-11207 A; Charlton Ogburn Jr., *The Marauders* (Woodstock, N.Y.: Overlook Press, 1959), 226.
129. *Growth, Development and Operating Procedures of the Air Supply and Evacuation System*, Northern Combat Area Command Front, Burma Campaign, 1943–1945, Fort Leavenworth Research Library Collection, N-11207 B.

130. "War Department to CG U.S. Army Forces China Burma India," April 15, 1944, Franklin D. Roosevelt Presidential Library, box 80.
131. Dod, *The Corps of Engineers in the War against Japan*, 463.
132. *G-4 Periodic Report, Period Ending 30 September 1944*, Headquarters, U.S. Forces, India-Burma Theater, Fort Leavenworth Research Library Collection, N-4429, enclosure 17.
133. Ogburn, *The Marauders*, 1.
134. Tuchman, *Stilwell and the American Experience in China, 1911–1944*, 415.
135. Gary J. Bjorge, *Merrill's Marauders: Combined Operations in Northern Burma in 1944* (Fort Leavenworth, Combat Studies Institute, 1996), 43.
136. Hunter, *Galahad*, 49.
137. Hunter, *Galahad*, 30.
138. Eldridge, *Wrath in Burma*, 166.
139. Ogburn, *The Marauders*, 251.

CHAPTER 5. DIRECTING ALLIES IN YUNNAN

1. Radio Message, July 2, 1944, Marshall to Stilwell, "Eyes Alone" Correspondence of General Joseph W. Stilwell, National Archives and Records Administration, Microfilm Publication M1419, reel 4.
2. Wesley Frank Craven and James Lea Cate, *The Army Air Forces in World War II: Volume IV: The Pacific: Matterhorn to Nagasaki, June 1944 to August 1945* (Washington, D.C.: Office of Air Force History, 1983), 213–14.
3. Charles Romanus and Riley Sunderland, *Stilwell's Mission to China* (Washington, D.C.: U.S. Army Center of Military History, 1953), 38.
4. *The Salween Campaign: China, May 1944–January 1945*, G. B. Coverdale, Fort Leavenworth Research Library Collection, Command and General Staff College, N-2253.74, 3; Journal for 1943, John C. H. Lee letter to Stilwell, War Department orders, and Domestic Disturbances Conference manual, 1917/1945, Joseph Warren Stilwell Papers, Hoover Institution Library and Archives, https://digitalcollections.hoover.org/objects/62938/journal-for-1943-john-c-h-lee-letter-to-stilwell-war-dep.
5. Philip Jowett, *Soldiers of the White Sun: The Chinese Army at War, 1931–1949* (Atglen, Pa.: Schiffer Military History, 2011), 125–29.
6. Daniel Jackson, *Famine, Sword, and Fire: The Liberation of Southwest China in World War II* (Atglen, Pa.: Schiffer Publishing, 2015), 64; Marc Gallicchio, "The Other China Hands: U.S. Army Officers and America's Failure in China, 1941-1950," *Journal of American-East Asian Relations* 4, no. 1 (1995): 52.
7. Jackson, *Famine, Sword, and Fire*, 65.
8. Chang Jui-Te, "The National Army from Whampoa to 1949," in *A Military History of China*, ed. David A. Graff and Robin Higham (Lexington: University of Kentucky Press, 2002), 203.

9. G-1 periodic report, June 4, 1944, Joseph Warren Stilwell Papers, Hoover Institution Library and Archives, https://digitalcollections.hoover.org/objects/62922/g1-periodic-report.
10. Alfred E. Cornebise, *Soldier Extraordinaire: The Life and Career of Brig. Gen. Frank "Pinkie" Dorn (1901–81)* (Fort Leavenworth, Kan.: Combat Studies Institute Press, 2019), 124.
11. Claire Lee Chennault, *Way of a Fighter: The Memoirs of Claire Lee Chennault* (New York: G. P. Putnam, 1949), 275.
12. "New Delhi to AGWAR," October 29, 1943, Franklin D. Roosevelt Presidential Library, Map Room 300, box 80.
13. Riley Sunderland and Charles F. Romanus, eds., *Stilwell's Personal File: China-Burma-India, 1942–1944* (Wilmington DE: Scholarly Resources, 1976), 508.
14. Cornebise, *Soldier Extraordinaire*, 120.
15. Ting Guo, *Surviving Violent Conflicts: Chinese Interpreters in the Second Sino-Japanese War 1931–1945* (London: Palgrave Macmillan, 2016), 45–46; Jackson, *Famine, Sword, and Fire*, 65.
16. Mary E. Condon-Rall and Albert E. Cowdery, *Medical Service in the War against Japan* (Washington, D.C.: U.S. Army Center of Military History, 1998), 315.
17. Romanus and Sunderland, *Stilwell's Mission to China*, 292.
18. Romanus and Sunderland, *Stilwell's Mission to China*, 297.
19. Ambassador Walter E. Jenkins Jr., interview, February 20, 1991, 4, Association for Diplomatic Studies and Training, Foreign Affairs Oral History Project.
20. Romanus and Sunderland, *Stilwell's Mission to China*, 351.
21. Romanus and Sunderland, *Stilwell's Mission to China*, 300.
22. Romanus and Sunderland, *Stilwell's Mission to China*, 352–53.
23. "Status of Chinese Forces in Yunnan" (no date, likely early 1944), Frank Dorn Papers, Stanford University, Hoover Institution Archives, box 1, 1.
24. Yang Chenguan, "Guojun weiwan cheng de junshi shiwu daige (1943–1945) yi guojun meishi zhuangbeihua budui wei zhongxin de shentan," *Zhonghua junshi xue huiyi huikan* 10 (April 1995), 166–68; Charles F. Romanus and Riley Sunderland, *Stilwell's Command Problems* (Washington, D.C.: U.S. Government Printing Office, 1955), 334.
25. *The Salween Campaign: China, May 1944–January 1945.*
26. Romanus and Sunderland, *Stilwell's Command Problems*, 298.
27. Peiji Tang, *Kangzhan shiqi de duiwai guanxi* [Foreign relations during the Sino-Japanese War] (Beijing: Beijing Yanshan chubanshe, 1997), 318–19.
28. Wenzhao Tao, *Kangri zhanzheng shiqi Zhongguo duiwai guanxi* [Foreign relations during the Sino-Japanese War era] (Beijing: Zhongguo shehui kexue chubanshe, 2009), 310; Romanus and Sunderland, *Stilwell's Command Problems*, 310.
29. *The Papers of George Catlett Marshall*, ed. Larry I. Bland and Sharon Ritenour Stevens (Lexington, Va.: The George C. Marshall Foundation, 1981–). Electronic version based on *The Papers of George Catlett Marshall*, vol. 4, *"Aggressive and Determined Leadership," June 1, 1943–December 31, 1944* (Baltimore: The Johns Hopkins University

Press, 1996) (hereafter Marshall, vol. 4), 408; Romanus and Sunderland, *Stilwell's Command Problems*, 312–13.
30. John Paton Davies Jr., *China Hand: An Autobiography* (Philadelphia: University of Pennsylvania Press, 2012), 184; Marshall, vol. 4, 413–14.
31. Cornebise, *Soldier Extraordinaire*, 140.
32. *Burma Operations Record, 33rd Army Operations*, Japanese Monograph No. 148, Assistant Chief of Staff G-2, USARJ, August 1960, 9.
33. Asano Toyomi, "Japanese Operations in Yunnan and North Burma," in *The Battle for China: Essays on the Military History of the Sino-Japanese War of 1937–1945*, ed. Mark Peattie, Edward J. Drea, and Hans van de Ven (Stanford, Calif.: Stanford University Press, 2011), 366; *Burma Operations Record, 33rd Army Operations*, Japanese Monograph No. 148, Assistant Chief of Staff G-2, USARJ, August 1960, 42; William Slim, *Defeat into Victory* (New York: David McKay Company, Inc., 1961), 276.
34. *Burma Operations Record, 33rd Army Operations*, Japanese Monograph No. 148, Assistant Chief of Staff G-2, USARJ, August 1960, 44.
35. Lai Cheng-liang, "The Battle of the Salween River" (U.S. Army Command and General Staff College, Student Paper, 1947), 2.
36. "Status of Chinese Forces in Yunnan" (no date, likely early 1944), Frank Dorn Papers, Stanford University, Hoover Archives, box 1, 3; Cornebise, *Soldier Extraordinaire*, 126; Jackson, *Famine, Sword, and Fire*, 97.
37. Hsu Long-hsuen and Chang Ming-kai, *History of the Sino-Japanese War* (Taipei: Chung Wu Publishing, 1971), 409.
38. Hsu and Chang, *History of the Sino-Japanese War*, 398, 409.
39. *The Salween Campaign: China, May 1944–January 1945*, 7; Donald Q. Harris, "Organizing Artillery Battalions in China," *Field Artillery Journal* 35, no. 6 (June 1945): 323.
40. Joseph Stilwell, *The Stilwell Papers*, ed. Theodore H. White (New York: Sloane and Associates, 1948), 263–64.
41. Romanus and Sunderland, *Stilwell's Command Problems*, 334.
42. *Supply of Chinese Forces*, R-12980, Headquarters, United States Army Forces CBI, Fort Leavenworth Research Library Collection, January 1, 1944, 11.
43. Cornebise, *Soldier Extraordinaire*, 136.
44. Romanus and Sunderland, *Stilwell's Command Problems*, 339–40.
45. Romanus and Sunderland, *Stilwell's Command Problems*, 335.
46. "CG U.S. Army Forces China Burma India to War Department," May 14, 1944, Franklin D. Roosevelt Presidential Library, Map Room 0486, box 81; Hsu and Chang, *History of the Sino-Japanese War*, 409.
47. Memorandum for General Hsiao I-Hsu, Field Headquarters, Y Force Operations Staff, May 18, 1944, Frank Dorn Papers, Hoover Archives, Stanford University, box 1.
48. "CG U.S. Army Forces China Burma India to War Department," May 31, 1944, Franklin D. Roosevelt Presidential Library, Map Room 0486, box 81.

49. Karl C. Dod, *The Corps of Engineers in the War against Japan* (Washington, D.C.: U.S. Army Center of Military History, 1987), 459.
50. Jackson, *Famine, Sword, and Fire*, 124–25; Gallicchio, "The Other China Hands," 59–60.
51. P. M. Judson, "The Operations of the Fifty-Third Army, CEF, Culminating in the Battle for Muse and Tachingshan 3 Dec 44–27 Jan 45" (U.S. Army Command and General Staff College, Student Paper, 1947), 2.
52. Romanus and Sunderland, *Stilwell's Command Problems*, 352.
53. *Burma Operations Record, 33rd Army Operations*, Japanese Monograph No. 148, Assistant Chief of Staff G-2, USARJ, August 1960, 50; Memorandum for General Hsiao I-Hsu, Field Headquarters, Y Force Operations Staff, May 18, 1944, Frank Dorn Papers, Hoover Archives, Stanford University, box 1.
54. Jackson, *Famine, Sword, and Fire*, 127.
55. Romanus and Sunderland, *Stilwell's Command Problems*, 353–54.
56. Romanus and Sunderland, *Stilwell's Command Problems*, 355.
57. G-4 report Western Front, June 18, 1944, Joseph Warren Stilwell Papers, Hoover Institution Library and Archives, https://digitalcollections.hoover.org/objects/62933/g4-report-western-front.
58. Romanus and Sunderland, *Stilwell's Command Problems*, 355.
59. Joseph Tussman, Oral History interview, University of California, Berkeley, Bancroft Library, October 21, 2004, 62.
60. Jackson, *Famine, Sword, and Fire*, 136.
61. "CG U.S. Army Forces in China Burma India to War Department," June 19, 1944, Franklin D. Roosevelt Presidential Library, Map Room 0488, box 81.
62. Hsu and Chang, *History of the Sino-Japanese War*, 411.
63. *Burma Operations Record, 33rd Army Operations*, Japanese Monograph No. 148, Assistant Chief of Staff G-2, USARJ, August 1960, 94; G-2 periodic report, June 11, 1944, Joseph Warren Stilwell Papers, Hoover Institution Library and Archives, https://digitalcollections.hoover.org/objects/62929/g2-periodic-report; Hsu and Chang, *History of the Sino-Japanese War*, 410.
64. Condon-Rall and Cowdery, *Medical Service in the War against Japan*, 315; Romanus and Sunderland, *Stilwell's Command Problems*, 391.
65. Donovan Webster, *The Burma Road: The Epic Story of the China-Burma-India Theater in World War II* (New York: HarperCollins, 2004), 275.
66. *Chinese Operations on Salween Front*, Field Headquarters, Y Force Operations Staff, N-3571, August 11, 1944, Fort Leavenworth Research Library Collection, 4.
67. *The Salween Campaign: China, May 1944–January 1945*, 13; Frank Dorn, *Walkout: With Stilwell in Burma* (New York: Thomas Y. Crowell Co., 1971), 94.
68. *Burma Operations Record, 33rd Army Operations*, Japanese Monograph No. 148, Assistant Chief of Staff G-2, USARJ, August 1960, 99; "CG U.S. Army Forces China Burma India to War Department," September 15, 1944, Franklin D. Roosevelt Presidential Library, Roosevelt Map Room Files, Map Room 0490, box 82.

69. Judson, "The Operations of the Fifty-Third Army, CEF," 2.
70. *Burma Operations Record, 33rd Army Operations,* Japanese Monograph No. 148, Assistant Chief of Staff G-2, USARJ, August 1960, 81.
71. Benshu Xie, *Minguo jinglü, Dianjun fengyun* [The first half of the twentieth century: Yunnan military history] (Kunming: Yunnan renmin chubanshe, 2004), 286.
72. Romanus and Sunderland, *Stilwell's Command Problems*, 395.
73. *The Salween Campaign: China, May 1944–January 1945*, 12; Romanus and Sunderland, *Stilwell's Command Problems*, 396.
74. Lloyd E. Eastman, *Seeds of Destruction: Nationalist China in War and Revolution, 1937–1949* (Stanford, Calif.: Stanford University Press, 1984), 145.
75. Lai, "The Battle of the Salween River," 6; Romanus and Sunderland, *Stilwell's Command Problems*, 397.
76. "Chinese Operations on Salween Front," Field Headquarters, Y Force Operations Staff, N-3571, August 11, 1944, Fort Leavenworth Research Library Collection, 7.
77. Webster, *The Burma Road*, 274; "Chinese Operations on Salween Front," Field Headquarters, Y Force Operations Staff, N-3571, August 11, 1944, Fort Leavenworth Research Library Collection, 5.
78. He Yingqin, *Banian kangzhan* [Eight years of war against Japan] (Taipei: Zaiban, 1969), 232; *Burma Operations Record, 33rd Army Operations,* Japanese Monograph No. 148, Assistant Chief of Staff G-2, USARJ, August 1960, 88; *The Salween Campaign: China, May 1944–January 1945*, 12.
79. Xie, *Minguo jinglü, Dianjun fengyun*, 287; Jackson, *Famine, Sword, and Fire*, 158.
80. Hsu and Chang, *History of the Sino-Japanese War*, 410; *Burma Operations Record, 33rd Army Operations,* Japanese Monograph No. 148, Assistant Chief of Staff G-2, USARJ, August 1960, 90; Romanus and Sunderland, *Stilwell's Command Problems*, 398.
81. Toyomi, "Japanese Operations in Yunnan and North Burma," 370; "CG U.S. Army Forces, China Burma India to War Department, June 30, 1944, Franklin D. Roosevelt Presidential Library, Map Room 0488, box 81.
82. Cornebise, *Soldier Extraordinaire*, 145.
83. Chang Rui-te, "The Nationalist Army on the Eve of the War," in *The Battle for China: Essays on the Military History of the Sino-Japanese War of 1937–1945*, ed. Mark Peattie, Edward J. Drea, and Hans van de Ven (Stanford, Calif.: Stanford University Press, 2011), 91.
84. George W. Thomas, interview, Rutgers Oral History Archives for World War II, October 7, 1995, 22–23.
85. Ting, *Surviving Violent Conflicts*, 69; John C. H. Lee letter to Stilwell, War Department orders, and Domestic Disturbances Conference manual, 1917/1945, Journal for 1943, Joseph Warren Stilwell Papers, Hoover Institution Library and Archives, https://digitalcollections.hoover.org/objects/62938/journal-for-1943-john-c-h-lee-letter-to-stilwell-war-dep.

86. Message to Ferris from Dorn, Eyes Alone, June 26, 1944, "Eyes Alone" Correspondence of General Joseph W. Stilwell, National Archives and Records Administration, Microfilm Publication M1419, reel 4.
87. Slim, *Defeat into Victory*, 277.
88. Judson, "The Operations of the Fifty-Third Army, CEF," 6.
89. G-1, G-2, G-3, and G-4 reports, 1944/06-25/1944-07-17, Joseph Warren Stilwell Papers, Hoover Institution Library and Archives, https://digitalcollections.hoover.org/objects/62937/g1-g2-g3-and-g4-reports.

CHAPTER 6. SUPPORTING LOCAL ALLIES

1. Joseph Stilwell, *The Stilwell Papers*, ed. Theodore H. White (New York: Sloane and Associates, 1948), 256.
2. Riley Sunderland and Charles F. Romanus, eds., *Stilwell's Personal File: China-Burma-India, 1942–1944* (Wilmington, Del.: Scholarly Resources, 1976), 2114; Charles F. Romanus and Riley Sunderland, *Stilwell's Command Problems* (Washington, D.C.: U.S. Government Printing Office, 1955), 320.
3. *History of the India-Burma Theater, Vol. I*, December 6, 1945, Combined Arms Research Library, Fort Leavenworth Research Library Collection, WWII Operational Documents, no. 4709, 23.
4. Mary E. Condon-Rall and Albert E. Cowdery, *Medical Service in the War against Japan* (Washington, D.C.: U.S. Army Center of Military History, 1998), 316.
5. Radio Message, November 22, 1943, Dorn to Stilwell, "Eyes Alone" Correspondence of General Joseph W. Stilwell, National Archives and Records Administration, Microfilm Publication M1419, reel 2.
6. Radio Message, November 28, Dorn to Stilwell, "Eyes Alone" Correspondence of General Joseph W. Stilwell, National Archives and Records Administration, Microfilm Publication M1419, reel 2.
7. Memorandum for the President, Cordell Hull, December 2, 1943, Franklin D. Roosevelt Presidential Library, PSFA 0268, China, 1943.
8. The Ambassador in China (Gauss) to the Secretary of State, Chungking, January 14, 1944, in *Foreign Relations of the United States, 1944*, vol. 6, *China* (Washington, D.C.: Government Printing Office, 1967), document 7.
9. The Ambassador in China (Gauss) to the Secretary of State, Chungking, January 18, 1944, in *Foreign Relations of the United States, 1944*, vol. 6, *China* (Washington, D.C.: Government Printing Office, 1967), document 8.
10. Romanus and Sunderland, *Stilwell's Command Problems*, 298.
11. Letter from Chiang Kai-shek to Franklin D. Roosevelt, February 3, 1944, "Eyes Alone" Correspondence of General Joseph W. Stilwell, National Archives and Records Administration, Microfilm Publication M1419, reel 3; Paraphrase of Telegram Sent to Secretary of State, U.S. Embassy, Chungking, February 12, 1944, "Eyes Alone" Correspondence of General Joseph W. Stilwell, National Archives and

Records Administration, Microfilm Publication M1419, reel 3; Michael J. Green, *By More than Providence: Grand Strategy and American Power in the Asia Pacific Since 1783* (New York: Columbia University Press, 2017), 214; H. H. Arnold, Memorandum for the Chief of Staff, Subject: Rate of Exchange with Chinese, February 18, 1944, George Marshall correspondence on China and India, ProQuest History Vault. Folder: 003255-008-0346 Date: Jan 1, 1944–Jun 30, 1944, Papers of George C. Marshall: Selected World War II Correspondence; Romanus and Sunderland, *Stilwell's Command Problems*, 300.

12. Dayna Barnes, "Plans and Expectations: The American News Media and Postwar Japan," *Japanese Studies* 34, no. 3 (2014): 6.
13. Hsu Long-hsuen and Chang Ming-kai, *History of the Sino-Japanese War* (Taipei: Chung Wu Publishing, 1971), 423.
14. Claire Lee Chennault, *Way of a Fighter: The Memoirs of Claire Lee Chennault* (New York: G. P. Putnam, 1949), 262.
15. Lloyd E. Eastman, *Seeds of Destruction: Nationalist China in War and Revolution, 1937–1949* (Stanford, Calif.: Stanford University Press, 1984), 143.
16. The Consul at Kweilin (Ringwalt) to the Ambassador in China (Gauss), May 30, 1944, in *Foreign Relations of the United States, 1944*, vol. 6, *China* (Washington, D.C.: Government Printing Office, 1967), document 80.
17. Hsi-Sheng Chi, *Nationalist China at War: Military Defeats and Political Collapse, 1937–1945* (Ann Arbor: University of Michigan Press, 1982), 102.
18. Radio Message Stilwell to Marshall, March 30, 1944, ProQuest History Vault, Folder: 003255-008-0346, Date: Jan 1, 1944–Jun 30, 1944, Papers of George C. Marshall: Selected World War II Correspondence; Romanus and Sunderland, *Stilwell's Command Problems*, 303–4.
19. Tao Wenzhao, *Kangri zhanzheng shiqi Zhongguo duiwai guanxi* [Foreign relations during the Sino-Japanese War era] (Beijing: Zhongguo shehui kexue chubanshe, 2009), 312; Message to Ferris to Stilwell, Eyes Alone, June 25, 1944, "Eyes Alone" Correspondence of General Joseph W. Stilwell, National Archives and Records Administration, Microfilm Publication M1419, reel 4; Barbara Tuchman, *Stilwell and the American Experience in China, 1911–1945* (New York: Macmillan Publishers, 1970), 464.
20. *The Papers of George Catlett Marshall*, ed. Larry I. Bland and Sharon Ritenour Stevens (Lexington, Va.: The George C. Marshall Foundation, 1981–). Electronic version based on *The Papers of George Catlett Marshall*, vol. 4, *"Aggressive and Determined Leadership," June 1, 1943–December 31, 1944* (Baltimore: The Johns Hopkins University Press, 1996) (hereafter Marshall, vol. 4), 249–50.
21. H. P. Willmott, *Grave of a Dozen Schemes: British Naval Planning and the War against Japan, 1943–1945* (Annapolis, Md.: Naval Institute Press, 1996), 49–65.
22. Wesley F. Craven and James L. Cate, *The Army Air Forces in World War II: Volume IV: The Pacific: Guadalcanal to Saipan, August 1942 to July 1944* (Washington, D.C.: Office of Air Force History, 1983), 497–98; Tuchman, *Stilwell and the American Experience in*

China, 1911–1944, 428–31; Christopher Thorne, *Allies of a Kind: The United States, Britain, and the War against Japan, 1941–1945* (New York: Oxford University Press, 1978), 410; Marshall, vol. 4, 298–99.
23. Albert C. Wedemeyer, Oral History Interview, February 28, 1973, 13–14, Senior Officers Debriefing Program, Army Heritage and Education Center, Carlisle, PA.
24. "Chiefs of Staff to Joint Staff Mission," February 28, 1944, Franklin D. Roosevelt Presidential Library, Map Room 0484, box 80.
25. Radio Message, From CG, U.S. Army (Marshall) to CG, USAF in CBI (Stilwell), March 2, 1944, "Eyes Alone" Correspondence of General Joseph W. Stilwell, National Archives and Records Administration, Microfilm Publication M1419, reel 3; Marshall, vol. 4, 321–23.
26. Radio Message Stilwell to Marshall, March 7, 1944, George Marshall correspondence on China and India, ProQuest History Vault, Folder: 003255-008-0346 Date: Jan 1, 1944–Jun 30, 1944, Papers of George C. Marshall: Selected World War II Correspondence; Tuchman, *Stilwell and the American Experience in China, 1911–1944*, 437.
27. The Ambassador in China (Gauss) to the Secretary of State, Chungking, February 9, 1944, in *Foreign Relations of the United States, 1944*, vol. 6, *China* (Washington: Government Printing Office, 1967), document 17.
28. Memorandum of Conversation, Military-Political Problems in the China-Burma-India Theater," February 23, 1944, ProQuest History Vault, Folder: 003249-002-0360, Records of the War Department's Operations Division, 1942–1945, Part 1. World War II Operations, Series B, Pacific Theater.
29. Chi, *Nationalist China at War*, 73–74.
30. *Army Operations in China, January 1944–August 1945*, Japanese Monograph 72, Headquarters, U.S. Army Forces Far East, 18.
31. Romanus and Sunderland, *Stilwell's Command Problems*, 306.
32. *Report: The President and U.S. Aid to China*, November 18, 1944, U.S. Army Center of Military History Geographic Files, China-Burma-India, 32.
33. Sunderland and Romanus, *Stilwell's Personal File*, 1817.
34. Craven and Cate, *The Army Air Forces in World War II: Volume IV*, 541.
35. Romanus and Sunderland, *Stilwell's Command Problems*, 315.
36. Maj. Gen. Claire L. Chennault to President Roosevelt, Headquarters 14th Air Force [in China], April 19, 1944, in *Foreign Relations of the United States, 1944*, vol. 6, *China* (Washington: Government Printing Office, 1967), document 53.
37. Romanus and Sunderland, *Stilwell's Command Problems*, 308.
38. Instructions to Commanding General, Army Air Forces in China-Burma-India, on air support of Pacific Operations, Joint Chiefs of Staff, JCS 839, April 28, 1944, page 2, ProQuest History Vault, Folder: 003183-010-0736 Date: Apr 28, 1944–Apr 28, 1944, Records of the Joint Chiefs of Staff, Part 1: 1942–1945, The Pacific Theater.
39. Craven and Cate, *The Army Air Forces in World War II: Volume IV*, 544; *Army Operations in China, January 1944–August 1945*, Japanese Monograph 72, Headquarters, U.S. Army

Forces Far East, 63; "Director Intelligence Chungking (Navy) to CNO," May 8, 1944, Franklin D. Roosevelt Presidential Library, Map Room 486a, box 81; Tang Tsou, *America's Failure in China, 1941–1950* (Chicago: University of Chicago Press, 1963), 112.
40. Wang Chaoguang, "The Dark Side of the War: Corruption in the Guomindang Government during World War II," *Journal of Modern Chinese History* 11, no. 2 (2017): 254–55.
41. Eastman, *Seeds of Destruction*, 139.
42. Hsi-sheng Chi, "The Military Dimension, 1942–1945," in *China's Bitter Victory: The War with Japan 1937–1945*, ed. James C. Hsiung and Steven I. Levine (Armonk, N.Y.: M. E. Sharpe, Inc., 1992), 171; Jonathan Fenby, *Chiang Kai-shek and the China He Lost* (London: Free Press, 2003), 417.
43. War Cabinet, W.P. 44 (631), November 8, 1944, United Kingdom, National Archives, Reference # CAB 66/57/31, 1–4.
44. Romanus and Sunderland, *Stilwell's Command Problems*, 366.
45. Wesley Frank Craven and James Lea Cate, *The Army Air Forces in World War II: Volume V: The Pacific: Matterhorn to Nagasaki, June 1944 to August 1945* (Washington, D.C.: Office of Air Force History, 1983), 220; Romanus and Sunderland, *Stilwell's Command Problems*, 369; Tuchman, *Stilwell and the American Experience in China; 1911–1945*, 458–59.
46. Craven and Cate, *The Army Air Forces in World War II: Volume V*, 221.
47. Joseph Bykofsky and Harold Larson, *The Transportation Corps: Operations Overseas* (Washington, D.C.: Center of Military History, 1990), 591–93.
48. Chennault, *Way of a Fighter*, 290–91.
49. Ronald H. Spector, *Eagle against the Sun: The American War with Japan* (New York: Random House, 1985), 366–67; Romanus and Sunderland, *Stilwell's Command Problems*, 326.
50. "CG U.S. Army Forces China Burma India Forward Echelon to War Department," June 5, 1944, Franklin D. Roosevelt Presidential Library, Roosevelt Map Room Files, Map Room 0487, box 81, 3.
51. Marshall, vol. 4, 466–67.
52. Romanus and Sunderland, *Stilwell's Command Problems*, 362–63.
53. Romanus and Sunderland, *Stilwell's Command Problems*, 364.
54. The Ambassador in China (Gauss) to the Secretary of State Chungking, June 15, 1944, in *Foreign Relations of the United States*, vol. 6, *China*, document 93.
55. "U.S. Military Attaché, Chungking to War Department," June 28, 1944, Franklin D. Roosevelt Presidential Library, Map Room 0488, box 81.
56. Maurice Matloff, *Strategic Planning for Coalition Warfare, 1943–1944* (Washington, D.C.: Government Printing Office, 1999), 441–42.
57. John Paton Davies Jr., *China Hand: An Autobiography* (Philadelphia: University of Pennsylvania Press, 2012), 188.
58. Jay Taylor, *The Generalissimo: Chiang Kai-shek and the Struggle for Modern China* (Cambridge, Mass.: Belknap, 2009), 277.

59. Romanus and Sunderland, *Stilwell's Command Problems*, 382; Marshall, vol. 4, 503–6.
60. Joseph E. Persico, *Roosevelt's Centurions: FDR and the Commanders He Led to Victory in World War II* (New York: Random House, 2013), 418–19; Message to Stilwell from Marshall, Eyes Alone, July 2, 1944, "Eyes Alone" Correspondence of General Joseph W. Stilwell, National Archives and Records Administration, Microfilm Publication M1419, reel 4.
61. *Report on Official Trip to China-Burma-India from 5 August to 17 October 1944*, Chief, Overseas Branch, Supply Division, February 2, 1945, Fort Leavenworth Command and General Staff College, 1.
62. Message, Washington to Chungking, July 6, 1944, "Eyes Alone" Correspondence of General Joseph W. Stilwell, National Archives and Records Administration, Microfilm Publication M1419, reel 5; Runming Tang, *Kangzhan shiqi Chongqing junshi* [Chongqing military affairs during the Sino-Japanese War] (Chongqing: Chongqing chubanshe, 1995), 186.
63. Peiji Tang, *Kangzhan shiqi de duiwai guanxi* [Foreign relations during the Sino-Japanese War] (Beijing: Beijing Yanshan chubanshe, 1997), 328–29.
64. George Marshall correspondence with Albert C. Wedemeyer, July 7, 1944, ProQuest History Vault, Folder: 003255-039-0766 Date: Jan 1, 1944–Jul 31, 1944, Papers of George C. Marshall: Selected World War II Correspondence; Fenby, *Chiang Kai-shek*, 423.
65. Romanus and Sunderland, *Stilwell's Command Problems*, 385–86.
66. Marshall, vol. 4, 508–10.
67. Hu Pu-Yu, *A Brief History of the Sino-Japanese War, 1937–1945* (Taipei: Chung Wu Publishing, 1974), 226.
68. Albert C. Wedemeyer, *Wedemeyer Reports!: An Objective, Dispassionate Examination of World War II, Postwar Policies, and Grand Strategy* (New York: Henry Holt and Co., 1958), 275; Tuchman, *Stilwell and the American Experience in China; 1911–1945*, 472.
69. Romanus and Sunderland, *Stilwell's Command Problems*, 372.
70. Hu, *A Brief History of the Sino-Japanese War*, 227; Hsu and Chang, *History of the Sino-Japanese War*, 425.
71. Huang, Qiang, *Hengyang kangzhan si shi ba tian* [Hengyang's 48 day battle]. (Taipei: Zaiban, 1977), 80–92; *Army Operations in China, January 1944–August 1945*, Japanese Monograph 72, Headquarters, U.S. Army Forces Far East, 84; Hsu and Chang, *History of the Sino-Japanese War*, 423, 525; Chi, *Nationalist China at War*, 77; Chennault, *Way of a Fighter*, 297.
72. Craven and Cate, *The Army Air Forces in World War II: Volume V*, 223; Romanus and Sunderland, *Stilwell's Command Problems*, 400–401; F. F. Liu, *A Military History of Modern China* (Princeton, N.J.: Princeton University Press, 1956), 220.
73. Peter Chen-main Wang, "Chiang Kai-shek's Faith in Christianity: The Trial of the Stilwell Incident," *Journal of Modern Chinese History* 8, no. 2 (2014): 204.
74. Taylor, *The Generalissimo*, 272.

75. Message to Stilwell from Hearn, Eyes Alone, July 20, 1944, "Eyes Alone" Correspondence of General Joseph W. Stilwell, National Archives and Records Administration, Microfilm Publication M1419, reel 4.
76. Message to Hearn from Lindsey, Eyes Alone, July 21, 1944, "Eyes Alone" Correspondence of General Joseph W. Stilwell, National Archives and Records Administration, Microfilm Publication M1419, reel 4.
77. Message to Lindsey and Chennault from Hearn, Eyes Alone, July 24, 1944, "Eyes Alone" Correspondence of General Joseph W. Stilwell, National Archives and Records Administration, Microfilm Publication M1419, reel 4.
78. Romanus and Sunderland, *Stilwell's Command Problems*, 402.
79. Eastman, *Seeds of Destruction*, 29.
80. Chi, *Nationalist China at War*, 114.
81. Romanus and Sunderland, *Stilwell's Command Problems*, 408.
82. Tuchman, *Stilwell and the American Experience in China; 1911–1945*, 475; Romanus and Sunderland, *Stilwell's Command Problems*, 409.
83. Romanus and Sunderland, *Stilwell's Command Problems*, 410.
84. Tuchman, *Stilwell and the American Experience in China; 1911–1945*, 380.
85. T'ien-wei Wu. "Contending Political Forces," in *China's Bitter Victory: The War with Japan 1937–1945*, ed. James C. Hsiung and Steven I. Levine (Armonk, N.Y.: M. E. Sharpe, Inc., 1992), 411.
86. Message Stilwell to Marshall, August 10, 1944, George Marshall correspondence on China and India, ProQuest History Vault, Folder: 003255-008-0364, Date: July 1, 1944–Aug 31, 1944, Papers of George C. Marshall: Selected World War II Correspondence; "CG U.S. Army Forces China Burma India to War Department," August 10, 1944, Franklin D. Roosevelt Presidential Library, Roosevelt Map Room Files, Map Room 0490, box 82.
87. "CG U.S. Army Liaison Section, Ceylon to War Department," August 16, 1944, Franklin D. Roosevelt Presidential Library, Roosevelt Map Room Files, Map Room 0490, box 82.
88. Message to Hearn from Stilwell, Eyes Alone, August 10, 1944, "Eyes Alone" Correspondence of General Joseph W. Stilwell, National Archives and Records Administration, Microfilm Publication M1419, reel 4.
89. Tuchman, *Stilwell and the American Experience in China; 1911–1945*, 455.
90. "CG U.S. Army Forces China Burma India to War Department," August 21, 1944, Franklin D. Roosevelt Presidential Library, Roosevelt Map Room Files, Map Room 0490, box 82; Message to Gauss from Ringwalt, Eyes Alone, August 18, 1944, "Eyes Alone" Correspondence of General Joseph W. Stilwell, National Archives and Records Administration, Microfilm Publication M1419, reel 4.
91. "Dissident Movement in Southwest China," Memorandum for the President, August 28, 1944, Franklin D. Roosevelt Presidential Library, Map Room 0491, box 82.

92. Eric Larrabee, *Commander in Chief: Franklin Delano Roosevelt, His Lieutenants, and Their War* (New York: Simon & Schuster, 1988), 575–76.
93. Letter from Vice President Henry A. Wallace to President Franklin D. Roosevelt, July 10, 1944, Franklin D. Roosevelt Presidential Library, China, July–December 1944, Presidential Secretary Files 0270, box 27.
94. Spector, *Eagle against the Sun*, 367–68.
95. Romanus and Sunderland, *Stilwell's Command Problems*, 414.
96. Letter to General Patrick J. Hurley from President Franklin D. Roosevelt, August 18, 1944, Franklin D. Roosevelt Presidential Library, China, July–December 1944, Presidential Secretary Files 0270, box 27.
97. Elliott Roosevelt, ed., *The Roosevelt Letters: Being the Personal Correspondence of Franklin Delano Roosevelt, Vol. III* (London: George G. Harrap and Co., 1952), 506.
98. Romanus and Sunderland, *Stilwell's Command Problems*, 417.
99. Romanus and Sunderland, *Stilwell's Command Problems*, 421.
100. The World War II Diaries of Joseph W. Stilwell, 1944, transcribed 2005, 245, Hoover Institution Archives.
101. Taylor, *The Generalissimo*, 284; Romanus and Sunderland, *Stilwell's Command Problems*, 423.
102. From Chungking (de Wiart) to Foreign Office, September 8, 1944, United Kingdom, National Archives, Reference FO 954-7A-182.
103. Romanus and Sunderland, *Stilwell's Command Problems*, 428.
104. Message to Marshall from Stilwell, Eyes Alone, September 12, 1944, "Eyes Alone" Correspondence of General Joseph W. Stilwell, National Archives and Records Administration, Microfilm Publication M1419, reel 1.
105. Letter from Chiang Kai-Shek to President Franklin D. Roosevelt, September 19, 1944, Franklin D. Roosevelt Presidential Library, China, July–December 1944, Presidential Secretary Files 0270, box 27.
106. Tang, *Kangzhan shiqi de duiwai guanxi*, 334; President Roosevelt to Generalissimo Chiang Kai-shek, September 16, 1944, in *Foreign Relations of the United States*, vol. 6, *China*, document 146; Marshall, vol. 4, 584–86.
107. The World War II Diaries of Joseph W. Stilwell, 1944, transcribed 2005, Hoover Institution Archives, 251; Romanus and Sunderland, *Stilwell's Command Problems*, 453.
108. Major General Patrick J. Hurley to President Roosevelt, October 10, 1944, in *Foreign Relations of the United States*, vol. 6, *China*, document 155.
109. William D. Leahy, *I Was There* (New York: Whittlesey House, 1950), 271.
110. Davies, *China Hand*, 188.
111. John F. Melby, interview, June 16, 1989, 18, The Association for Diplomatic Studies and Training, Foreign Affairs Oral History Project.
112. Radio Message Marshall to Wedemeyer, October 23, 1944, George Marshall correspondence with Albert C. Wedemeyer, ProQuest History Vault, Folder:

003255-039-0800 Date: Oct 1, 1944–Oct 31, 1944, Papers of George C. Marshall: Selected World War II Correspondence.
113. Joint Chiefs of Staff Message, October 24, 1944, George Marshall correspondence with Albert C. Wedemeyer, ProQuest History Vault, Folder: 003255-039-0800 Date: Oct 1, 1944–Oct 31, 1944, Papers of George C. Marshall: Selected World War II Correspondence.
114. James L. Durrence, "Ambassador Clarence E. Gauss and United States Relations with China, 1941–1944" (PhD diss., University of Georgia, 1971), 227–28.
115. Michael Schaller, "The Command Crisis in China: A Road Not Taken," *Diplomatic History* 4, no. 3 (1980): 329.

CONCLUSION

1. Larry I. Bland, ed., *George C. Marshall Interviews and Reminiscences for Forrest C. Pogue* (Lexington, Va.: George C. Marshall Foundation, 1996), October 29, 1956, 605.
2. Paul W. Carraway, Oral History Interview, March 16, 1971, 7, Senior Officers Oral History Program, Military History Institute.
3. Albert C. Wedemeyer, Oral History Interview, February 28, 1973, 22–23, Senior Officers Oral History Program, Army Heritage and Education Center, Carlisle, Pa.
4. Col. F. Hill, *Lessons from the CBI Theater*, Second Command Class, June 21, 1946, appendix C, Command and General Staff School, Fort Leavenworth Research Library Collection, Ike Skelton Combined Arms Research Library.
5. Lloyd E. Eastman, *Seeds of Destruction: Nationalist China in War and Revolution, 1937–1949* (Stanford, Calif.: Stanford University Press, 1984), 156.
6. Mike Jason, "What We Got Wrong in Afghanistan," *The Atlantic*, August 12, 2021, https://www.theatlantic.com/ideas/archive/2021/08/how-america-failed-afghanistan/619740/, accessed July 29, 2023.
7. Special Inspector General for Afghanistan Reconstruction, *What We Need to Learn: Lessons from Twenty Years of Afghanistan Reconstruction*, August 2021, 67, https://www.sigar.mil/pdf/lessonslearned/SIGAR-21-46-LL.pdf.
8. Walter C. Ladwig III, *The Forgotten Front: Patron-Client Relationships in Counterinsurgency* (Cambridge: Cambridge University Press, 2017), 293.
9. Ladwig, *The Forgotten Front*, 312.
10. Eli Berman and David A. Lake, eds., *Proxy Wars: Suppressing Violence through Local Agents* (Ithaca, N.Y.: Cornell University Press, 2019), 5.
11. John S. Service, interview for the Association for Diplomatic Studies and Training, Foreign Affairs Oral History Project, 1977, 183.
12. "Strictly Confidential Memorandum for the Ambassador [Gauss], John P. Davies," March 9, 1943, Franklin D. Roosevelt Presidential Library, Presidential Secretary files 0267, China, 1943.
13. John E. Shepard, "Warriors and Politics: The Bitter Lesson of Stilwell in China," *Parameters* 19, no. 1 (1989): 74.

14. Tang Tsou, *America's Failure in China, 1941–1950* (Chicago: University of Chicago Press, 1963), 94–95.
15. Dean Rusk, Interview D, Oral History Collection, University of Georgia, Richard B. Russell Library for Political Research and Studies, 1985, Part O, 13.
16. Fred Eldridge, *Wrath in Burma: The Uncensored Story of General Stilwell and International Maneuvers in the Far East* (New York: Doubleday, 1946), 200.
17. Special Inspector General for Afghanistan Reconstruction, *Reconstructing the Afghan National Defense and Security Forces: Lessons from the U.S. Experience in Afghanistan*, September 2017, 108–10. https://www.sigar.mil/pdf/lessonslearned/sigar-17-62-ll.pdf, accessed July 31, 2023.
18. Warren I. Cohen, *America's Response to China: A History of Sino-American Relations* (New York: Columbia University Press, 2010), 144.
19. Wenzhao Tao, *Kangri zhanzheng shiqi Zhongguo duiwai guanxi* [Foreign relations during the Sino-Japanese War era] (Beijing: Zhongguo shehui kexue chubanshe, 2009), 326.
20. Sally Burt, *At the President's Pleasure: FDR's Leadership of Wartime Sino-US Relations* (Boston: Brill, 2015), 96.
21. Henry L. Stimson and McGeorge Bundy, *On Active Service in Peace and War* (New York: Harper and Bros., 1948), 535.
22. Eric Larrabee, *Commander in Chief: Franklin Delano Roosevelt, His Lieutenants, and Their War* (New York: Simon & Schuster, 1988), 517.
23. Samuel P. Huntington, *The Soldier and the State: The Theory and Politics of Civil-Military Relations* (Cambridge, Mass.: Harvard University Press, 1957).
24. Peter D. Feaver, *Armed Servants: Agency, Oversight, and Civil-Military Relations* (Cambridge, Mass.: Harvard University Press, 2003), 18.
25. William E. Rapp, "Civil-Military Relations: The Role of Military Leaders in Strategy Making," *Parameters* 45, no. 3 (2015): 13–26, https://press.armywarcollege.edu/parameters/vol46/iss4/4/, accessed July 23, 2023; William E. Rapp, "Ensuring Effective Military Voice," *Parameters* 46, no. 4 (2016–2017): 13–25.
26. Risa Brooks, "Paradoxes of Professionalism: Rethinking Civil-Military Relations in the United States," *International Security* 44, no. 4 (2020): 44.
27. Brian Babcock-Lumish, "Uninformed, Not Uniformed: The Apolitical Myth," *Military Review* (September–October 2013), 51.
28. Babcock-Lumish, "Uninformed, Not Uniformed," 54–55.
29. Janine A. Davidson, Emerson T. Brooking, and Benjamin J. Fernandes, *Mending the Broken Dialogue: Civil-Military Relations and Presidential Decision-Making*, Council on Foreign Relations, December 2016, https://www.cfr.org/report/mending-broken-dialogue, accessed June 15, 2023.
30. Mark Thompson, "Here's Why the U.S. Military Is a Family Business," *Time*, March 10, 2016, https://time.com/4254696/military-family-business/, accessed July 29, 2023.

31. Paul D. Shinkman, "A Photo of a General's Family Highlights Civil-Military Concerns," *U.S. News and World Report*, May 2, 2019, https://www.usnews.com/news/national-news/articles/2019-05-02/a-photo-of-a-generals-family-highlights-civil-military-concerns, accessed July 31, 2023.
32. Matthew F. Cancian, "Officers Are Less Intelligent: What Does It Mean?" *Joint Forces Quarterly* 81, no. 2 (2016): 54, https://ndupress.ndu.edu/JFQ/Joint-Force-Quarterly-81/Article/702026/officers-are-less-intelligent-what-does-it-mean/, accessed July 31, 2023.
33. Arthur T. Coumbe, Steven J. Condley, and William L. Skimmyhorn, *Still Soldiers and Scholars? Analysis of Army Officer Testing*, Strategic Studies Institute, December 2017, 24–25, https://press.armywarcollege.edu/cgi/viewcontent.cgi?article=1000&context=monographs.
34. Kathleen Curtis, "Cadets in College: Top Majors for ROTC Students," Student Training and Education in Public Service (STEPS), August 31, 2021, https://www.publicservicedegrees.org/college-resources/college-rotc/.
35. Robert Scales, "O! The Damage 'Once an Eagle' Has Done to My Army – and Yes, It Is Partly My Fault," *Foreign Policy*, December 18, 2013, https://foreignpolicy.com/2013/12/18/o-the-damage-once-an-eagle-has-done-to-my-army-and-yes-it-is-partly-my-fault/, accessed July 23, 2023.

BIBLIOGRAPHY

ARCHIVES
Association for Diplomatic Studies and Training: Oral History Collection
    Emory C. Swank
    Everett Drumright
    Frank N. Burnett
    Henry Byroade
    John A. Lacey
    John F. Melby
    John S. Service
    Joseph A. Yager
    Kenneth P. Landon
    Larue R. Lutkins
    Louise S. Armstrong
    Ralph N. Clough
    Walter E. Jenkins Jr.
    William McAfee
Franklin Delano Roosevelt Presidential Library
    Map Room Papers
    Presidential Secretary Files
Guoshiguan (National Archives Administration). Taipei, Taiwan. Academia Historica.
    Jiang Zhongzheng zongtong wenwu (President Chiang Kai-shek Files)
Harry S. Truman Presidential Library, Independence, Missouri
    Oral History Interviews
        Ralph Block
        Edwin A. Locke
        John S. Service
        Phillip D. Sprouse
        Arthur N. Young
Hoover Institution Archives, Stanford, California
    Alvin Franklin Richardson Papers
    Frank Dorn Papers
    Haydon L. Boatner Papers

Joseph W. Stilwell Papers
Millard Preston Goodfellow Papers
Lutheran Seminary. Midwest China Oral History and Archives Collection
    Arie Gaalswyk
    Dillard M. Eubank
    John Foster
    Morris B. Depass
    Nathan Ma
    Paul C. Domke
National Archives and Records Administration (U.S.), College Park, Maryland
    "Eyes Alone" Correspondence of General Joseph W. Stilwell, January 1942–October 1944 (Microfilm), M1419
    Records of the U.S. State Department, Office of Chinese Affairs, 1945–1955 (Microfilm)
    RG 218 Records of the Joint Chiefs of Staff
    RG 334.5.3 Records of the Joint U.S. Military Advisory Group to the Republic of China (JUSMAG China)
    RG 493.5 Records of Headquarters U.S. Forces, China Theater (HQ USF CT) 1941–46
    RG 59 General Records of the Department of State
National Museum of the Pacific War: Oral History Collection
    John L. Bates Jr.
    Harold D. Clevenger
    Richard M. Young
National Park Service
    Eisenhower National Historic Site
ProQuest History Vault
    Records of the War Department's Operations Division, 1942–1945
Rutgers University, Oral History Archives of World War II
    George W. Thomas Oral History Interview
Scholarly Resources, Microfilm Collections
    The War against Japan
    Wartime Conferences of the Combined Chiefs of Staff
United Kingdom, National Archives, Kew
    Cabinet Office Papers
    Foreign Office Papers
    War Cabinet Papers
U.S. Air Force Official History Office
    The Army Air Forces in World War II. 7 vols. Edited by Wesley F. Craven and James L. Cate. Washington, D.C.: Office of Air Force History, 1983.

The Fourteenth Air Force to 1 October 1943. Assistant Chief of Air Staff, Intelligence, Historical Division. Army Air Forces Historical Office, July 1945.

U.S. Army Center of Military History

Report: The President and U.S. Aid to China. November 18, 1944. Geographic Files, China-Burma-India.

U.S. Army Combat Studies Institute, Fort Leavenworth, Kansas

U.S. Army Command and General Staff College, Fort Leavenworth, Kansas

U.S. Army, Fort Leavenworth Research Library Collection

Activation of Service of Supply in China-Burma-India, December 11, 1944.

Advantages of Air Transport. Headquarters China-Burma-India, October 20, 1944.

Air Supply-Operations, Personnel and Material. Headquarters, U.S. Army Forces CBI, October 24, 1944.

Airfields in China, Engineer Section, Fourteenth Air Force, May 7, 1945.

Allocation of Air and Truck Tonnage in Support of Combat and Construction Forward to Ledo Base. Headquarters, U.S. Forces India-Burma Theater, November 29, 1944.

Anglo-Chinese Relations at Lashio. March 21–April 25, 1942, Headquarters, U.S. Forces in China-Burma-India, May 15, 1942.

Burma: Observations on Air Invasion of Myitkyina Airfield. Headquarters Eastern Air Command, July 21, 1944.

Chihkiang Campaign, 10 April–3 June 1945. Twenty Fourth Statistical Control Unit, July 9, 1945.

China Theater Activities, Headquarters. Army Air Forces China Theater, September 6, 1945.

China's Role in the Recapture of Burma. Major Chen Ju-Hwa, Republic of China Army, 1947.

Chinese Operations on Salween Front. Field Headquarters, Y Force Operations Staff, August 11, 1944.

Combined Operations Training in India. Joint Intelligence Collection Agency, CBI/SEA, May 24, 1944.

Cost Estimate: Ledo Road, Office of Chief of Engineers, January 1946.

Development of Close Air Support Technique in North Burma. Headquarters, Tenth Air Force, September 5, 1944.

Development of Joint Air Ground Operations in North Burma. Headquarters, 10th Air Force, January 1945.

Fuel Consumption Figures. G-4, Headquarters China-Burma-India, December 1, 1944.

G-4 Periodic Report: Quarter Ending 30 September 1944. Headquarters, U.S. Army Forces CBI, n.d.

Growth, Development and Operating Protocols of Air Supply and Evacuation System. Northern Combat and Command Front, Headquarters U.S. Forces India-Burma Theater, 1945.

History of Combat in the India-Burma Theater. October 25, 1944–June 15, 1945, Headquarters, U.S. Army Forces, India-Burma Theater, 1945.

History of India-Burma Theater. October 25, 1944–June 23, 1945, Headquarters, U.S. Army Forces, India-Burma Theater, December 6, 1945.

History of the India-Burma Theater, Vol. I. December 6, 1945, Combined Arms Research Library, Fort Leavenworth, WWII Operational Documents, No. 4709.

History of the Northern Combat Area. Photograph, Vol. I–III, War Department Special Staff, Historical Division, 1945.

History of the Northern Combat Area Command. China-Burma-India Theater and India-Burma Theater, October 1943–June 1945.

Information on Some Aspects of Japanese Intelligence Organizations in China. Sino Translation and Interrogation Center, Headquarters, U.S. Forces China Theater, January 8, 1945.

Interrogation Reports. Sino Translation and Interrogation Center, Headquarters, U.S. Forces China Theater, August 17, 1945.

Ledo Road, Photograph Collection. Planning Division, Office of the Director of Plans and Operations, Army Service Forces, War Department.

Ledo-Kunming Road: Maximum Capabilities and Requirements. Planning Division, Office of the Director of Plans and Operations, War Department, January 16, 1945.

Lessons from the CBI Theater. Second Command Class, June 21, 1946, Command and General Staff School, Fort Leavenworth. Ike Skelton Combined Arms Research Library.

Maj. Gen. Haydon Boatner Historical Material. WWII Operational Documents. No. 16436.

Motor Transport Operation in China. Headquarters, U.S. Army Forces, China-Burma-India, n.d.

Notes on Duties with the Chinese Expeditionary Force. Brig. Gen. John Bowerman, n.d., in "Analysis of Boatner Materials."

Notes on Merrill Expedition, 1944. Joint Intelligence Coordination Agency, China-Burma-India, September 27, 1944. N-3405.

Organization and Functions of the Staff. Headquarters, China-Burma-India Air Service Command, January 20, 1944.

Organizational Charts of General Stilwell's Field Headquarters. Headquarters, U.S. Forces, India-Burma Theater, November 4, 1944.

Preliminary Report on Myitkyina Operations. Headquarters, Forward Command Post, Chinese Army in India, May 18, 1944.

Report of Chinese Engineer Operations on the Salween Front. Headquarters China-Burma-India, October 11, 1944.

Report of Mr. John S. Service, The Communist Problem in China. Headquarters, U.S. Forces, China Theater, April 23, 1945.

Report Summarizing the Activities of U.S. Army Medical Department Units Assigned to Northern Combat Area Command during the Northern and Central Burma Campaigns. Office of the Surgeon, Northern Combat Area Command, July 28, 1945.

Report on Official Trip to China-Burma-India from 5 August to 17 October 1944. Chief, Overseas Branch, Supply Division, February 2, 1945.

Salween Campaign: China, May 1944–January 1945. Colonel G. B. Coverdale. Command and General Staff College, N-2253.74.

Standing Orders for Troops Arriving at Bombay, Service of Supply. Headquarters China-Burma-India, January 9, 1944.

Stilwell Road Report. Colonel A. C. Welling, Theater Engineer, August 14, 1945, Fort Leavenworth Library, R-10889.

Study of Transport Requirements. Headquarters, Northern Combat Area Command, December 20, 1944.

Supply of Chinese Forces. Headquarters, U.S. Army Forces China-Burma-India, January 1, 1944.

Stilwell Road Report. Headquarters, U.S. Forces, India-Burma Theater, August 14, 1945.

Tactics and Strategy of the Japanese Army in the Burma Campaign from November 1943 to September 1944. Joint Intelligence Collection Agency, CBI/SEA, October 23, 1944.

War Zone Familiarization: China-Burma-India Theatre of Operations. Troop Carrier Command, August 28, 1944.

U.S. Army Heritage and Education Center, Carlisle, Pa.
- Paper Collections
    - Hayden L. Boatner
    - J. Calvin Frank
    - Alvan C. Gillem Jr.
    - Edward E. MacCorland
    - Willis B. Scudder
- Photograph Collections
    - Gerard J. Casius Photograph Collection
    - John C. Arrowsmith Photograph Collection
- Senior Officers Debriefing Program
    - Gen. Paul L. Freeman
    - Gen. Albert C. Wedemeyer
    - Lt. Gen. Paul W. Carraway

U.S. Army Japanese World War II Monograph Collection

Army Operations in China, January 1944–August 1945. Japanese Monograph 72, Headquarters, U.S. Army Forces Far East.

Burma Operations Record: 18th Division Operations in the Hukawng Area. Japanese Monograph 131, 1949, U.S. Army Center of Military History, Fort McNair, Washington, D.C.

Burma Operations Record: 15th Army Operations in Imphal Area and Withdrawal to Northern Burma. Japanese Monograph 134. Headquarters, United States Army, Japan. P. 60.

Burma Operations Record, 33rd Army Operations, Japanese Monograph No. 148, Assistant Chief of Staff G-2, USARJ, August 1960.

U.S. Army Office of the Judge Advocate General

U.S. Army Office of the Surgeon General

U.S. Army Training and Doctrine Command

Army Regulation 34-1. *Interoperability*, April 9, 2020.

U.S. Army War College, Carlisle, Pa.

United States Department of Defense, Joint Chiefs of Staff History Office

Rearden, Steven L. *Council of War: A History of the Joint Chiefs of Staff, 1942–1991.* 2012.

World War II Strategy Conferences Document Collections

Arcadia Conference (Washington, D.C.) December 24, 1941–January 14, 1942

Post-Arcadia Conference (Washington, D.C.), January 23–May 19, 1942

Casablanca Conference (Morocco), January 14–24, 1943

Trident Conference (Washington, D.C.), May 12–25, 1943

Quadrant Conference (Quebec City, Canada), August 14–24, 1943

Sextant Conference (Cairo, Egypt), Eureka Conference (Tehran, Iran), and the Second Cairo Conference (Egypt), November 22–December 7, 1943

Octagon Conference (Quebec City, Canada), September 12–16, 1944

Organizational Developments of the Joint Chiefs of Staff, 1942–2013

United States Department of State. *Foreign Relations of the United States.* Washington, D.C.: U.S. Government Printing Office.

1942, vol. V: China. 1956

1943, vol. V: China. 1962

1944, vol. VI: China. 1967

1945, vol. VII: China. 1969

University of California, Berkeley: Bancroft Library

Papers of Joseph Tussman

Virginia Military Institute: Military Oral History Project

Michnewich, Alexander

Wisconsin Veterans Museum: Oral History Collection

Richard Bates

Roman A. Carpenter

Donald R. Denman

Kenneth Johnson

Leonard Madaus

Raymond Olson

Donald L. Paulson
Frank J. Remington
Claude Williams

ARTICLES AND BOOKS

Ackerson, Steven J. *Detachment 101 and North Burma: Historical Conditions for Future Unconventional Warfare Operations.* Command and General Staff School, Fort Leavenworth, 2016.

Adams, Thomas Knight. "Military Doctrine and Organization Culture of the United States Army." PhD dissertation, Syracuse University, 1990.

Allen, Louis. *Burma: The Longest War, 1941–45.* London: Phoenix Press, 2000.

Anders, Leslie. *The Ledo Road: General Joseph W. Stilwell's Highway to China.* Norman: University of Oklahoma Press, 1965.

Arnold, H. H. *Global Mission.* New York: Harper and Brothers, 1949.

Babb, Joseph G. "The Harmony of Yin and Yank: The American Military Advisory Effort in China, 1941–1951." PhD dissertation, Kansas State University, 2012.

Babcock-Lumish, Brian. "Uninformed, Not Uniformed: The Apolitical Myth." *Military Review*, September–October 2013. Accessed July 31, 2023. https://www.army upress.army.mil/Portals/7/military-review/Archives/English/MilitaryReview _20131031_art009.pdf.

Bai Chongxi. *Bai Chongxi xiansheng fangwen jilu* [Oral history of General Bai Chongxi]. Taipei: Zhongyang Yanjiu Suo, 1989.

———. *Military Education and Training in China.* Shanghai: International Publishers, 1946.

Barber, Charles H. "China's Political Officer System." *Military Review* 33, no. 4 (July 1953): 10–21.

———. "Military Assistance Advisory Group Formosa." *Military Review* 34, no. 9 (Dec. 1954): 53–59.

Barnes, Dayna. "Plans and Expectations: The American News Media and Postwar Japan." *Japanese Studies* 34, no. 3 (2014): 325–42.

Bedeski, Robert. *State-Building in Modern China: The Kuomintang in the Prewar Period.* Berkeley: Center for Chinese Studies, Research Monograph 18, 1981.

Belden, Jack. *Retreat with Stilwell.* Garden City, N.Y.: Blue Ribbon Books, 1944.

Bell, Raymond E. Jr. "A Combined Effort: Chinese and American Tanks in Burma, 1944–1945." *On Point* 17, no. 3 (Winter 2012): 34–42.

Berman, Eli, and David A. Lake, eds. *Proxy Wars: Suppressing Violence through Local Agents.* Ithaca, N.Y.: Cornell University Press, 2019.

Bidwell, Shelford. *The Chindit War: Stilwell, Wingate, and the Campaign in Burma, 1944.* New York: Macmillan, 1979.

Bjorge, Gary J. *Merrill's Marauders: Combined Operations in Northern Burma in 1944.* Fort Leavenworth, Kan.: Combat Studies Institute, 1996.

Bland, Larry I., ed., *George C. Marshall Interviews and Reminiscences for Forrest C. Pogue*. Lexington, Va.: George C. Marshall Foundation, 1996.

Bland, Larry I., and Sharon Ritenour Stevens, eds. *The Papers of George Catlett Marshall*. Lexington, Va.: The George C. Marshall Foundation, 1981–. Electronic version based on *The Papers of George Catlett Marshall*, vol. 3, *"The Right Man for the Job," December 7, 1941–May 31, 1943*. Baltimore: The Johns Hopkins University Press, 1991; vol. 4, *"Aggressive and Determined Leadership," June 1, 1943–December 31, 1944*. Baltimore: The Johns Hopkins University Press, 1996.

Boye, F. W. "Operating with a Chinese Army Group." *Military Review* 27, no. 2 (May 1947): 3–8.

Brooks, Risa. "Paradoxes of Professionalism: Rethinking Civil-Military Relations in the United States," *International Security* 44, no. 4 (2020): 7–44.

Burt, Sally. "The Ambassador, the General, and the President: FDR's Mismanagement of Interdepartmental Relations in Wartime China." *Journal of American–East Asian Relations* 19, no. 3/4 (2012): 288–310.

———. *At the President's Pleasure: FDR's Leadership of Wartime Sino-US Relations*. Boston: Brill, 2015.

Byers, Adrian R. *Air Supply Operations in the China-Burma-India Theater between 1942 and 1945*. Command and General Staff School, Fort Leavenworth, 2010.

Bykofsky, Joseph, and Harold Larson. *The Transportation Corps: Operations Overseas*. Washington, D.C.: Center of Military History, 1990.

Calvert, Michael. *Prisoners of Hope*. Havertown, Pa: Pen and Sword, 2004.

Cancian, Matthew F. "Officers Are Less Intelligent: What Does It Mean?" *Joint Forces Quarterly* 81, no. 2 (2016). Accessed July 31, 2023. https://ndupress.ndu.edu/JFQ/Joint-Force-Quarterly-81/Article/702026/officers-are-less-intelligent-what-does-it-mean/.

Chan, Won-Loy. *Burma, the Untold Story*. Novato, Calif.: Presidio Press, 1986.

Chang, C. S. *Logistical Service of Chinese Army in the Last War*. Command and General Staff School, Fort Leavenworth, 1947.

Chang, Gordon H. *Fateful Ties: A History of America's Preoccupation with China*. Cambridge, Mass.: Harvard University Press, 2015.

Chang, Jui-Te. "Nationalist Army Officers during the Sino-Japanese War, 1937–1945." *Modern Asian Studies* 30, no. 4 (Oct. 1996): 1033–56.

———. "The National Army from Whampoa to 1949." In *A Military History of China*, edited by David A. Graff and Robin Higham, 193–210. Lexington: University of Kentucky Press, 2002.

———. "Chiang Kai-shek's Coordination by Personal Directive." In *China at War: Regions of China, 1937–45*, edited by Stephen R. Mackinnon, Diana Lary, and Ezra F. Vogel, 65–89. Stanford, Calif.: Stanford University Press, 2007.

———. "The Nationalist Army on the Eve of the War." In *The Battle for China: Essays on the Military History of the Sino-Japanese War of 1937–1945*, edited by Mark Peattie,

Edward J. Drea, and Hans van de Ven , 83–104. Stanford, Calif.: Stanford University Press, 2011.

Chen Du. *Guomindang gaoji jiangling zhuanlue* [Guomindang Senior Officer Biographies]. Beijing: Zhongwen chubanshe, 2005.

Chen Jian. "The Myth of America's 'Lost Chance' in 'China: A Chinese Perspective in Light of New Evidence,'" *Diplomatic History* 21, no. 1 (Winter 1997): 77–86.

Chen, Li. "The Chinese Army in the First Burma Campaign." *Journal of Chinese Military History* 2 (2013): 43–73.

Chennault, Claire Lee. *Way of a Fighter: The Memoirs of Claire Lee Chennault.* New York: G. P. Putnam, 1949.

Chi, Hsi-sheng. *Nationalist China at War: Military Defeats and Political Collapse, 1937–1945.* Ann Arbor: University of Michigan Press, 1982.

———. "The Military Dimension, 1942–1945." In *China's Bitter Victory: The War with Japan 1937–1945*, edited by James C. Hsiung and Steven I. Levine. Armonk, N.Y.: M. E. Sharpe, Inc., 1992.

Chiang Kai-shek. *The Collected Wartime Messages of Generalissimo Chiang Kai-shek, 1937–1945.* New York: Kraus Reprint, 1969.

Chu Hongyuan. *Sun Liren yanlun xuanji* [Collected works of Sun Li-jen]. Taipei: Zhongyang yanjiuyuan jundai yanjiusuo. 2000.

Churchill, Winston S. *The Second World War: The Hinge of Fate.* Boston: Houghton Mifflin Co., 1950.

———. *Closing the Ring.* Boston: Houghton Mifflin Co., 1951.

Coakley, Robert W., and Richard Leighton, *Global Logistics and Strategy, 1943–1945.* Washington, D.C.: U.S. Army Center of Military History, 1989.

Coble, Parks M. "China's 'New Remembering' of the Anti-Japanese War of Resistance, 1937–1945." *China Quarterly* 190 (June 2007): 394–410.

———. *China's War Reporters: The Legacy of Resistance against Japan.* Cambridge, Mass.: Harvard University Press, 2015.

Coe, Douglas. *The Burma Road.* New York: J. Messney Publishers, 1946.

Coffman, Edward. "The American 15th Infantry Regiment in China, 1912–1938: A Vignette in Social History." *Journal of Military History* 58, no. 1 (January 1994): 57–74.

———. *The Regulars: The American Army, 1898–1941.* Cambridge, Mass.: Harvard University Press, 2004.

Cohen, Warren I. *America's Response to China: A History of Sino-American Relations.* New York: Columbia University Press, 2010.

Collier, Harry. *Organizational Changes in the Chinese Army, 1895–1950.* Taipei: Office of the Military Historian, 1969.

Condon-Rall, Mary, and Albert E. Cowdery. *Medical Service in the War against Japan.* Washington, D.C.: U.S. Army Center of Military History, 1998.

Cornebise, Alfred E. *Soldier Extraordinaire: The Life and Career of Brig. Gen. Frank "Pinkie" Dorn (1901–81).* Fort Leavenworth, Kan.: Combat Studies Institute Press, 2019.

Coulombe, David P. *Learning on the Move: OSS Detachment 101 Special Operation in Burma.* Command and General Staff School, Fort Leavenworth, 2015.

Coumbe, Arthur T., Steven J. Condley, and William L. Skimmyhorn. *Still Soldiers and Scholars? Analysis of Army Officer Testing.* Strategic Studies Institute, December 2017. https://press.armywarcollege.edu/cgi/viewcontent.cgi?article=1000&context=monographs.

Cox, Samuel J. *The China Theater, 1944–1945: A Failure of Joint and Combined Operations Strategy.* U.S. Army Command and Staff College, 1980.

Craft, Stephen G. *V. K. Wellington Koo and the Emergence of Modern China.* Lexington: University Press of Kentucky, 2004.

Cray, Ed. *General of the Army: George C. Marshall, Soldier and Statesman.* New York: W. W. Norton and Co., 1990.

Curtis, Kathleen. "Cadets in College: Top Majors for ROTC Students." Student Training and Education in Public Service (STEPS), August 2021. Accessed June 15, 2023. https://www.publicservicedegrees.org/college-resources/college-rotc/.

Dallek, Robert. *Franklin D. Roosevelt and American Foreign Policy, 1932–1945.* New York: Oxford University Press, 1979.

Davidson, Janine A., Emerson T. Brooking, and Benjamin J. Fernandes. *Mending the Broken Dialogue: Civil-Military Relations and Presidential Decision-Making.* Council on Foreign Relations, December 2016. Accessed June 15, 2023. https://www.cfr.org/report/mending-broken-dialogue.

Davies, John Paton Jr. *Dragon by the Tail: American, British, Japanese, and Russian Encounters with China and One Another.* New York: W. W. Norton and Co., 1972.

———. *China Hand: An Autobiography.* Philadelphia: University of Pennsylvania Press, 2012.

Denning, Margaret B. *The Sino-American Alliance in World War II: Cooperation and Dispute among Nationalists, Communist, and Americans.* New York: P. Lang, 1986.

Diehl, Samuel J. *Army Health System Support in the Forgotten Theater: China-Burma-India, 1942–1944.* Command and General Staff School, Fort Leavenworth, 2019.

Dod, Karl C. *The Corps of Engineers in the War against Japan.* Washington, D.C.: U.S. Army Center of Military History, 1987.

Dorn, Frank. *Walkout: With Stilwell in Burma.* New York: Thomas Y. Crowell Co., 1971.

Drea, Edward. *The Battle for China: Essays on the Military History of the Sino-Japanese War of 1937–1945.* Stanford, Calif.: Stanford University Press, 2011.

Dreyer, Edward L. *China at War, 1901–1949.* New York: Longman Press, 1995.

Du Yuming and Song Xilan. *Yuanzheng yinmian kangzhan* [The Burma Expeditionary Army's campaign]. Beijing: Zhongguo wenshi chubanshe, 2015.

Dunlop, Richard. *Behind Japanese Lines: With the OSS in Burma.* New York: Rand McNally and Co., 1979.

Durrence, James L. "Ambassador Clarence E. Gauss and United States Relations with China, 1941–1944." PhD dissertation, University of Georgia, 1971.

Eastman, Lloyd. *The Abortive Revolution: China under Nationalist Rule, 1927–1937*. Cambridge, Mass.: Harvard University Press, 1974.

———. *Seeds of Destruction: Nationalist China in War and Revolution, 1937–1949*. Stanford, Calif.: Stanford University Press, 1984.

Ehrman, James M. "Ways of War and the American Experience in the China-Burma-India Theater, 1942–1945." PhD dissertation, Kansas State University, 2006.

Eldridge, Fred. *Wrath in Burma: The Uncensored Story of General Stilwell and International Maneuvers in the Far East*. New York: Doubleday, 1946.

Elleman, Bruce. *Modern Chinese Warfare, 1795–1989*. London: Routledge Press, 2001.

Fairbank, John K. *Dangerous Acquaintances, New York Times Book Review*, May 17, 1979.

Feaver, Peter D. *Armed Servants: Agency, Oversight, and Civil-Military Relations*. Cambridge, Mass.: Harvard University Press, 2003.

Feis, Herbert. *The China Tangle: The American Effort in China from Pearl Harbor to the Marshall Mission*. Princeton, N.J.: Princeton University Press, 1953.

Fellowes-Gordon, Ian. *The Battle for Naw Seng's Kingdom: General Stilwell's North Burma Campaign and Its Aftermath*. London: Leo Cooper Press, 1971.

Fenby, Jonathan. *Chiang Kai-shek and the China He Lost*. London: Free Press, 2003.

Fitzgerald, Stephen K. *Magic and Ultra in the China-Burma-India Theater*. Command and General Staff School, Fort Leavenworth, 1991.

Gaither, John B. *Galahad Redux: An Assessment of the Disintegration of Merrill's Marauders*. Command and General Staff School, Fort Leavenworth, 1975.

Gallicchio, Marc. "The Other China Hands: U.S. Army Officers and America's Failure in China, 1941–1950." *Journal of American-East Asian Relations* 4, no. 1 (Spring 1995): 49–72.

———. "Colouring the Nationalists: The African-American Construction of China in the Second World War." *International History Review* 20, no. 3 (Sept. 1998): 571–96.

Gallup Organization. Gallup Poll (AIPO), Feb. 1940 [survey question]. USGALLUP.40-185.QK04. Gallup Organization [producer]. Cornell University, Ithaca, N.Y.: Roper Center for Public Opinion Research, iPOLL [distributor]. Accessed September 9, 2019.

———. Gallup Poll, Sept. 1943 [survey question]; National Opinion Research Center, University of Chicago. Foreign Affairs Survey, Aug. 1945 [survey question]. USNORC.450133.R02G. National Opinion Research Center, University of Chicago [producer]. Cornell University, Ithaca, N.Y.: Roper Center for Public Opinion Research, iPOLL [distributor]. Accessed September 9, 2019.

Garver, John W. "China's Wartime Diplomacy." In *China's Bitter Victory: The War with Japan 1937–1945*, edited by James C. Hsiung and Steven I. Levine. Armonk, N.Y.: M. E. Sharpe, Inc., 1992.

Gao Yongguang. "Woguo junshi yuanxiao zhengzhi jiaoyu kecheng zhi yanjiu-jundui yu guojia, jundui yu shehui guanxi quexiang de neirong fenxi." PhD dissertation, Guoli zhengzhi daxue, 1999.

Gibson, Michael. "Chiang Kai-Shek's Central Army, 1924–1938." PhD dissertation, George Washington University, 1985.

Graff, David A., and Robin Higham, eds. *A Military History of China*. Boulder, Colo.: Westview Press, 2002.

Green, Michael J. *By More than Providence: Grand Strategy and American Power in the Asia Pacific since 1783*. New York: Columbia University Press, 2017.

Grieve, William G. *The American Military Mission to China, 1941–1942: Lend-Lease Logistics, Politics and the Tangles of Wartime Cooperation*. Jefferson, N.C.: McFarland and Co., 2014.

Guo, Ting. *Surviving in Violent Conflicts: Chinese Interpreters in the Second Sino-Japanese War, 1931–1945*. London: Palgrave Macmillan, 2016.

Guojun jianjun shi [History of the National Army]. Taipei: jiayu bu, 1965.

Haith, Michael C. *Partner Operations in North Burma: Assessing By, With, and Through*. Command and General Staff School, Fort Leavenworth, 2019.

Han Yongli. *Zhanshi Meiguo dazhan lüeyu Zhongguo kangri zhanzheng (1941–1945 nian)* [The United States wartime grand strategy and China's anti-Japanese theater, 1941–1945]. Wuhang: Wuhan daxue chubanshe, 2003.

Hantzis, Steven J. *Rails of War: Supplying the Americans and Their Allies in China-Burma-India*. Lincoln: University of Nebraska Press, 2017.

Harris, Donald Q. "Organizing Artillery Battalions in China." *Field Artillery Journal* 35, no. 6 (June 1945): 323.

Hart, John N. *The Making of an Army "Old China Hand": A Memoir of Colonel David D. Barrett*. Berkeley, Calif.: Institute of East Asian Studies, 1985.

Hastings, Michael. "The Runaway General: The Profile that Brought Down McChrystal," *Rolling Stone*, June 22, 2010. Accessed June 15, 2023. https://www.rollingstone.com/politics/politics-news/the-runaway-general-the-profile-that-brought-down-mcchrystal-192609/.

Hayes, Grace Person. *The History of the Joint Chiefs of Staff in World War II: The War against Japan*. Annapolis, Md.: Naval Institute Press, 1982.

He Husheng. *Banian kangzhan Zhong de jiang jieshi, 1937–1945* [Chiang Kai-shek and the Eight Year War against Japan]. Taipei: Fengyun shidai, 2013.

He Yingqin. *Banian kangzhan* [Eight years of war against Japan]. Taipei: Zaiban, 1969.

He Zelin. *Chen Cheng xiansheng congjun shiliao xuanji : zhengjun jiyao* [Documentary collection of Chen Cheng's military history: Army reorganization and training]. Taipei: guoshiguan, 2010.

Heiferman, Ronald I. "The Cairo Conference: A Turning Point in Sino-American Relations." PhD dissertation, New York University, 1990.

———. *The Cairo Conference of 1943: Roosevelt, Churchill, Chiang Kai-shek, and Madame Chiang*. Jefferson, N.C.: McFarland, 2011.

Hibbert, George. "Reminiscences of the China Theater." *Military Review* 26, no. 12 (March 1947): 22–28.

Hogan, David W. Jr. "MacArthur, Stilwell, and Special Operations in the War against Japan." *Parameters* 25, no. 1 (Spring 1995): 104–15.

———. *U.S. Army Special Operations in World War II*. Washington, D.C.: Government Printing Office, 1992.

Holdings and Opinions, *Board of Review, Branch Office of the Judge Advocate General, China-Burma-India*. Vol. 3. Washington, D.C.: Office of the Judge Advocate General, 1946.

Hopkins, James E. T. *Spearhead: A Complete History of Merrill's Marauder Rangers*. Baltimore: Galahad Press, 2000.

Hopkins, James, Henry G. Stelling, and Tracy S. Voorhees. "The Marauders and the Microbes." In *Crisis Fleeting: Original Reports on Military Medicine in India and Burma in the Second World War*, edited by Walter Stone, 307–10. Washington, D.C.: Office of the Surgeon General, 1969.

Hsiung, James, and Steven I. Levine. *China's Bitter Victory: The War with Japan, 1937–1945*. Armonk, N.Y.: M. E. Sharpe Inc., 1992.

Hsu Long-hsuen and Chang Ming-kai. *History of the Sino-Japanese War*. Taipei: Chung Wu Publishing, 1971.

Hu Pu-Yu. *A Brief History of the Sino-Japanese War (1937–1945)*. Taipei: Chung Wu Publishing, 1974.

Huang Chan-Kuei. *The Logistical Organization of the Chinese Army*. Command and General Staff School, Fort Leavenworth, 1947.

Huang Qiang. *Hengyang kangzhan si shi ba tian* [Hengyang's 48-day battle]. Taipei: Zaiban, 1977.

Huang, Ray. "Letter from Nanking." *Military Review* 28, no. 9 (December 1948): 24–30.

Hunter, Charles N. *Galahad*. San Antonio: Naylor Co., 1963.

Huntington, Samuel P. *The Soldier and the State: The Theory and Politics of Civil-Military Relations*. Cambridge, Mass.: Harvard University Press, 1957.

Jackson, Daniel. *Famine, Sword, and Fire: The Liberation of Southwest China in World War II*. Atglen, Pa.: Schiffer Publishing, 2015.

James, D. Clayton. "American and Japanese Strategies in the Pacific War." In *Makers of Modern Strategy: From Machiavelli to the Nuclear Age*, edited by Peter Paret, 703–732. Princeton, N.J.: Princeton University Press, 1986.

Janowitz, Morris. *The Professional Soldier: A Social and Political Portrait*. New York: The Free Press, 1960.

Jason, Mike. "What We Got Wrong in Afghanistan." *The Atlantic*, August 12, 2021. Accessed July 29, 2023. https://www.theatlantic.com/ideas/archive/2021/08/how-america-failed-afghanistan/619740/.

Johnson, Matthew D. "Propaganda and Sovereignty in Wartime China: Morale Operations and Psychological Warfare under the Office of War Information." *Modern Asian Studies* 45, no. 2 (March 2011): 303–44.

Joiner, Lynne. *Honorable Survivor: Mao's China, McCarthy's America, and the Persecution of John S. Service*. Annapolis, Md.: Naval Institute Press, 2009.

Jones, Walter S. "Chinese Liaison Detail." In *Crisis Fleeting: Original Reports on Military Medicine in India and Burma in the Second World War*, edited by Walter Stone, 69–132. Washington, D.C.: Office of the Surgeon General, 1969.

Jowett, Phillip S. *Soldiers of the White Sun: The Chinese Army at War, 1931–1949*. Atglen, Pa.: Schiffer Military History, 2011.

Judson, P. M. "The Operations of the Fifty-Third Army, CEF, Culminating in the Battle for Muse and Tachingshan 3 Dec 44 – 27 Jan 45." U.S. Army Command and General Staff College, Student Paper, 1947.

Kaufman, David A. "31st Signal Battalion." *On Point* 18, no. 3 (Winter 2013): 23–27.

Kesaris, Paul. *U.S. Military Intelligence Reports: China 1911–1941*. Frederick, Md.: University Publications of America, 1983.

Kikuchi, Kazutaka. *Chūgoku kōnichi gunjishi: 1937–1945: A History of China's War against Japan: 1937–1945*. Tokyo: Yushisha, 2009.

Kinnison, Henry L. *The Deeds of Valiant Men: A Study in Leadership, The Marauders in North Burma, 1944*. Command and General Staff School, Fort Leavenworth, 1993.

Kinzley, Judd. "The Power of the 'Stockpile': American Aid and China's Wartime Everyday." *Journal of Modern Chinese History* 13, no. 1 (2019): 169–88.

Kirby, S. Woodburn. *The War against Japan, Vol. II: India's Most Dangerous Hour.* London: Her Majesty's Stationery Office, 1958.

Kleiner, Sam. *The Flying Tigers: The Untold Story of the American Pilots Who Waged a Secret War against Japan*. New York: Penguin Books, 2019.

Ladwig, Walter C. III. *The Forgotten Front: Patron-Client Relationships in Counterinsurgency.* Cambridge: Cambridge University Press, 2017.

Lai Cheng-liang. "The Battle of the Salween River." U.S. Army Command and General Staff College, Student Paper, 1947.

Lai, Jinzhi. *History of the Sino-Japanese War*. Taipei: U.S. Army Office of Military History, 1967.

Larrabee, Eric. *Commander in Chief: Franklin Delano Roosevelt, His Lieutenants, and Their War.* New York: Simon & Schuster, 1988.

Lary, Diana, and Stephen MacKinnon. *Scars of War: The Impact of Warfare on Modern China*. Vancouver: University of British Columbia Press, 2001.

Lathrop, Alan K. "The Employment of Chinese Nationalist Troops in the First Burma Campaign." *Journal of Southeast Asian Studies* 12, no. 2 (Sept. 1981): 403–32.

Leahy, William D. *I Was There*. New York: Whittlesey House, 1950.

Li, Zongren. *The Memoirs of Li Tsung-Jen*. Boulder, Colo.: Westview Press, 1979.

Liang, Chin-tung. *General Stilwell in China, 1942–1944: The Full Story.* New York: St. John's University Press, 1972.

Lin Wei. *Kangzhan yuanzheng riji* [The expedition diaries of General Lin Wei-wen]. Taipei: Minguo li shi wen hua xue she, 2019.

Liu An-chi. *Liu Anchi xiansheng fangwen jilu* [Oral history of General Liu Anchi]. Taipei: Zhongyang Yanjiu Suo, 1991.

Liu, F. F. "The Nationalist Army of China: An Administrative Study of the Period 1924–1946." PhD dissertation, Princeton University, 1951.

———. *A Military History of Modern China*. Princeton, N.J.: Princeton University Press, 1956.

Lohbeck, Donald. *Patrick J. Hurley*. Chicago: Henry Regnery Co., 1956.

Luo Man. *Lanying bingtuan: Zhongguo yuanzheng jun mian yin xie zhan ji* [The Blue Eagles: China's Expeditionary Force in Burma and India]. Taipei: Xing Guang Publishers, 1991.

Luo Youlun. *Luo Youlun xiansheng fangwen jilu* [Oral history of General Luo Youlun]. Taipei: Zhongyang Yanjiu Suo, 1994.

Lysaght, Patrick B. *The School of Hard Knocks: The Development of Close Air Support in Burma during the Second World War*. Command and General Staff School, Fort Leavenworth, 2015.

MacKinnon, Stephen R. "The Sino-Japanese Conflict, 1931–1945." In *A Military History of China*, edited by David A. Graff and Robin Higham, 211–228. Lexington: University of Kentucky Press, 2002.

MacKinnon, Stephen, Diana Lary, and Ezra Vogel. *China at War: Regions of China, 1937–1945*. Stanford, Calif.: Stanford University Press, 2007.

Matloff, Maurice. *Strategic Planning for Coalition Warfare, 1943–1944*. Washington, D.C.: Government Printing Office, 1999.

Matloff, Maurice, and Edwin Snell. *Strategic Planning for Coalition Warfare, 1941–1942*. Washington, D.C.: Government Printing Office, 1999.

McMichael, Scott R. *A Historical Perspective on Light Infantry*. Combat Studies Institute, Fort Leavenworth, 1987.

McGee, George A. *The History of the 2nd Battalion, Merrill's Marauders*. Self-published, 1987.

McLaughlin, John J. *General Albert C. Wedemeyer: America's Unsung Strategist in World War II*. Philadelphia: Casemate Publishing, 2012.

McLynn, Frank. *The Burma Campaign: Disaster into Triumph, 1942–1945*. New Haven, Conn.: Yale University Press, 2011.

Merrill's Marauders (February–May 1944). Military Intelligence Division, U.S. War Department, 1945, 8–9.

Miles, Milton E. *A Different Kind of War: The Little-Known Story of the Combined Guerrilla Forces Created in China by the U.S. Navy and the Chinese during World War II*. Garden City, N.Y.: Doubleday, 1967.

Millett, John D. *The Organization and Role of the Army Service Forces*. Washington, D.C.: Office of the Chief of Military History, Department of the Army, 1954.

Mitter, Rana. *Forgotten Ally: China's World War II, 1937–1945*. Boston: Houghton Mifflin, 2013.

———. "Identities and Alliances: China's Place in the World after Pearl Harbor, 1941–1945." In *Beyond Pearl Harbor: A Pacific History*, edited by Beth Bailey and David Farber, 102–120. Lawrence: University Press of Kansas, 2019.

Morton, Louis. "Army and Marines on the China Station: A Study in Military and Political Rivalry." *Pacific Historical Review* 29, no. 1 (1960): 51–73.

———. *Strategy and Command: The First Two Years*. Washington, D.C.: Government Printing Office, 2014.

Mountbatten, Vice Admiral, Earl of Burma. *Report to the Combined Chiefs of Staff by the Supreme Allied Commander, Southeast Asia: 1943–1945*. London: His Majesty's Stationery Office, 1951.

Muscalino, Micah. *The Ecology of War in China: Henan Province, the Yellow River, and Beyond, 1938–1950*. Cambridge: Cambridge University Press, 2016.

Noble, Dennis. *The Eagle and the Dragon: The United States Military in China, 1901–1937*. New York: Greenwood Press, 1990.

Ogburn, Charlton Jr. *The Marauders*. Woodstock, N.Y.: Overlook Press, 1959.

Peers, William R., and Dean Brelis. *Behind the Burma Road*. Boston: Little Brown and Co., 1963.

Pei, Jean, and William Wang. *Under the Same Army Flag: Recollections of the Veterans of the World War II*. Beijing: Wuzhou zhuanbo chubanshe, 2005.

Peng, Chen-Kai. *Proposals for Improvement of the Chinese Army Supply System*. Command and General Staff School, Fort Leavenworth, 1949.

Persico, Joseph E. *Roosevelt's Centurions: FDR and the Commanders He Led to Victory in World War II*. New York: Random House, 2013.

Peterkin, W. J. *Inside China, 1943–1945: An Eyewitness Account of America's Mission to Yenan*. Baltimore: Gateway Press, 1992.

Plating, John D. "Keeping China in the War: The Trans-Himalayan 'Hump' Airlift and Sino-US Strategy in World War II." PhD dissertation, The Ohio State University, 2007.

Pogue, Forrest C. *George C. Marshall: Ordeal and Hope*. New York: Viking Press, 1965.

Prefer, Nathan. *Vinegar Joe's War: Stilwell's Campaigns for Burma*. Novato, Calif.: Presidio Press, 2000.

Rapp, William E. "Civil-Military Relations: The Role of Military Leaders in Strategy Making." *Parameters* 45, no. 3 (2015): 13–26.

———. "Ensuring Effective Military Voice." *Parameters* 46, no. 4 (2016–2017). Accessed July 23, 2023. https://press.armywarcollege.edu/parameters/vol46/iss4/4/.

Rasor, Eugene L. *The China-Burma-India Campaign, 1931–1945: Historiography and Annotated Bibliography*. Westport, Conn.: Greenwood Press, 1998.

Rayburn, Joel D., and Frank K. Sobchak. *The U.S. Army in the Iraq War – Volume 1: Invasion – Insurgency – Civil War, 2003–2006*. Carlisle, Pa.: U.S. Army War College Press. Accessed July 31, 2023. https://press.armywarcollege.edu/monographs/386/.

Richard B. Russell Library for Political Research and Studies, Interview D. Dean Rusk Oral History Collection, University of Georgia.

Ritter, Jonathan Templin. *Stilwell and Mountbatten in Burma: Allies at War, 1943–1944*. Denton: University of North Texas Press, 2017.

Romanus, Charles, and Riley Sunderland. *Stilwell's Mission to China*. Washington, D.C.: U.S. Army Center of Military History, 1953.

———. *Stilwell's Command Problems*. Washington, D.C.: U.S. Government Printing Office, 1955.

———. *Time Runs Out in CBI*. Washington, D.C.: U.S. Government Printing Office, 1958.

Roett, Brice U. *The US Strategic Logistics Plan in the CBI Theater and Its Contemporary Significance*. Command and General Staff School, Fort Leavenworth, 2016.

Rooney, David. *Stilwell the Patriot: Vinegar Joe, the Brits and Chiang Kai-Shek*. London: Greenhill Books, 2005.

Roosevelt, Elliott, ed. *The Roosevelt Letters: Being the Personal Correspondence of Franklin Delano Roosevelt, Vol. III*. London: George G. Harrap and Co., 1952.

Sacca, John Wanda. "Like Strangers in a Foreign Land: Chinese Officers Prepared at American Military Colleges, 1904–1937." *Journal of Military History* 70 (July 2006): 703–42.

Sacquety, Troy J. *The OSS in Burma: Jungle War against the Japanese*. Lawrence: University Press of Kansas, 2013.

Sapozhnikov, B. G. *The China Theatre in World War II, 1939–1945*. Moscow: Progress Publishers, 1985.

Scales, Robert. "O! The Damage 'Once an Eagle' Has Done to My Army – and Yes, It Is Partly My Fault." *Foreign Policy*, December 18, 2013. Accessed July 23, 2023. https://foreignpolicy.com/2013/12/18/o-the-damage-once-an-eagle-has-done-to-my-army-and-yes-it-is-partly-my-fault/.

Scardina, Hayden D. *Stilwell's North Burma Campaign: A Case Study in Multinational Mission Command*. Command and General Staff School, Fort Leavenworth, 2017.

Schaller, Michael. "SACO! The United States Navy's Secret War in China." *Pacific Historical Review* 44, no. 4 (Nov. 1975): 527–53.

———. *The U.S. Crusade in China, 1938–1945*. New York: Columbia University Press, 1979.

———. "The Command Crisis in China, 1944: A Road Not Taken." *Diplomatic History* 4, no. 3 (Summer 1980): 327–31.

Schoppa, Keith. *In a Sea of Bitterness: Refugees during the Sino-Japanese War*. Cambridge, Mass.: Harvard University Press, 2011.

Scott, Robert L. *Flying Tiger: Chennault of China*. New York: Doubleday, 1959.

Seagrave, Gordon S. *Burma Surgeon*. New York: W. W. Norton and Co., 1943.

———. *Burma Surgeon Returns*. New York: W. W. Norton and Co., 1946.

Shelton, William W. *What Is Mine Is Yours: The Art of Operational Integration*. Command and General Staff School, Fort Leavenworth, 2016.

Shepard, John E. "Warriors and Politics: The Bitter Lesson of Stilwell in China." *Parameters* 19, no. 1 (March 1989): 61–75.

Shinkman, Paul D. "A Photo of a General's Family Highlights Civil-Military Concerns." *U.S. News and World Report*, May 2, 2019. https://www.usnews.com/news/national-news/articles/2019-05-02/a-photo-of-a-generals-family-highlights-civil-military-concerns.

Slim, William. *Defeat into Victory*. New York: David McKay Company, Inc., 1961.

Smith, Nicol. *Burma Road*. New York: Bobbs-Merrill Company, 1940.

Spector, Ronald. *Eagle against the Sun: The American War with Japan*. New York: Random House, 1985.

Spence, Jonathan. *To Change China: Western Advisers in China, 1620–1960*. Boston: Little Brown and Co., 1969.

Special Inspector General for Afghanistan Reconstruction. *What We Need to Learn: Lessons from Twenty Years of Afghanistan Reconstruction*, August 2021. Accessed July 23, 2023. https://www.sigar.mil/pdf/lessonslearned/SIGAR-21-46-LL.pdf.

———. *Reconstructing the Afghan National Defense and Security Forces: Lessons from the U.S. Experience in Afghanistan*, September 2017. Accessed July 31, 2023. https://www.sigar.mil/pdf/lessonslearned/sigar-17-62-ll.pdf.

Spengler, Henry M. "American Liaison Groups." *Military Review* 27, no. 1 (April 1947): 61–64.

Spracher, William C. "The OSS in Support of the Chinese Communists." *American Intelligence Journal* 3, no. 3 (Winter 1980–81): 14–20.

Stilwell, Joseph. *The Stilwell Papers*. Edited by Theodore H. White. New York: Sloane and Associates, 1948.

Stimson, Henry L., and McGeorge Bundy. *On Active Service: In Peace and War*. New York: Harper and Bros., 1948.

Stoler, Mark A. *Allies and Adversaries: The Joint Chiefs of Staff, the Grand Alliance, and U.S. Strategy in World War II*. Chapel Hill: University of North Carolina Press, 2000.

Sun Jianzhong. *Guojun zhuangjia bin fazhan shi* [A history of the ROC armored forces]. Taipei: Guofang bus hi zhengbian yishi, 2005.

Sun Li-jen, and Shen Jingyong. *Zhongguo junhun: Sun Liren* [China's military hero: Sun Li-jen]. Taipei: Taiwan xuesheng shuju, 1993.

Sunderland, Riley, and Charles F. Romanus, eds. *Stilwell's Personal File: China-Burma-India, 1942–1944*. Wilmington, Del.: Scholarly Resources, 1976.

Sweeney, Red. *Ramgarh: Now It Can Be Told*. N.p., 1952.

Tai, Paul H., and Tai-chun Kuo, "Chiang Kai-Shek Revisited." *American Journal of Chinese Studies* 17, no. 1 (April 2010): 81–86.

Tang Peiji. *Kangzhan shiqi de duiwai guanxi* [Foreign relations during the Sino-Japanese War]. Beijing: Beijing Yanshan chubanshe, 1997.

Tanner, Harold. *The Battle for Manchuria and the Fate of China: Siping, 1946*. Bloomington: Indiana University Press, 2013.

———. *Where Chiang Kai-shek Lost China: The Liao-Shen Campaign, 1948*. Bloomington: Indiana University Press, 2015.

Tang Runming. *Kangzhan shiqi Chongqing junshi* [Chongqing military affairs during the Sino-Japanese War]. Chongqing: Chongqing chubanshe, 1995.

Tao Wenzhao. *Kangri zhanzheng shiqi Zhongguo duiwai guanxi* [Foreign relations during the Sino-Japanese War era]. Beijing: zhongguo shehui kexue chubanshe, 2009.

Taylor, Jay. *Generalissimo: Chiang Kai-shek and the Struggle for Modern China.* Cambridge, Mass.: Belknap, 2009.

Taylor, Joe G. *Air Interdiction in China in World War II.* Montgomery, Ala.: Air University, 1956.

———. *Air Supply in the Burma Campaigns.* Montgomery, Ala.: Air University, 1957.

Thompson, George R., and Dixie R. Harris. *The Signal Corps: The Outcome.* Washington, D.C.: U.S. Army Center of Military History, 1991.

Thompson, Henrietta. "Walk a Little Faster: Escape from Burma with General Stilwell in 1942." Master's thesis, University of Maine, 1992.

Thompson, Mark. "Here's Why the U.S. Military Is a Family Business." *Time*, March 10, 2016. Accessed July 29, 2023. https://time.com/4254696/military-family-business/.

Thorne, Christopher. *Allies of a Kind: The United States, Britain, and the War against Japan, 1941–1945.* New York: Oxford University Press, 1978.

Toyomi, Asano. "Japanese Operations in Yunnan and North Burma." In *The Battle for China: Essays on the Military History of the Sino-Japanese War of 1937–1945*, edited by Mark Peattie, Edward J. Drea, and Hans van de Ven, 361–385. Stanford, Calif.: Stanford University Press, 2011.

Tsou, Tang. "The Historians and the Generals." *Pacific Historical Review* 31, no. 1 (Feb. 1962): 41–48.

———. *America's Failure in China, 1941–1950.* Chicago: University of Chicago Press, 1963.

Tuchman, Barbara. *Stilwell and the American Experience in China, 1911–1945.* New York: Macmillan Publishers, 1970.

Tunner, Willaim H. *Over the Hump.* New York: Duell, Sloane and Pearce, 1964.

United States Relations with China: With Special Reference to the Period 1944–1949. United States Department of State. Washington, D.C.: U.S. Government Printing Office, 1949.

van De Ven, Hans. "Stilwell in the Stocks: The Chinese Nationalists and the Allied Powers in the Second World War." *Asian Affairs* 34, no. 3 (2003): 243–59.

———. *War and Nationalism in China, 1925–1945.* London: Routledge, 2003.

———. *Warfare in Chinese History.* Boston: Brill, 2000.

Wang, Chaoguang. "The Dark Side of the War: Corruption in the Guomindang Government during World War II." *Journal of Modern Chinese History* 11, no. 2 (2017): 249–63.

Wang, Jingbin. "No Lost Chance in China: The False Realism of American Foreign Service Officers, 1943–1945." *Journal of American-East Asian Relations* 17, no. 2 (2010): 118–45.

Wang, Peter Chen-Main. "Revisiting US–China Wartime Relations: A Study of Wedemeyer's China Mission." *Journal of Contemporary China* 18, no. 59 (March 2009): 233–47.

———. "Chiang Kai-shek's Faith in Christianity: The Trial of the Stilwell Incident." *Journal of Modern Chinese History* 8, no. 2 (2014): 194–209.

Wang Zhenhua. *Kangzhan shiqi waiguo dui Hua junshi yuanzhu* [Military aid to China during the anti-Japanese war]. Taipei: Huanqiu shuju, 1987.

Warnock, A. Timothy. "The Chinese American Composite Wing: A Case Study of the Versatility of the Composite Concept." *Air Power History* 39, no. 3 (Fall 1992): 21–30.

Watson, Mark Skinner. *Chief of Staff: Prewar Plans and Preparations*. Washington, D.C.: Government Printing Office, 2003.

Webster, Donovan. *The Burma Road: The Epic Story of the China-Burma-India Theater in World War II*. New York: HarperCollins, 2004.

Wedemeyer, Albert C. *Wedemeyer Reports!: An Objective, Dispassionate Examination of World War II, Postwar Policies, and Grand Strategy*. New York: Henry Holt and Co., 1958.

———. *Wedemeyer on War and Peace*. Stanford, Calif.: Hoover Institution Press. 1987.

Wen Haxiong. *Wen Haxiong xiansheng fangwen lilu* [Oral history of General Wen Haxiong]. Taipei: Zhongyang Yanjiu Suo, 1997.

Whitson, William W. *Chronology of Military Campaigns in China, 1895–1950*. N.p., 1967.

———. *Military Campaigns in China, 1942–1950*. Taipei: U.S. Army Office of Military History, 1966.

Willmott, H. P. *Grave of a Dozen Schemes: British Naval Planning and the War against Japan, 1943–1945*. Annapolis, Md.: Naval Institute Press, 1996.

Worthing, Peter. *A Military History of Modern China: From the Manchu Conquest to Tian'anmen Square*. Westport, Conn.: Praeger, 2007.

Wu, Shih-weh. "History, Organization and Operation of the Armored School and Chinese Military Academy." Military Monograph, Advanced Officers Class #1, The Armored School, Fort Knox, February 25, 1947.

Wu, T'ien-wei. "Contending Political Forces." In *China's Bitter Victory: The War with Japan 1937–1945*, edited by James C. Hsiung and Steven I. Levine. Armonk, N.Y.: M. E. Sharpe, Inc., 1992.

Xie Benshu, *Minguo jinglü, Dianjun fengyun* [The first half of the twentieth century: Yunnan military history]. Kunming: Yunnan renmin chubanshe, 2004.

Xu, Guangqiu. "Americans and Chinese Nationalist Military Aviation, 1929–1949." *Journal of Asian History* 31, no. 2 (1997): 155–80.

———. "The Issue of US Air Support for China during the Second World War, 1942–45." *Journal of Contemporary History* 36, no. 3 (July 2001): 459–84.

Yang Chenguan. "Guojun weiwan cheng de junshi shiwu daige (1943–1945) yi guojun meishi zhuangbeihua budui wei zhongxin de shentan." *Zhonghua junshi xue huiyi huikan* 10 (April 1995): 166–68.

Yang Tianshi. *Zhaoxun zhenshi de Jiang Jieshi: Jiang Jieshi riji jiedu* [Looking for the real Chiang Kai-shek: An interpretation of his diary]. 2 vols. Hong Kong: Sanlian shudian, 2008.

Yang, Y. K. *The Supply Service of the Chinese Army*. Command and General Staff School, Fort Leavenworth, 1948.

Yin, Cao. "The Return of Chen Ching Lin: Chinese Deserters and Chinatowns in the British Raj, 1943–1946." *Journal of South Asian Studies* 44, no. 5 (2021): 888–902.

———. "Establishing the Ramgarh Training Center: The Burma Campaign, the Colonial Internment Camp, and the Wartime Sino-British Relations," *TRaNS: Trans-Regional and National Studies of Southeast Asia* 9 (2021): 1–10.

Yin Guoxiang. *Yin Guoxiang xiansheng fangwen jilu* [Oral history of General Yin Guoxiang]. Taipei: Zhongyang Yanjiu Suo, 1994.

Young, Kenneth R. "The Stilwell Controversy: A Bibliographical Review." *Military Affairs* 39, no. 2 (April 1975): 66–68.

Yu Da. *Yu da xiansheng fangwen jilu* [Oral history of General Yu Da]. Taipei: Zhongyang Yanjiu Suo, 1989.

Yu, Maochun. *OSS in China: Prelude to Cold War.* Annapolis, Md.: Naval Institute Press, 1996.

———. *The Dragon's War: Allied Operations and the Fate of China, 1937–1947.* Annapolis, Md.: Naval Institute Press, 2013.

Yue Bingnan. *Zheng jiemin jiangjun shengping* [The life of General Zhen Jiemin]. Taipei: Shiying, 2010.

Zhang Fakui. *Zhang Fakui koushu zi zhuan: Guomindang lujun zong siling huiyi lu* [Zhang Fakui oral history memoirs: Memories of a Guomindang general officer]. Beijing: Dandai zhongguo chubnshe, 2012.

Zhang Faqian. *Zhang Faqian xiansheng fangwen jilu* [Oral history of General Zhang Faqian]. Taipei: Zhongyang Yanjiu Suo, 1992.

Zhang Mingkai. *History of the Sino-Japanese War.* Taipei: Military History Bureau of the Ministry of National Defense, 1985.

Zhang Ruide. *Kangzhan shiqi de guojun renshi* [Anatomy of the Nationalist Army, 1937–1945]. Taipei: Zhongyang Yanjiu Suo, 1993.

Zhang, Xiaoming. "Toward Arming China: United States Arms Sales and Military Assistance, 1921–1941." PhD dissertation, University of Iowa, 1994.

Zheng Jinju. *Yi dai zhanshen: Sun Liren* [A generation's war hero: Sun Li-jen]. Taipei: Shuiniu chuban youxian gongsi, 2004.

Zheng, Yanqiu. "A Specter of Extraterritoriality: The Legal Status of U.S. Troops in China, 1943–1947." *Journal of American-East Asian Relations* 22, no. 1 (2015): 17–44.

Zhibingtang bianjibu. *Zhongguo yuan zheng jun Miandian zhan ji, 1942–1945* [A record of the China Expeditionary Army in Burma, 1942–1945]. Taipei: Zhibingtang wenhua chuanmei youxian gongsi, 2014.

Ziegler, Philip. *Mountbatten: The Official Biography.* New York: Harper & Row, 1986.

INDEX

Abrams, Creighton, 180
Afghanistan: desertion and retention in, 179; lack of clear mission for U.S. operations in, 23; lack of military interest in shaping mission in, 182; political aspects of, 177; unmanned drones for airpower in, 57; U.S. military in, 4, 175
Air Commando unit, Chindits in north Burma and, 102
aircraft: Chiang's Three Demands and, 60; Japanese losses in China theater and, 93–94; for Nationalist Chinese, 57–58; transport, American, for Chindits into north Burma, 101–2; transport, north Burma campaign and, 81; transport, supplies for north Burma campaign and, 102–3
airfield, Myitkyina, 122–3, 123–4, 125, 128–9
airpower: based in China, Dorn and, 133; invasion of Japan from China and, 82; Myitkyina capture and, 124; official Army histories on U.S. policies for, 13; Stilwell's and Army's role in CBI and, 5; Stilwell's plan to retake Burma and, 49; strategy conferences and, 63–70; as tactical threat to Stilwell's operations, 55
Alexander, Harold, 33, 36
Allied Chief of Staff for China Theater: *See* Stilwell, Joseph W.
Allied Councils of War, 75
allies, uncertain: ambiguous missions and, 178–83; Army involvement in military affairs of, 3; CBI theater and, 6–7; Stilwell's failures in cultivating, 51;

See also British; Chinese; north Burma campaign
Alsop, Joseph, 65, 177
American, British, Dutch, and Australian (ABDA) command, 32
American medical personnel, 128, 153
American military: advisers, arrive in Yunnan, 134–5; advisers, mixed success of, 150; institutional insulation from political awareness and, 8, 176; as negotiators, coordinators, and managers, 177; objective civilian control and, 184; operations, lack of clear mission for, 23; operations, north Burma campaign and, 81; operations, Sun Li-jen, Burma defense and, 35; political understanding and, 184–5; strategies for difficult tasks, 38–39; support, to Chinese operations, 134; units, acrimony due to north Burma campaign and, 129; Y Force offensive and, 141; on Y Force prospects in Burma, 149–50; *See also* military authority
American Military Mission to China (AMMISCA), 25, 33
American public: attitudes of, Stilwell not learning about, 176; Chiang Kai-shek and, 91; China support by, 30; doubts about China among, 156; military insulation from life of, 8; Stilwell's lack of understanding political attitudes of, 8–9; *See also* United States
American Revolution, 2, 175
American Volunteer Group (AVG), 33, 58, 60

251

America's Failure in China, 1941–1950 (Tsou), 14, 182
Anbar Awakening, 175, 179
Andaman Islands, Operation Buccaneer and, 88
Arakan coast, Burma, 81, 82, 88
Arcadia Conference (1941), 28
aristocratic connections, Mountbatten's, 82, 181
Army, U.S.: airpower advocates and, 57; British efforts in southeast Asia and, 75; CBI assessment, spring 1946, 1–2; in China, Dorn on mission of, 135; on fraternization in China, 59; on interoperability, 97; military affairs of foreign allies and, 3; as niche career removed from American political life, 185; north Burma campaign and, 98; Stilwell assessment in 1950s by official histories of, 12–14; on Stilwell in CBI theater, 177; Stilwell support by, 165–6; Stilwell's allies in, 84; Stilwell's failure to cultivate Gauss as ally and, 51; support of British Commonwealth and China by, 25; as Y Force personnel, 151; *See also* Joint Chiefs of Staff, U.S.; Stilwell, Joseph W.
Army Air Forces, U.S., 58–59, 60, 102. *See also* Chennault, Claire
Army Military Intelligence Division, U.S., 25
Army Services of Supply, U.S., 84, 163
Army War College, 11, 185
Arnold, Henry H. "Hap": on airpower in China problems, 62; Cairo Conference and, 90; at Casablanca Conference, 63; on Chennault and Stilwell, 60; post-Casablanca meeting with Chiang and, 66; support for Stilwell by, 68
Arrowsmith, John C., 103
Assam logistics corridor, 70, 85
Auchinleck, Claude, 84–85, 86, 88

B-24 bombers, 71
B-25 Mitchell medium bombers, 102, 147
B-29 bombers, 162
Babcock-Lumish, Brian, 184
Bai Chongxi, 52, 167, 168, 169
Baldwin, Hanson, 91
Behind Japanese Lines: With the OSS in Burma (Dunlop), 18
Behind the Burma Road (Peers), 18
Berman, Eli, 180
Bissell, Clayton L., 31–32, 59, 60, 61, 62
"Bitter Tea of General Joe, The" (*Time*), 129
Boatner, Hayden L.: disseminating orders (guidance) from, 78; Mountbatten's Burma plan and, 159; on Myitkyina capture, 125; as NCAC commanding general, 110; on Stilwell concentrating his forces, 127–8; on Stilwell's leadership style, 130; on Stilwell's staff, 73; training Chinese troops in India, 44, 45, 79–80
Brereton, Lewis H., 58–59, 60
British: acrimony due to north Burma campaign and, 129–30; CBI theater and, 1–2; Chiang isolation from, 41; on Chiang's *China's Destiny*, 91; on Chinese ground forces, 69; light infantry use by, 127; Marshall's negotiations with, CAI and, 80; Mogaung Valley and, 119; north Burma campaign and, 74–75, 80–82, 98; opposing north Burma road and pipeline, 84–86; political goals for Southeast Asia, 88; Stilwell at odds with, 32–33; Stilwell on retaking Burma and objectives of, 76–77; Stilwell's allies in military establishment of, 74–75; on Stilwell's behavior and demeanor, 158; Stilwell's critical attitude toward, 28; Stilwell's lack of authority and, 4–5; Stilwell's plan to retake Burma and, 48; Stilwell's relations with, 19–20; on Sun Li-jen and Burma defense, 35–36; suspicions about Chinese troops by, 33; U.S. as uncertain allies with, 6–7; U.S. manipulation (1941–1945) by, 13; *See also*

Chindits; Churchill, Winston; Mountbatten, Louis; Wingate, Orde
British Chiefs of Staff, 83
British Long-Range Patrol Groups, 97. *See also* Chindits
Brooke, Alan, 81, 92–93
Brooks, Risa, 184
brothels, in China, 59
Brown, Rothwell H., 99
Buccaneer, Operation, 88
Burma: American support for Stilwell's attack on, 48; CAI probing attacks into, 86–87; Churchill restructuring command in, 80–81; defense by U.S., British, and Chinese troops, 33–36; failure in, 31–36, 38; Japanese conquest of, 4, 18–19; Mountbatten's plan for, 158–9; retreat from, 36; SEAC and, 82; Stilwell on retaking, 68, 74–75; Stilwell resolving practical difficulties in, 76; Stilwell's attack reevaluated, 63; Stilwell's proposal to attack, 41–43; Trident Conference on operations in, 70; *See also* north Burma campaign
Burma Road: campaign to reopen, 20; CBI theater logistical difficulties and, 19; connector road t0 Ledo from, 49, 77, 84–85; supplies to be carried over, 27; Y Force and Japanese defense along, 140; Y Force to seize, 139; *See also* pipeline, in north Burma
Burma-India theater, creation of, 174
Burt, Sally, 183

CAI: *See* Chinese Army in India
Cairo Conference: Chiang's demands at, 72; Chinese military officers at, 92–93; demonstrating CBI capabilities at, 86–95; East Asian policy objectives and, 89; Stilwell performance at, 79; Stilwell's influence regained at, 75; Stilwell's leverage at, 80; Stilwell's political difficulties at, 5; Y Force training and, 138
Calvert, Colonel, 120
Canol Road, Canada, 84

Casablanca Conference, 63–64
CEF: *See* Chinese Expeditionary Force
Ceylon, SEAC and, 82
chain of command: American liaison officers training CAI and, 80; British, Mountbatten's use of, 181; CAI insulated from, 178; command relationships, 1943–1944 and, 83, 88; Marshall on Chennault and, 94; Stilwell and SEAC's, 159; Stilwell's appeals using, 67–68
Champion, Operation, 88, 89, 94. *See also* north Burma campaign
Changsha, Hunan Province, falls to Japanese, 167
Chao Chen-yu, 99
Chen Cheng, 78–79. *See also* Chinese Expeditionary Force
Chen Jian, 17–18
Chennault, Claire: aerial operations coordination and planning and, 133; air support and supplies for Xue Yue and, 167; as airpower advocate, 55–57; American policy in Asia debate between Stilwell and, 19; Bissell's and Stilwell's tensions with, 59; blaming bad weather on not stopping Japanese, 163; Burma defense and, 32; Cairo Conference and doubts about air program under, 93–94; CBI theater and, 5; Chiang on Air Task Force in China under, 66; as Chinese air force advisor, 58; Dorn and, 135–6; independent military advice to Chiang by, 161–2; north Burma campaign and, 102; political and media maneuvers of, 177; Roosevelt on airpower in China and, 69–70; Stilwell and influence of, 75; Stilwell criticism by, 12; Stilwell's command relationships, 1943–1944 and, 83; Stilwell's personality clash with, 57; *See also* Fourteenth Air Force
Chiang Kai-shek: accepts Stilwell's Burma attack proposal, 41–42, 77; on airpower and bombing, 56; on

airpower and north Burma offensive, 62–63; Allied chief of staff to, 45–46; American role in China and, 26; American special envoys and, 181; Cairo Conference and, 89, 90–91; CBI theater and personality of, 9; Chennault and, 58; on Chennault's airpower in China plan, 64, 67; China theater and, 21; Chinese Expeditionary Force and, 134; Chinese troops under Stilwell and, 33, 95; command relationships, 1943–1944, 83; Davies on, 15; declining faith in, 155–6; disputes with Lung Yun in Yunnan, 137; insulted by Brereton's orders to Suez, 60; Japan's Ichi-Go offensive and, 161, 164; KMT government collapse and flight of, 11; micromanagement of Burma defense by, 34–35, 36; on Mogaung Valley operations, 118; north Burma campaign and, 98, 158–9; opposing Army reforms in China, 74; opposition coalition against, 154, 168, 169; political influence at Cairo Conference, 92–93; post-Casablanca meeting with, 65–66; problematic statements by, 24; provisions on Stilwell commanding Chinese forces, 170–1; reactionary Nationalist Party elements and, 30; regional military leaders on government opposing, 168; as responsible for defeats, 163; revisionist school of historiographical writing on, 14; Roosevelt cooling toward, 152; Roosevelt on Stilwell's mission and, 172–4; Roosevelt's flawed assumptions about, 182–3; senior American officer role in CBI and, 23; Stilwell as Allied chief of staff for, 4, 31; on Stilwell as Chinese and American forces' commander, 166; Stilwell as Chinese army commander and, 172; Stilwell at odds with, 32–33; Stilwell on dealing with, 164; Stilwell on training Chinese military forces and, 39–40; on Stilwell's authority for north Burma campaign, 99; Stilwell's campaign in China and, 6; Stilwell's difficulties with, 20; Stilwell's mission and, 22; Stilwell's plan to retake Burma and, 50; on U.S. and Chinese Communists, 157–8; on visible attack on Japanese in China, 61; Xue Yue and orders from, 157; Y Force training and supplies, 138–9; Yunnan Province and, 134, 151; *See also* Meiling Soong; Three Demands, Chiang's

Chiang-chu, Burma, Y Force offensive and, 144

China: anti-Chiang government talks in, 168; increasing importance in CBI theater, 21; international planning conferences and, 5; Japan's Ichi-Go offensive and, 161; north Burma campaign and, 20; retreat from Yangtze River Valley, 155; Roosevelt on East Asia role of, 9; Stilwell and regional forces nominally recognizing Nationalists in, 51–53; U.S. influence via regional military leaders in, 156–7; U.S. political representatives in, 89; Z Force in, 153; *See also* Chiang Kai-shek; Chinese Communists; Hump airlift; Mao Zedong; People's Republic of China; Taiwan

China Hands: *See* Dorn, Frank; Timberman, Thomas

China Lobby, U.S., 11–12, 24

China Tangle, The (Feis), 13

China theater: creation of, 174; *See also* Stilwell, Joseph W.

China Training and Combat Command, 83

China-Burma-India (CBI) theater: airpower advocates in, 56–57; airpower results in, 71; American military understanding of, 24–25; Churchill restructuring command in, 80–81; Combined Chiefs limiting mission of, 165; Drum on mission to, 27; expanding New Delhi headquarters of, 46; flawed command structures, 31–36, 38; initial plans for, 23–31; Joint Chiefs abolish, 174;

lack of unity in, 50–52; Lend-Lease supplies and, 43–44; lessons of, 186; map of, 37; relational and diffused mission in, 7; shifting roles and eccentric personalities in, 57–63; Sino-American relationship and, 75; Somervell and Ledo Road for, 84–85; spring 1946 assessment of, 1–2, 3; Stilwell and engineering projects in, 76–77; Stilwell's appointment to, 28–29; Stilwell's command relationships, 1943–1944 in, 83; Stilwell's tenure in, 18–19

China's Destiny (Chiang Kai-shek), 91, 183

Chindits: Mogaung Valley and, 119; north Burma campaign and, 97, 98, 101–2; Wingate's death and, 120; Wingate's expectations for, 126–7; *See also* light infantry

Chinese: acrimony due to north Burma campaign and, 129; on American airpower, 57; at Cairo Conference, 92–93; CBI theater and, 1–2; as combat personnel in CBI theater, 7; hygiene and mental health, 128; north Burma campaign and, 98, 132; Stilwell's command authority over, 39–40; Stilwell's command of, 20; Stilwell's lack of authority and, 4–5; Stilwell's plan to retake Burma and, 50; suspicions about British troops by, 33; tactical behaviors of, 133; training in India, 41–43, 44–45; *See also* Chiang Kai-shek; Chinese Army in India; Chinese Communists; Chinese Expeditionary Force

Chinese air force, 58, 162

Chinese army, 92, 178–9. *See also* Chinese Expeditionary Force

Chinese Army in India (CAI): allied support for Stilwell and, 75–76; intensive, comprehensive advisory approach for, 153; low educational levels of, 109; military school system and, 135; Myitkyina capture and, 123, 124; probing attacks into Burma by, 86–87; Stilwell training, 44; Stilwell's command relationships, 1943–1944 and, 83; as tangible asset that Stilwell created, 95; total strength of, 99; training and developing, 77–80, 151; U.S. tactics, doctrine, operational behaviors and, 178

Chinese black market, 94

Chinese Communists, 156, 157–8, 171, 183

Chinese Expeditionary Force (CEF), 20–21, 77–79, 90, 140. *See also* Y Force

Chinese language, 10, 28

Chungking (Chongqing): AMMISCA office in, 25; Arnold's visit to, 66; congressional delegation visit to, 91; Ichi-Go offensive and, 164–5; Mao Zedong and, 156; radio messages to, 34; Wallace's visit to, 158; Wilkie's visit to, 61–62; Xue Yue outside the authority of, 157; *See also* Chiang Kai-shek; China; Currie, Lauchlin B.; Gauss, Clarence E.; Nationalist China

Churchill, Winston: on airpower in China, 69; Cairo Conference and, 89, 93; restructuring British command in India and Burma, 80–81; Roosevelt on military presence in China and, 26; Southeast Asia Command and, 82; Stilwell on retaking Burma and, 76; Tehran Conference and, 90; on unconventional operations, 100; as Wingate supporter, 101; *See also* British

Clark, Wesley, 181

Clausewitz, Carl von, 53

Cohen, Warren, 182–3

Cold War, military affairs of foreign allies and, 3

Combined Chiefs of Staff (CCS), U.S.–U.K.: Chiang Kai-shek at Cairo Conference and, 93; Chiang on adding China to, 40; command relationships, 1943–1944, 83; formation of, 28; on land route to China, 85; limiting CBI theater mission parameters, 165; Stilwell training Chinese troops in India and, 44; on Stilwell's appointment to CBI theater, 29

command and control, north Burma campaign and, 111
"Command Crisis in China, 1944, The: A Road Not Taken" (Schaller), 17
communications, north Burma campaign and, 111, 112
Communist Party, official Army histories of Stilwell and, 13
conditionality strategies, unilateral grants of support compared with, 180
Congress, U.S., 9, 30, 91, 176
Council on Foreign Relations, 185
cultural challenges: for Chinese interpreters, 150; to light infantry, 127
Culverin plan, 159
Currie, Lauchlin B., 41, 47

Dai Anlan, 35, 36
Dai Li, 30, 169, 170
Davies, John Paton, Jr.: on British and plan to retake Burma, 48; on Chinese and Allied war effort, 155–6; on Chinese Communists, 157; on lack of coordination in CBI theater, 160–1; Mountbatten's Burma plan and, 159; on policy inconsistencies for Stilwell, 181–2; as Stilwell advisor, 12; on Stilwell and CBI theater, 15; on Stilwell and Chennault bypassing Gauss, 51; on Stilwell and politics, 65; as Stilwell political advisor, 91; Stilwell's Cairo Conference plan and, 89–90; Stilwell's military staff and, 28; on unprepared Chinese military officers, 92
de Wiart, Carton, 172
desertion, uncertain allies and, 179
Dill, John, 28, 49, 94
Diplomatic History, 17
diseases, tropical: British brigades and, 119, 121; Chinese troops and, 119, 126; light infantry attitudes and, 127; Marauders and, 115, 117; Myitkyina attack and, 121–2, 123, 125; north Burma campaign and, 104, 106; poor medical care and, 124

distance, understanding senior policy debates and, 8
doctrinal differences, north Burma campaign and, 97, 98
Dorn, Frank: airpower based in China and, 133; Chennault and, 135–6; on opposition to Chiang coalition, 154; on Stilwell as scapegoat, 15–16; Stilwell's command relationships, 1943–1944 and, 83; on Wei Li-Huang, 141; Wei's offensive and, 146; on Y Force engineers, 143; on Y Force prospects in Burma, 149–50; on Y Force tactics, 141–2; Y Force training and, 78, 135
Dragon by the Tail: American, British, Japanese, and Russian Encounters with China and One Another (Davies), 15
drones, unmanned, airpower advocates on, 57
Drum, Hugh A., 26–27
Dunlop, Richard, 18
Dutch East Indies (Indonesia), 32

Eastman, Lloyd, 16
education, of officer corps, 185–6
18th Division, Japanese, 79, 104–5, 107, 113, 117
88th Division, Chinese, 145, 146
88th Regiment, Chinese, 122
87th Division, Chinese, 146
Eisenhower, Dwight D., 54, 183
Eldridge, Fred, 11
Eleventh Army Group, 83
11th Group Army, Chinese, 145, 148
11th Indian Infantry Brigade, British, 119
engineers and engineering: *See* military engineering
equipment for Chinese army, 136, 150–1. *See also* aircraft; landing craft
European theater, during World War II, 183

Fairbank, John K., 17
families, Army service among, 185

Index 257

Far East Air Force, U.S., 58–59
Feis, Herbert, 13, 14
field hospitals, 137, 147
Fifth Army, Chinese, 33–34, 37
54th Army, Chinese, 142, 143, 144
56th Division, Japanese, 139–40
53rd Division, Japanese, 120–1
53th Army, Chinese, 142, 143, 144
5307th Composite Unit (Provisional): clearing the Hukawng Valley and, 112; communications problems with, 127; flanking in the Hukawng Valley, 110–1; flanking in the Mogaung Valley, 114–5; Myitkyina capture and, 123, 125; organization of, 100–101; sickness and exhaustion and, 126; *See also* Hunter, Charles N.
1st Provisional Tank Group: clearing the Hukawng Valley and, 110, 112; fixing Japanese on Jambu Bum and, 114; Mogaung Valley and, 116; north Burma campaign and, 99, 125
flight crews, U.S., 98
Flying Tigers, 55–56, 58
Fong Hsien-chueh, 167
Foreign Affairs, 9
Fort Leavenworth, 1–2, 3–4, 10, 11
Fourteenth Air Force: aerial operations coordination and planning and, 133; Cairo Conference and doubts about effectiveness of, 93–94; in CBI theater, 71–72; Chennault as commander of, 66, 162; Japanese advances and, 172; Japan's Ichi-Go offensive and, 167; Stilwell and supplies for, 163; Stilwell on effects of, 70; Stilwell's command relationships, 1943–1944, 83; *See also* Chennault, Claire
IV war zone, China's, 167
Free Thais, 88
French in Indo-China, State Department advisors in CBI theater and, 88

Galahad (specialized unit), 100
Gandhi, Mahatma, 41

Gauss, Clarence E.: as ambassador to China, 22; on American efforts in China as problematic, 29–30; on Chiang's empty rhetoric, 164; on Chinese and Allied war effort, 48, 155; on Chinese attitude toward British, 41; leaves China, 174; Stilwell and Chungking role of, 50–51; Stilwell coordination with, 160
Giffard, George, 83
Great Britain: *See* British

Hamilton, Maxwell M., 47–48, 64–65
hammer and anvil attack, 110, 113
Hengyang, China, 167
historical accounts: academic reevaluation of, 16–17; official Army histories and, 13–14; political and personal passions in, 11–12; by political scientists, 12–13; professionally researched intelligence studies and, 18; revisionist school (1960s–1980s) and, 14–16; untapped resources and materials (1990s) and, 17–18
Ho Ying-chin, 139, 154
Hogan, David W., 18
Hopkins, Harry, 30–31, 62, 94
Hornbeck, Stanley, 47–48, 91
hospitals, military, 137, 147
Hu Hanmou, 154
Hukawng Valley, Burma: CAI attack down, 77; Chinese probing attacks into, 87; clearing, 110–3; Japanese blocking, 107–9, 110–1, 112–3; on north Burma campaign map, 107; road network through, 103, 105, 106
Hump airlift: Chennault and logistics of supplies via, 66–67; Chiang on diversion of transport aircraft from, 89; deliveries to Burma via, 42; difficulties of flying supplies over, 56; equipment for Chinese army carried over, 136; Fourteenth Air Force supplies and, 163; Myitkyina airfield and, 128–9; north Burma campaign and, 97; Roosevelt

on increasing deliveries by, 70; Roosevelt's faith in, 76; transport aircraft for Burma drive and, 81
Hunter, Charles N., 72, 115–6, 122–3, 127, 129–30
Huntington, Samuel, 184
Huo Kuei-chang, 141
Hurley, Patrick, 12, 171, 172, 173–4

Ichi-Go offensive, Japanese, 6, 161–4, 167–8, 170
illiteracy, Chinese units in Burma and, 109
Imphal, India: *See* Assam logistics corridor
India: airlifting supplies into east China from, 163; Chinese troops training in, 42–43, 53, 74–75; Churchill restructuring command in, 80–81; Japanese attack British in, 139; U.S. bombers for, 61; U.S. political representatives in, 89; *See also* Chinese Army in India
Indian Nationalist leaders, 41, 42
Indo-Chinese, State Department advisors and, 88
Inkangakwawng, Burma, 116
intelligence: CAI probing attacks into Burma and, 87; in CBI theater, 24–25; Mogaung Valley and, 115; professionally researched studies of, 18
International Security, 184
interoperability, Army definition of, 97
interpreters, 136, 150
Iraq, U.S. operations in: Anbar Awakening and, 175; Iraqi Counter Terrorism Service, 179; lack of clear mission for, 23; long-term national security goals and, 4; political aspects of, 177; subjective and undefined orders for, 54; unmanned drones for airpower and, 57
Italy, aircraft for Nationalist Chinese and, 58

Jackson, Michael, 181
Jambu Bum, 105, 111, 113, 114, 116, 118
Janowitz, Morris, 8
Japan, Allies' invasion plans for, 82

Japanese: advances into China, 172; aircraft losses in China theater and, 93–94; airpower in CBI theater and, 71–72; on Allied logistics for north Burma campaign, 103; attack British in India, 139; in Burma, 76; Burma conquest by, 4, 18–19, 35; CBI theater and, 2; Chennault on airpower against, 55–56; China's political affairs and, 152; and clearing the Hukawng Valley, 110–1; in Hukawng Valley blocking Allies, 107–8, 109, 112–3; Ichi-Go offensive, 6, 161, 163, 167–8, 170; logistics, north Burma campaign and, 106; Manchuria invasion and China invasion by, 23–24; Mogaung Valley and, 116, 117, 118–9, 120–1; Myitkyina defense and, 122, 123; probing attacks into Burma by, 32; resisting CAI probing attacks into Burma, 87; resisting north Burma campaign, 96–97; Tengchong offensive and, 147–8; Y Force offensive and, 143
Jenkins, Walter E., Jr., 137
Joint Chiefs of Staff, U.S.: abolishes CBI theater, 174; on airpower in China, 70; CBI theater and, 29; on Chinese forces at Cairo Conference, 92; limiting CBI theater mission parameters, 165; Marshall on Stilwell's plan and, 64; reshaping Stilwell's mission, 163–4; Stilwell–Mountbatten rift and, 159–60; Stilwell's command relationships, 1943–1944, 83; Stilwell's plan to retake Burma and, 49, 77
Joint Forces Quarterly, 185
Joint History Office, U.S., 29
Jones, Walter S., 109–10
jungle training, of Chinese troops in India, 43

Kachin tribe: American OSS officers arming and organizing, 104; CBI theater and, 6; Mogaung Valley and, 115; Myitkyina capture plan and, 122; north

Burma campaign and, 98; reporting to NCAC, 110
Kaoli-kung (Gaoligong) mountains, 141, 142–3
Karzai, Hamid, 180
King, Ernest, 68, 90
Kipling, Rudyard, 33
KMT (Kuomintang) party: Chiang on Soviets' clash with, 161; Chinese government and, 154–5; Chinese government collapse and, 11; historical assessment of, 16; Long Yun and, 134; opposition government talks and, 168; Whampoa Academy of, 92; Xue Yue and, 52; *See also* Chiang Kai-shek
Korea and Korean War, 4, 11–12, 177, 180
Kosovo conflict, blocking airport access to Russians and, 181
Kumon Mountains, 121, 122, 125

Ladwig, Walter, 180
Lake, David, 180
landing craft, 81
Larrabee, Eric, 183
League of Democratic Parties, 168
Leahy, William D., 68
Ledo Road, Burma, 49, 77, 84–85
Lend-Lease Act (1941), 25
Lend-Lease supplies, 43, 47, 171
Li Tsung-jen, 52, 169
Liao Yaoxiang, 44, 79, 99, 111–2, 118
light footprint approach, 149, 153, 154–5
light infantry, 126–8. *See also* Chindits
Lindsay, Malcolm F., 153, 167, 168
Lippman, Walter, 47
Liu, F. F., 12
Lo Chin-ying, 36
local regional leaders: seeking U.S. assistance, 179; *See also* regional forces
Lodge, Henry Cabot, 91
logistics: American, Chinese distribution of, 150; Chennault's lack of interest in, 66–67; clearing the Hukawng Valley and, 113; Fourteenth Air Force supplies and, 163; north Burma campaign and, 81, 102–3, 106; Stilwell on aid to Chinese forces and, 180; to supply China overland, 77; U.S. Army officers supporting Stilwell and, 84; Wheeler as SEAC G-4 and, 88; Y Force offensive and, 146; Z Force and, 153
Lohbeck, Donald, 12
Long Yun, 134
Longling, Burma, 140, 141, 142, 143, 145–6
Long-Range Patrol Groups, British: *See* Chindits
lost chance narrative, 16, 17–18
Luce, Henry, 24
Lung Yun, 52, 137, 154, 168

M3A3 Stuart tanks, 99–100
MacArthur, Douglas, 89
Magruder, John L., 25, 29
Malaya, SEAC and, 82
al-Maliki, Nouri, 180
Mamian pass, 143, 144
Manchuria, Japanese invasion of, 23
Mao Pang-tzo, 58
Mao Zedong, 16, 156
maps, 24, 37, 107, 142
Marauders: *See* Merrill's Marauders
Marshall, George C.: American military presence in China and, 26–27; Cairo Conference and, 90; at Casablanca Conference, 63–64; on CBI theater accomplishments, 50; Chennault and chain of command issues and, 94; on Chennault's airpower in China plan, 62, 67, 70; on Chiang's Three Demands, 46; on Chinese at Cairo Conference, 93; combat units to Stilwell and, 100; denies Stilwell request for resources and support, 38–39; Hurley as Chiang's personal representative and, 171; on limiting China theater operations, 164; on McHugh's criticism of Army in CBI theater, 51; on Mountbatten and SEAC, 82; on

Myitkyina capture, 121; negotiations with British, CAI and, 80; nominates Stilwell for CBI theater, 27–28; Roosevelt's rejection of, 17; Somervell and, 84; on Stilwell and politics in China, 166; on Stilwell in CBI theater, 177; Stilwell support by, 158, 165–6; Stilwell–Mountbatten rift and, 160; Stilwell's plan to retake Burma and, 48–49, 64; on supplies for Y Force, 139; support for Stilwell by, 68

McChrystal, Stanley, 73, 180, 186

McConville, James C., 185

McHugh, James M., 51, 62

media, American, 129, 176

medical evacuation, north Burma campaign and, 102

medical role in China, 135, 153

Mei-ling Soong, 52, 58, 62, 166. *See also* Chiang Kai-shek

Melby, John F., 174

Merrill, Frank D.: clearing the Hukawng Valley and, 112; heart attack of, 115–6, 122; Myitkyina attack and, 123; Stilwell's leadership and, 130; as trusted Stilwell staff member, 101

Merrill's Marauders: clearing the Hukawng Valley and, 110; flanking in the Hukawng Valley, 112–3; flanking in the Mogaung Valley, 116, 117; Mogaung Valley and, 114–5; Myitkyina capture and, 121–2, 123, 124; north Burma campaign and, 96; Stilwell's handling criticized in U.S., 129; Wingate's expectations for, 127

Mexico, Army campaign against, 2

military advisory and assistance, 6

military authority: initial CBI theater plans and, 23–24; Japanese attack on Pearl Harbor and, 26; scope in CBI theater of, 22–23; Stilwell's lack of clear mission and, 4–5; *See also* American military

military engineering: American battalions, 123, 124, 126; in CBI theater, 76–77; in China, Americans and, 135, 140, 143–4, 149; clearing the Hukawng Valley and, 112; road building and, 103–4, 106–8; Somervell and, 75

Military Review, 184

missionaries, in China, 24

missions, ambiguous: CBI theater and, 6–7; in China, 24–27; flawed command structures and, 31–36, 38; since Stilwell's, 54; Stilwell nominated as CBI theater commander and, 28–31; Stilwell's redefining of, 39–43, 53; U.S. military and, 7–8

Mitchell, William "Billy," 31

Mogaung Valley: British and Chinese capture, 124; Chindits and, 119–20; Chinese divisions and, 117–9; final push to secure, 120–1; flanking attacks and, 114–6; Marauders and, 116–7

monsoon rains, 105–6, 123–4, 147

Montagnards, 179

Mountain Artillery Regiment, Japanese, 104–5

Mountbatten, Louis: on Boatner's dispatch to Washington, 159; British chain of command and, 181; CAI probing attacks into Burma and, 86–87; Cairo Conference and, 94–95; CBI theater and personality of, 9; on Chiang Kai-shek, 90–91; Myitkyina attack and, 130; north Burma campaign and, 98; road building and, 89; as SEAC commander, 82, 87–88; Stilwell, Somervell and Ledo Road and, 86; on Stilwell out of SEAC area, 165; Stilwell's difficulties with, 20, 158; on supplies for Y Force, 139

Musette Bag General: *See* Stilwell, Joseph W.

Myanmar: *See* Burma

Myitkyina, Burma: campaign to seize, 5–6; casualties in capture of, 125; Chindits and blocking of, 119; Chinese and, 123, 124, 125; conclusion of battle over, 171; Kachin and, 122; on map,

142; Marauders and attack on, 117, 121–2, 123, 124; Mogaung Valley and, 114; north Burma campaign and, 96, 97; race to, 121–5; Y Force opening Allied route to, 139

Naga Hills, Burma, 87
National Archives, 10
national army, American Army bias against regional forces and, 175
National Military Council, China's, 172
Nationalist China: academic reevaluation of, 16–17; army, doctors for, 135; Chiang's micromanagement of military and, 35; as corrupt government, 27; crippling military problems of, 25; Japanese invasions of China and political support for, 23–24; postwar close relationship with U.S. envisioned with, 64–65; Stilwell on training military forces of, 39–40; *See also* Chiang Kai-shek
nation-building, American military missions and, 23
Native Americans, 2
Navy, U.S., 51
Nazis, Chiang Kai-shek and, 24
New York Times, 129
Nhpum Ga, Burma, 107, 115–6
Nimitz, Chester, 89
9/11 attacks, 184
9th Military Region, China's, 52, 167
Nixon, Richard, 16
north Burma campaign: acrimony among British, Chinese, and U.S. units, 129–31; airfield capture and, 128–9; American combat unit for, 100–101; British and U.S. military and, 74–75; British Chindits and aircraft for, 101–2; British opposing, 81; Chiang approves use of Chinese troops in, 95; Chiang on, 62–63; Chiang's failures at Cairo regarding, 93; Chinese and U.S. forces for, 96; Chinese Army in India and, 98–99; difficult terrain and Allied plan for, 105–6, 111; Hukawng Valley clearing, 110–3; initial plans and capabilities, 98–106; interoperability challenges, 97; Kachin tribe and, 104; light infantry use in, 127–8; logistics, 102–3, 106; maps, 37, 107, 142; Mogaung Valley and, 114–21; Myitkyina attack and, 121–5; plans for, 20–21; political considerations and, 125–6; preliminary engagements along Tarung River, 106–10; road network, 103–4; Somervell and logistics for, 84–85; Stilwell–Mountbatten rift over, 158–60; U.S. media criticism of Stilwell and, 129; *See also* Burma Road; Champion, Operation; diseases, tropical; Tarzan, Operation
Northern Combat Area Command (NCAC): Chindits and, 120; on Marauders holding Nhpum Ga, 115–6; Mogaung Valley as logistics barrier for, 118; Myitkyina capture plan, 121; OSS mobilizing Kachin and, 115; Stilwell's command relationships, 1943–1944, 83; supervision of Chinese forces and, 110

objective civilian control, 184
Odierno, Raymond T., 73
officers, decline in average test scores of, 185
Ogburn, Charleton, 130–1
111th Indian Infantry Brigade, British, 119–20
150th Regiment, Chinese, 122–3
112th Indian Infantry Brigade, British, 87
orders, subjective and undefined, 54
Osborne, William, 114–5, 116
OSS (Office of Strategic Services) officers, 99, 104, 110, 115
OSS in Burma, The: Jungle War against the Japanese (Sacquety), 18

P-40 fighters, 124, 147
P-51 Mustang fighter-bombers, 102

Parameters, 182
Pearl Harbor, Japanese attack on, 26
Peers, William R., 18
Peng Ke-li, 108
People's Republic of China, 10. *See also* Chinese Communists; Mao Zedong
Pershing, John, 2–3
Persian Gulf, coalition forces in, 183
personalizing aid, problems with, 180
Petraeus, David, 180
Philippine Scouts, 39
Philippines, 164
Pick, Lewis A., 103
pilot training, in China, 58
Pingda, Burma, 143, 145
pipeline, in north Burma, 75–76, 84–85, 103–4
policy inconsistencies, Stilwell's ambiguous assignment and, 181
political advisors, 91, 170, 176
political considerations or issues: American military and, 184–5; Army understanding context of, 3; British chain of command and, 180–1; CBI theater and, 2; Chinese, Yunnan campaign and, 132–4; Chinese Army in India and, 76; military commanders and, 177; narrow skills and insights of Stilwell's staff and, 72–73; north Burma campaign and, 125–6; opposition to Chiang coalition and, 168–9; professional military as above, 8; Stilwell, American policy in Asia debate and, 19, 64–69; Stilwell on State Department advisors on his command staff and, 88–89; Stilwell–Mountbatten rift and, 160–1; Stilwell's and U.S. lack of understanding, 7–8; Stilwell's authority and influence reduced due to, 71; Stilwell's lack of awareness regarding, 176, 182, 186; Stilwell's lack of involvement in critical discussions and, 172; Stilwell's light footprint approach and, 154–5; of tactical decisions for north Burma campaign, 106; training Chinese troops in India and, 80

political scientists, Stilwell assessment in 1950s by, 12–13
political training, for American military officers, 3
political-military policymaking, 186

Quadrant Conference (Quebec), 82, 85, 87, 100

Ramgarh, India training center: for Chinese troops, 42–43, 53, 74–75, 76, 165–6, 176; Stilwell personnel supporting training in, 44–45
Rangoon (Yangon), 25, 26, 33
Rapp, William, 184
Red Army, 157. *See also* Chinese Communists
regional forces, 51–53, 156–7, 168, 175. *See also* Bao Chongxi; Li Tsung-jen; local regional leaders
Rhee, Syngman, 180
Ridgway, Matthew, 180
road network, 84–86, 89, 103–4, 105, 106–8, 114. *See also* Burma Road; Ledo Road
Rolling Stone, 73
Roosevelt, Franklin D.: academic reevaluation of, 17; on airpower and bombing, 5, 56; on American military presence in China, 26; American policy in Asia debate and, 19; Asian policies of, 182–3; Cairo Conference and, 89, 90; Chennault letter to, 61, 62; Chennault on airpower in China and, 94; Chennault's airpower requests to, 67; Chiang Kai-shek at Cairo Conference and, 91–92, 93; on Chiang opposition, 170; Chiang overplays his hand with, 40–41; on Chiang's Three Demands, 48; on Chinese and SEAC, 81–82; on Chinese collapse potential, 68–69; Chinese troops under Stilwell and, 33; cooling toward Chiang, 152; doubts about China by, 156; on Hurley as Chiang's personal representative, 171; military policy and, 30; senior

American officer role in CBI and, 23; on Stilwell as Chinese and American forces' commander, 166; on Stilwell at Trident Conference, 69; Stilwell on aid to Chinese forces and, 180; Stilwell on being undercut by, 79; Stilwell on retaking Burma and, 76; Stilwell recalled by, 174; Stilwell's campaign in China and, 6; Stilwell's lack of understanding political attitudes of, 8–9; Stilwell's mission in China and, 172–3; on supplies for Y Force, 138, 139; on unconventional operations, 100; on U.S. military mission to N. China, 157–8; vague direction from, 53; as Wingate supporter, 101; Y Force training and, 137–8; *See also* White House
Rusk, Dean, 182
Ryukyu Islands, 164

Sacquety, Troy, 18
Salween River: Chinese forces ensconced on, 132; crossing challenges, 140; Ho Ying-chin on moving across, 139; Japanese to stop Chinese at, 105; Roosevelt on Chiang's attack across, 172–3; Roosevelt on Y Force and, 139; Stilwell's attention on, 171; Y Force into Burma over, 140, 143–4
Scales, Bob, 186
Schaller, Michael, 16–17, 174
Schwarzkopf, Norman, 183
Scott, Robert, 59–60
Seagrave, Gordon, 11
2d Army, Chinese, 142, 143, 145
Seeds of Destruction: Nationalist China in War and Revolution, 1937–1945 (Eastman), 16
Service, John Stewart, 170
71st Army, Chinese, 142, 143, 146
77th Indian Infantry Brigade, British, 119, 120–1
76th Division, Chinese, 145
Shaduzup, Burma, 107, 115, 118
Shanghai conflict between China and Japan, 23

Shweli Valley, 144, 145
Sino-Japanese War (1937–1945), 18, 57–58
16th Indian Infantry Brigade, British, 119–20
Sixth Army, Chinese, 33–34, 37
65th Infantry Regiment, Chinese, 99, 111, 116
64th Infantry Regiment, Chinese, 99
Sixty-Sixth Army, Chinese, 33–34, 37
66th Infantry Regiment, Chinese, 99, 111
Sky, Emma, 73
Slim, William: dispute between Stilwell and British subordinates and, 120; on evacuation from Burma, 36; on Stilwell developing Chinese forces for Burma campaign, 77; Stilwell's command relationships, 1943–1944, 83; on Stilwell's plan to retake Burma, 50; on Sun Li-jen, 35; on training Chinese in India, 45; on Y Force training, 150
smuggling, Fourteenth Air Force and, 94
Somervell, Brehon B., 75, 84–86
Songshan Mountain, 140, 142, 148–9, 151
South Vietnam, 7, 175, 177, 180. *See also* Vietnam War
Southeast Asia Command (SEAC): Churchill on creation of, 81–82; combat units to Stilwell from, 100; Combined Chiefs on mission of, 165; command relationships, 1943–1944 and, 88; Mountbatten as supreme commander of, 82, 87; Stilwell and chain of command in, 83, 159; Stilwell's command relevance to, 98
Southwestern Government of Joint Defense, 168, 169
Soviet Union, 58
Spahn, Carlos G., 148
Spain, Army campaigns against, 2
Spanish-American War, 175
special envoys, 41, 42, 46–47, 181
Special Forces, British, 120
Sri Lanka: *See* Ceylon
staff, military, 8, 72–73

Stalin, Joseph, 26, 90
State Department, 46, 51, 88–89, 157, 170
Stilwell, Joseph W., Jr., 72–73, 115
Stilwell, Joseph W.: airpower advocates and, 56–57; allies in British military establishment, 74–75, 80–82; allies in U.S. military establishment, 74–75, 84–86, 88; American policy in Asia debate between Chennault and, 19; on authority in training Chinese troops, 79; AVG and, 58; background for CBI theater, 27–28; on British and Chinese, 53; on Burma attack to Chiang, 41–43; CAI force training and development by, 77–80; Cairo Conference and, 89–90, 94, 95; CBI tenure of, 18–19; CBI theater and dismissal of, 1–2; CBI theater mission and, 165–6; chain of command appeals by, 67–68; Chennault's failings blamed on, 66–67; on Chennault's independent advice to Chiang, 161–2; Chennault's personality clash with, 57–63; Chiang Kai-shek at odds with, 32–33; Chiang on China mission of, 173–4; Chiang's provisions on commanding Chinese forces by, 170–1; China's political affairs and, 152; on Chinese capabilities in Burma, 108; on Chinese in Burma defense, 34–35; on Chinese national army, 175; Chinese tank battalions and, 128; command relationships, 1943–1944, 83, 88; flanking maneuvers and, 111; Fourteenth Air Force supplies and, 163; Hurley's initial meetings with Chiang and, 172; intelligence reports (1930s) by, 25; Japan's Ichi-Go offensive and, 168; Joint Chiefs reshaping mission of, 163–4; lack of clear mission and authority for, 4–5, 22–23; leveraging Washington for supplies and organization, 43–50; light footprint plan for Yunnan by, 149, 154–5; light infantry problems for, 127–8; lingering issues for, 50–52; maneuvering the Chinese into decisions, 38–43; Mountbatten, Somervell and Ledo Road and, 86; Mountbatten and SEAC and, 82, 87–88; Mountbatten rift over north Burma campaign with, 158–60; nominated CBI commander, 27–31; north Burma campaign and, 97–98; overall performance as CBI theater commander, 176; political and personal passions in historiography of, 11–12; political perspective shortcomings, 8–9, 64–69, 72; on Roosevelt, 64, 69, 70; Roosevelt recalls, 174; senior American officer role in CBI and, 23; separation of military and political spheres by, 184; on Southwestern Government of Joint Defense, 168, 169; staff with narrow skills and insights for, 72–73; on transactional way to deal with Chiang, 164; walkout from Burma and, 36, 38; on Wei's offensive, 146; on Wingate's block position concept, 119; X Force and rising stature of, 152–3; Yunnan allies and, 132–3; *See also* China-Burma-India (CBI) theater; historical accounts

Stilwell and the American Experience in China, 1911–1945 (Tuchman), 14–15
Stilwell's Command Problems (U.S. Army), 13
Stilwell's Mission to China (U.S. Army), 13
Stimson, Henry: on American role in China, 26–27; on Chiang Kai-shek, 91; on Chiang's Three Demands, 46; Hurley as Chiang's personal representative and, 171; revised opinion of Chiang by, 40–41; on Roosevelt's use of personal representatives, 41; on Stilwell at Trident Conference, 69; on Stilwell's need for political support, 183
Sultan, Dan, 165
Sumatra, SEAC and, 82
Sun Li-jen, 35–36, 44, 79, 87, 98–99, 118–9
Sun Tzu, 53

Sung Hsi-lian (Song Xilian), 141, 146–7
supplies, 138–9. *See also* logistics
surgical hospitals, portable, 137

Taiwan, 10, 164
Tanai River, 87
Tanaka Shinichi, 105, 106–7, 112
tanks, Allied, 99–100, 110, 111, 112
Tao Wenzhao, 183
Tarung River, 87, 105, 106–10
Tarzan, Operation, 88
Tatangtzu pass, 143, 144
Taylor, Jay, 167–8
Tehran Conference, 90
telephone network, 104
Tengchong, Burma, 140, 141, 142, 143, 147–8
Tenth Air Force, U.S., 59, 61
10th Army, Chinese, 167
Thieu, Nguyen van, 180
30th Division, Chinese, 99
38th Division, Chinese: Burma defense and, 35; Japanese in Hukawng Valley and, 108–9, 112–3; Mogaung Valley and, 114–5, 117–8; north Burma campaign and, 96, 97; protecting engineers building the road, 106–8; recovering from combat losses and illness, 111; regiments, battalions, and firepower of, 98–99; training in India, 42–43, 79
39th Division, Chinese, 142
Three Demands, Chiang's, 40–41, 46, 51, 60
Timberman, Thomas, 168–9
Time, 129
Time Runs Out in CBI (U.S. Army), 13
"Too Much Wishful Thinking about China" (Baldwin), 91
transactional policies, 164, 180
Trident Conference: airpower in China and, 70, 72, 81; Chennault and Stilwell and, 67–69; Chennault's memoirs on, 69; Chiang on enemy attacks on air offensive before, 162; programs without specific dates identified at, 87; Quadrant Conference and, 82; Stilwell on his authority after, 79; Stilwell rebuilding his position after, 76–77; Stilwell's influence diminished at, 75; Y Force training and, 137–8
Tsou, Tang, 14, 182
Tuchman, Barbara, 14–15
XXth Group Army, Y Force's, 141, 142–3, 144–5, 147–8
22nd Division, Chinese: clearing the Hukawng Valley and, 110, 113; fixing Japanese on Jambu Bum and, 114; Mogaung Valley and, 115–6, 117–8; north Burma campaign and, 96, 97; regiments, battalions, and firepower of, 99; training in India, 42–43, 79
200th Division, Chinese, 35

U-Go, Operation, Japanese, 139
unilateral grants of support, conditionality strategies compared with, 180
United Kingdom: Lend-Lease Act and, 25; *See also* British
United States: British as uncertain allies with, 6–7; Chennault and Chinese aircraft purchases in, 58; military operations for economic and political advantage of, 3; national interests, Stilwell's lack of understanding, 7; public support for China in, 30; training Chinese troops in India and, 43; training personnel for Y Force, 136; *See also* Army, U.S.
United States Military Academy (West Point), 185
U.S. Army Special Operations in World War II (Hogan), 18
U.S. Crusade in China, The, 1938–1945 (Schaller), 16–17

Vietnam War: CBI and Stilwell studies in light of, 9–10; desertion and retention during, 179; revisionist school of historiographical writing and, 14–16;

U.S. military operations and, 4; *See also* South Vietnam
Vincent, John Carter, 65
volunteers, for north Burma campaign, 100. *See also* American Volunteer Group

Walawbum, Burma, 110–1, 112, 113
Walkout: With Stilwell in Burma (Dorn), 15–16
Wallace, Henry, 158, 170
War Department, 19, 39, 40, 61, 88
Washington, D.C. Conference (1942), 28
Washington, D.C. Conference (1943), 63
Wavell, Archibald, 32, 34, 39, 49
weapons, 78–79, 138, 141, 162–3. *See also* logistics
Wedemeyer, Albert C.: in CBI, Army assessment of, 13; Mountbatten on replacing Stilwell with, 165; north Burma campaign and, 158–9; on Stilwell and SEAC chain of command, 159; Stilwell assessment and, 12; on Stilwell in CBI theater, 177–8
Wedemeyer Reports! 12
Wei Li-Huang, 141, 145–7, 148
Whampoa Academy, KMT's, 92, 157
Wheeler, Raymond A., 31–32, 88
White, Theodore, 11
White House, 46, 182. *See also* Roosevelt, Franklin D.
Willkie, Wendell, 61–62
Wingate, Orde, 100–101, 102, 119, 120, 126–7
Wood, Walter, 79
Wrath in Burma (Eldridge), 11
Wu Tiecheng, 92

X Force, 43, 152–3, 165–6. *See also* Chinese Army in India
XI Army, Y Force, 141
Xue Yue: in Hunan Province, 134; Japan's Ichi-Go offensive and, 167, 168; as 9th Military Region commander, 52; opposition to Chiang coalition and, 154; U.S. military assistance to, 157

Y Force: American role in developing, 78; campaign map, 142; Chinese receptiveness to training, 144–5; code books recovered by Japanese, 140; establishing, 134; initial plans for, 132; interpreters for, 136; Longling offensive, 141, 143, 145–6; short-term training programs for, 136; Songshan offensive, 148–9; supplies and weapons for, 138–9; Tengchong offensive, 147–8; training, 137–8, 165–6; training and liaison techniques for, 135, 150, 153; *See also* Chinese Expeditionary Force
Yangtze River Valley, 155
Young, Richard M., 34, 36, 38
Yu, Maochun, 18
Yunnan Province, China: campaign map, 24; CEF training in, 77–79; Chinese airpower, tactical model, and organizational culture in, 133–4; offensive into Burma from, 20–21; Stilwell's campaign in, 6; Stilwell's shaping campaign from, 132–3
Yuzo Matsuyama, 139–40

Z Force, 153, 167
Zhang Fakui, 154, 168

ABOUT THE AUTHOR

ERIC SETZEKORN works for the U.S. federal government and is also an adjunct faculty member at George Mason University and the University of Maryland, Global Campus. After service in the U.S. Army and the intelligence community, he received his PhD from George Washington University. He has published more than two dozen academic articles with publications such as *Parameters*, the *Journal of American–East Asian Relations*, and the *Journal of Military and Strategic Studies*. He has also published two books: *The Rise and Fall of an Officer Corps: The Republic of China Military, 1942–1955* (2018), and *Arming East Asia: Deterring China in the Early Cold War* (Naval Institute Press, 2023).

THE NAVAL INSTITUTE PRESS is the book-publishing arm of the U.S. Naval Institute, a private, nonprofit, membership society for sea service professionals and others who share an interest in naval and maritime affairs. Established in 1873 at the U.S. Naval Academy in Annapolis, Maryland, where its offices remain today, the Naval Institute has members worldwide.

Members of the Naval Institute support the education programs of the society and receive the influential monthly magazine *Proceedings* or the colorful bimonthly magazine *Naval History* and discounts on fine nautical prints and on ship and aircraft photos. They also have access to the transcripts of the Institute's Oral History Program and get discounted admission to any of the Institute-sponsored seminars offered around the country.

The Naval Institute's book-publishing program, begun in 1898 with basic guides to naval practices, has broadened its scope to include books of more general interest. Now the Naval Institute Press publishes about seventy titles each year, ranging from how-to books on boating and navigation to battle histories, biographies, ship and aircraft guides, and novels. Institute members receive significant discounts on the Press' more than eight hundred books in print.

Full-time students are eligible for special half-price membership rates. Life memberships are also available.

For more information about Naval Institute Press books that are currently available, visit www.usni.org/press/books. To learn about joining the U.S. Naval Institute, please write to:

Member Services
U.S. Naval Institute
291 Wood Road
Annapolis, MD 21402-5034
Telephone: (800) 233-8764
Fax: (410) 571-1703
Web address: www.usni.org